THE PRICE OF THE TICKET

TRANSGRESSING BOUNDARIES

Studies in Black Politics and Black Communities
Cathy Cohen and Fredrick C. Harris, Series Editors

The Price of the Ticket

Barack Obama and the Rise and Decline of Black Politics

Fredrick C. Harris

OXFORD
UNIVERSITY PRESS

OXFORD
UNIVERSITY PRESS

Oxford University Press is a department of the University of Oxford.
It furthers the University's objective of excellence in research,
scholarship, and education by publishing worldwide.

Oxford   New York
Auckland   Cape Town   Dar es Salaam   Hong Kong   Karachi
Kuala Lumpur   Madrid   Melbourne   Mexico City   Nairobi
New Delhi   Shanghai   Taipei   Toronto

With offices in
Argentina   Austria   Brazil   Chile   Czech Republic   France   Greece
Guatemala   Hungary   Italy   Japan   Poland   Portugal   Singapore
South Korea   Switzerland   Thailand   Turkey   Ukraine   Vietnam

Oxford is a registered trade mark of Oxford University Press
in the UK and certain other countries.

Published in the United States of America by
Oxford University Press
198 Madison Avenue, New York, NY 10016

Library of Congress Cataloging-in-Publication Data
Harris, Fredrick C.
The price of the ticket : Barack Obama and the rise and decline of Black politics / Fredrick
C. Harris.
   p.   cm. — (Transgressing boundaries : studies in Black politics and Black communities)
Includes bibliographical references and index.
ISBN 978-0-19-973967-7 (cloth); 978-0-19-932523-8 (pbk) 1. African Americans—Politics
and government—20th century. 2. African Americans—Politics and government—21st
century. 3. African American political activists—History—20th century. 4. African
American politicians—History—20th century. 5. Obama, Barack—Relations with
African Americans. 6. United States—Politics and government—1945–1989. 7. United
States—Politics and government—1989– I. Title.
E185.615.H288   2012
323.1196′073—dc23   2012001114

9 8 7 6 5 4 3 2 1

Printed in the United States of America
on acid-free paper

For Nigel

Yes: we have lived through avalanches of tokens and concessions but white power remains white.
And what it appears to surrender with one hand it obsessively clutches in the other.

—James Baldwin

Contents

Preface to the Paperback Edition

ON NOVEMBER 6, 2012, President Barack Obama was reelected as president of the United States, winning comfortably in the popular vote and decisively in the Electoral College. Black voters came out in record numbers. For the first time in the recorded history of voter turnout in presidential elections, black voter turnout exceeded white turnout, giving Obama victories in critical swing states such as Ohio, Pennsylvania, and Virginia that allowed him to recapture the presidency. But despite the high level of voter enthusiasm among black voters, blacks' higher-than-average participation did not translate into any promises of policies directed at challenging the persistence of racial inequality. Nor did the Obama campaign reflect on what it had done—or could not do—on behalf of black communities during his first term or what the president would do in a second term.

The absence of discussions about policies that would arrest the persistence of racial inequality was glaring. Though Obama campaign videos for other key constituencies clarified the president's stance on issues affecting particular constituencies, the campaign's video that targeted black voters lacked policy substance. For instance, campaign spots conveyed to supporters of Israel how

Obama stood on Middle East policy, liberal women were told that the president had their back when it came to their reproductive rights, and Latino voters were reassured that the president supported immigration reform.

Yet campaign videos targeting black voters did not mention any policy issues specific to black communities. While, for instance, a campaign video targeting Latino voters heralded Obama's for "supporting small businesses in the Latino community" and the president's fight "to make sure that people brought here as children have an opportunity to earn a pathway to citizenship," the video targeted to black voters emphasized the need for voters and volunteers for the campaign to sign up and "say you're ready to make history again." It appears that the 2012 campaign—as did Obama's 2008 campaign—appealed to blacks' racial pride to reelect the nation's first black president rather than to policies that it had enacted or promised to enact to stem the persistence of racial inequality.

Most assume that black voters are sophisticated when they choose whether to support black candidates who proclaim racial neutrality in their approach to governance and policy. However, it is becoming increasingly apparent that black voters should become just as sophisticated when it comes to setting policy agendas to challenge the persistence of racial inequality. The either-or proposition of universal policies or targeted policies to address inequality is far too simplistic given the multiple issues facing black communities. The idea that policies that help everyone—what is described by policymakers as universalism—will trickle down to meet the systematic needs of black communities and that targeted policies toward minorities—which lack the political will of the majority—should be taken off the table is a shortsighted approach to race and policymaking. Indeed, a singular focus on universalism surrenders to the false notion of a color-blind society where race no longer matters.

This is also true when it comes to blacks' choosing which political strategies to pursue when advocating for policy issues that are particular to their communities. The tension in the approach boils down to whether blacks should work in coalitions with others around universal causes or go it alone as an independent constituency advocating for policies that target their communities. Depending on the issue and the level of support from non-black groups, it is ideal for blacks to use both strategies. Not every issue facing black communities fits under the rubric of universalism. Whether to use a universalist or targeted approach should depend on the issue at hand and what opportunities are available for building multiracial coalitions around specific policy issues. For instance, issues such as access to health care or tuition-free education at public colleges and universities are clearly issues that will benefit everyone, thus offering opportunities for blacks to build coalitions with other groups that have a stake in similar policies.

But what should be the political strategy for issues that overwhelmingly disproportionately affect blacks such as mass incarceration? What, for instance, would a national anti-racial profiling act—a law that would ban prohibit police from profiling individuals because of their race—look like under the principle of universalism? Does the principle of color-blindness in advocating issues and policies that are rooted in racial bias actually continue to perpetuate racial inequality by ignoring it or burying it under the rug? And does ignoring the persistence of racial inequalities capitulate to the idea that the United States has become a color-blind society, a concept that declares that race does not—or should not—matter in law and policymaking?

Defenders of the president's silence on racial inequality often make the claim that issues like high levels of black unemployment and criminal justice reform should focus on grassroots activism at the state and local level rather than trying to convince the White House to place these issues on its list of policy priorities. As the argument goes, a focus on local activism will create change from the bottom up, allowing issues to move their way to national politics and, as a consequence, set a the national agenda around community-focused issues. While activism should be encouraged on all levels of government, asking blacks to pursue such a narrow strategy amounts to what I would describe as African-American exceptionalism. That is to say, every other issue constituency within the political system can be encouraged to present their policy objectives—especially constituencies that are part of the president's electoral coalition—directly to the president except black voters.

This exceptionalism is grounded in the false—and disingenuous—idea that just because the president "happens to be black" that black voters and other advocates of racial equality should not expect the president to respond to policy issues aimed directly at addressing the persistence of racial inequality. Those supporting the idea of exceptionalism are asking black voters and black political elites to suspend their right as citizens to advocate for group-specific issues on the national level and to strictly focus their grievances and concerns on the state and local level.

There are some issues particular to black communities, the most loyal constituency of the Democratic Party, that should not require a full-fledged grassroots effort for the president to act. As pivotal voters in the president's reelection, black voters should not have to strictly pursue their policy objectives through the levers of local and state government. Some of those policy objectives ought to be expressed directly through the White House by either using executive action, prioritizing legislative objectives to Congress, or deploying the bully pulpit. This direct action has worked for other constituencies and it should work for advocates of racial equality. For instance, when women's reproductive rights were under attack by Republicans in Congress and in state legislatures there were no clarion calls for a renewed feminist movement to get the president to act. Advocates for women's reproductive rights expected and received a direct response from the White House.

This exceptionalist stance in black politics partly accounts for Obama's unusual silence on issues of race and poverty during his first term. During his first two years as president, Obama spoke less on issues of race than any other Democratic president since

1961. And in State of the Union addresses during the same time period, the president spoke less about the poor or poverty than any president Democrat in the White House since 1948. If the doctrine of exceptionalism continues into Obama's second term, advocates of racial inequality will have difficulty asking future presidential candidates—and presidents—to directly address the persistence of racial inequality. Republican and Democratic presidents alike now have the ability to simply wave off black demands for policy intervention by proclaiming that they—like Obama—have to be president for "all the people" not just for black Americans.

A long-standing problem with coalitions in black politics is that black political elites—specifically leaders of national civil rights organizations and black elected officials—have not engaged enough in a practice that is fundamental to the success of coalition politics: generating support from their partners for organizing and for issues that disproportionately affect black communities. This is known as reciprocity. While black organizations and leaders in the past four years have been called to endorse and advocate in behalf of other issue constituencies such as LGBT issues and immigration reform, these coalition partners have not been as vocal when it comes to particular issues facing black communities. This is especially the case with the issue of race and criminal justice reform. For this reason, blacks also have to engage in independent politics—that is, building coalitions within the black community and expanding to other affected constituencies and sympathizers—if there is to be any chance of placing such issues on the political agenda.

The political opportunities for black voters to press the Obama administration on issues specific to their communities appear to be dim in the president's second term. It is unlikely that Democrats will regain the House after the 2014 midterm election, and there is a possibility that Republicans will regain control of the Senate after the midterm. If both the House and Senate are led by Republicans, President Obama will spend his last two years as a lame duck president vetoing bills. If Democrats retain the Senate, the status quo remains intact and the president will get few of his domestic initiatives—whether they are targeted to address racial inequality or not—through a Republican-dominated House and a hopelessly contentious Senate. If advocates of racial equality who remained silent during the president's first term were gambling that the president in would focus on racial inequality in his second term, they may have gambled badly.

While other issue constituencies—particularly Latinos who pushed the president on stopping deportations and the LGBT community's pressure on the president to do away with the military's "don't ask, don't tell" policy and to take a stand for marriage equality—struck while the iron was hot, advocates of racial equality sat mum and kept hoping for a better day ahead. Certainly, concerns about the Right's exploitation of racial conflict drove most of the timidity, but few acknowledged that the Right has always opposed policies that would benefit blacks, a reality that had not muted activism in the past. Indeed, despite the president's silence on issues regarding racial inequality, anti-black sentiments in public opinion increased over the course of his first term and the president's support from white voters from 2008 to 2012 actually declined from a remarkable 45% to a dismal 37%. While anti-Latino sentiments increased as well during Obama's first term—increasing even more than for blacks—Latinos as a constituency were still able to gain traction on policies that were specific to their communities, despite the polarized political environment the president had to navigate.

Black political elites who remained silent or who operated as apologists for the president's silence and inaction are partly to blame. The political activist Al Sharpton, whose Janus-faced rumblings about the need for black leaders to organize and push for an agenda and his simultaneous criticism of blacks who have taken the president to task for his inaction and silence, has contributed to the present inertia on setting an agenda that focuses on challenging racial inequality. Sharpton's—and others'—duplicity in this regard may have protected the Obama administration from the sting of black critics, and demonized them as "race traitors" in the process. But the duplicity had the effect of sending negative signals to other black political elites and black voters who care about racial inequality that raising these issues would make it more difficult for the president to govern and damage his prospects for reelection.

The first six months of his second term have been met with Supreme Court decisions that severely weakened the 1965 Voting Rights Act and made it more difficult for colleges and universities to use race in college admissions. And the not-guilty verdict of George Zimmerman, who as a community crime watcher killed Trayvon Martin, an unarmed black teen, has sparked a renewed concern about racial profiling and the need for criminal justice reform. Nearly a week after the verdict the president used the bully pulpit to speak freely about the problems of racial profiling of black men and proposed some modest reforms to address racial bias in the criminal justice system. And the Attorney General has called for discretion in the mandatory sentencing of low-level and non-violent crimes that send thousands of black men and women to prison each year. Hopefully, this renewed attention to racial inequality in national politics will continue throughout Obama's second term and not fade in the abyss of cheap talk. The price of the persistence of racial inequality to American society is far too high for silence.

Preface

IN 1971, A BRITISH journalist noted during a televised interview with Muhammad Ali that the boxer was the second most prominent American after President Richard Nixon. The journalist followed the pronouncement by asking the world's heavyweight champion whether he would like to be president. Ali answered with an emphatic "no." "Too dangerous," the boxer quipped. Ali's concern about being the president of the United States was not only because of the potential violence that might be directed against him for being a black man holding the most powerful position in the world. His resistance also was due to the extraordinary challenges that would likely confront him as the nation's first black president.*

"Like in other words," Ali informed the journalist, there's "a ship, people are dancing on the ship, a lot of money is on the ship, a lot of food is on the ship, and I cannot integrate on the ship, I can't have equality on the ship . . . I'm just in the galley working, and I could never get up and see the captain of the ship." Ali explained while rubbing his forehead, "Now all of the sudden the man tells me 'Say, come on down, Ali, out of the galley. Hi, I want

* "Muhammad Ali on the First Black President," interview with Michael Parkinson, 1971. Available on YouTube.

you to have something to drink. What do you want?'" Ali continued. "Giving me the number one spot, from the galley to the
number one spot . . . This ship must be sinking," Ali surmised as a
burst of laughter rose from the studio audience. "Why is he so nice
to me now? What moves him to call me up here? Black men have
been mayors, now one might be president. America is in too much
trouble, I don't want that job now."

Ali's comedic reflection on the circumstances that would likely
produce the nation's first black president is prophetic. With the
election of Barack Obama as the forty-fourth president of the
United States, one could easily draw the conclusion that black
America reached the pinnacle of political empowerment—a journey that has taken blacks from one of the most marginalized
groups in American history (alongside Native Americans) to a key
constituency that helps elect a man of African descent to lead the
nation. But the economic conditions of the nation that greeted
Obama after he was inaugurated and the "race-neutral" political
rhetoric that helped catapult him into the White House put the
significance of Obama's election for black America in doubt. Far
from black America gaining greater influence in American politics,
Obama's ascendency to the White House actually signals a decline
of a politics aimed at challenging racial inequality head-on.

Scholars, journalists, and political analysts who have commented on race and politics in the wake of Obama's rise to the
presidency view his success as either an illustration of American
progress in race relations or view Obama as any other president
who—whether Democrat or Republican—represents the interests
of the rich and powerful. The only difference, these critics argue,
is that the new head of state has a black face.

Both supporters and critics of Obama have tried to deconstruct
his lack of attention to racial issues and policies by speculating on
the president's inner thoughts. Some have argued that Obama's
biracial heritage accounts for his ambivalence on racial issues.
Others believe that the president is reluctant to speak out on
racial issues because he does not want to be branded an "angry

black man." And still others think that the president is embracing a stealth strategy—quietly supporting black issues behind the scenes, out of the sight of right-wing detractors.

As if reading tea leaves for clues, these commentators search the pages of Obama's autobiography to find rationalizations for one point or the other. Some commentators even try to decipher Obama's use of alleged cultural cues—gestures he makes during speeches, his occasional use of black slang and "dialect," or the swagger in his walk—to argue that Obama sends signals to black voters to reassure them that he is one of them.

This book goes beyond the armchair psychologizing of Obama that too often passes for serious political analysis. Trying to dig into the inner thoughts of the president's view on race is best left to presidential historians who, as time passes, will have the benefit of primary sources and the distance of time to reflect on Obama's views. This book instead does what political scientists—and particularly historically conscious political scientists—do best. It places Obama's race-neutral campaign strategy and approach to governing within the context of history, politics, and policy. The book takes as its premise that Obama, just as any other president or candidate for the White House, makes strategic choices about what issues to prioritize, what constituencies receive more or less attention, and what risks are to be taken when pushing forward a policy agenda.

My analysis returns discussions about Obama's presidency to a fundamental question that still holds resonance in black politics today: What is the best strategy for black communities to pursue their political interests? This question has been a central concern of black politics since the early 1970s, during the transition of the civil rights and Black Power movements to the practices of mainstream American politics. Two views have come to dominate the answer to the question of strategy, coalition politics and independent black politics.

The coalition-politics perspective calls on black voters to build coalitions with whites and other racial and ethnic groups to develop support for issues and policies that help most everyone. The independent-black-politics perspective presses blacks to work independently of other groups to push for community interests with the aim toward building support with other groups around both universal policies and community-specific issues. The long-standing debate about whether coalition politics or independent black politics is the best electoral strategy for blacks is largely absent from recent writings about the state of black politics.

In the age of Obama, coalition politics—alongside race-neutral campaign strategies that are adopted by black candidates running in majority-white jurisdictions—has marginalized policy discussions about racial inequality. Proponents of "race-neutral" universalism fail to acknowledge that policies that help everyone—what can be described as a trickle-down approach to eradicating poverty and social inequality—are not enough to correct the deep-rooted persistence of racial inequality. In many ways, the majority of black voters have struck a bargain with Obama. In exchange for the president's silence on community-focused interests, black voters are content with a governing philosophy that helps "all people" and a politics centered on preserving the symbol of a black president and family in the White House.

Indeed, the symbol of a black president is not a trivial matter. No one recognizes the power of Obama's symbolism, particularly for black youth, more than I do. It hit me a year into Obama's term, when my then two-and-a-half-year-old son asked his preschool teacher to pen the following letter: "Dear Daddy. I miss Daddy. I want an ice cream and daddy said later. I want an ice cream but daddy [said] no. It's time to go to school. President Obama loves me." It is often difficult to tell what goes on in the minds of toddlers, but clearly Obama's image as a man of color in the White House captured my son's imagination, as well as the pride of millions of blacks in the United States and beyond. Yet, the grand bargain granting black pride in exchange for silence on race-specific issues and the marginalization of targeted policies by the Obama administration have left much to be desired.

This book is organized into three sections. The first two chapters chart the evolutionary forces within black politics that cleared the path for Obama's ascendency to the White House. The chapter "Clash of Ideas" takes a look back at the presidential campaigns of Shirley Chisholm in 1972 and Jesse Jackson in 1984 and 1988. The analysis reveals how coalition politics and independent black politics have been contested terrain in black electoral politics for more than forty years.

The chapter "Chicago: The Political Capital of Black America" examines the evolutionary stages of black politics that developed in Chicago. In particular, the chapter reconstructs the story of Harold Washington's successful campaign for mayor in 1983. Driven by independent black politics, Washington's mostly black coalition in 1983 and in 1987 (when he was reelected), set the stage for the rise of more coalition-driven black politics that led to Carol Moseley Braun and Barack Obama being elected to the United States Senate.

The next two chapters consider ideological fissures in black politics. "Entering the Land of Milk and Honey" places the Reverend Jeremiah Wright's controversial remarks about "God damn America" within the context of the fading influence of black liberation theology and the rising popularity of the prosperity gospel in Afro-Christianity. As the religious parallel to independent black politics, black liberation theology has given divinely sanctioned support to black electoral politics, as well as a theological framework that guides black churchgoers to challenge racial inequality. The prosperity gospel, a religious worldview that is silent on issues about racial inequality, provides, to some degree, a theological cover for the coalition-universalism wing of black politics. Though their goals differ, the prosperity gospel offers ideological support for universalism because both worldviews subscribe to the idea that black progress is possible by blacks "moving beyond race."

The chapter "Respectability as Public Philosophy" explores what has come to be known as the politics of respectability. For quite some time now, the century-old black middle-class ideology has been crafted by black elites as a public philosophy aimed directly at policing the black poor. The chapter places Obama's so-called tough love speeches to blacks within this tradition and argues that the rhetoric of respectability helped Obama capture the support of white working-class voters and moderate voters who needed assurance that the candidate would not support policies aimed toward the (black) poor.

The two final chapters address the practice and the consequences of race-neutral campaign strategies. "Wink, Nod, Vote" charts the origins of race-neutral campaign strategies among black politicians back to the early 1980s. Attempting to build biracial or multiracial coalitions, race-neutral black candidates—particularly those running as the first viable candidates for high-level offices—bent over backward to avoid discussing racism or express their views on policies designed to address racial inequality.

This silence by race-neutral black politicians led to an informal wink-and-nod agreement between race-neutral black candidates and black voters who supported them. Though some voters may assume that the candidates will address race-specific issues once elected to office, black voters get in return an advocate—as in the case of Obama—who supports policies that "help everyone" and the symbolism of having one of their own in office.

The concluding chapter "The Price of the Ticket" considers how Obama's race-neutral approach to governing and policymaking—as well as black voters' and black elites' refusal to pressure the president to address community interests—has incurred a political price for black Americans. The chapter raises questions about the marginalization of blacks' community interests, especially when compared alongside the Obama administration's attention to other constituencies such as the gay and lesbian movement and the Tea Party.

The nation's concession to the election of Barack Obama as president of the United States comes with an implicit agreement that the forces that keep racial inequality intact will not be directly challenged. While some might argue that universal policies would ultimately dismantle racial inequality by casting a wide net across black America, this one-dimensional approach to policymaking will not catch all the social ills facing black communities. Targeted efforts are needed. To paraphrase James Baldwin, the nation has, in one hand, surrendered to progress with the election of a black man to the highest seat of power in the land. But in the other hand, the nation still "obsessively clutches" the resources and the goodwill needed to rightly attend to the long-term and persistent problem of racial inequality. For black America—and its leaders—the dispiriting silence to this reality is the price paid for the election of the nation's first black president.

Acknowledgments

I AM FORTUNATE TO have family, friends, students, and colleagues who have been helpful to the development of this book. The idea for this project evolved from a marathon discussion with colleagues who study African American politics during meetings of the American Political Science Association in 2008. I also got ideas for this book during exchanges with the exceptionally engaging students at Columbia who took my undergraduate seminar on African American Politics in the fall of 2008 and my undergraduate seminar on Twentieth-Century African American Political Thought in the spring of 2009. I am particularly indebted to Claytoya Tugwell whose enthusiasm over the course of both seminars kept me on my toes and helped me think about many arguments for this book.

Conversations with Marcellus Blount, Anthea Butler, Cathy Cohen, Belinda Edmondson, Georgia Ellard, Curtis Foy, Farah Griffin, Charlene Harris, Randall Kennedy, Robert Lieberman, Naomi Long, Darrell Moore, Ernest Morrell, Mike Muse, Alondra Nelson, Courtney Nottage, Andrea Simpson, Valeria Sinclair-Chapman, Claude Steele, Dorothy Steele, Kendall Thomas, and Dorian Warren helped me to more critically analyze my arguments. I would also like to thank Richard Iton, Todd Shaw, and an anonymous reviewer for Oxford University Press for providing detailed comments on key chapters. I want to especially thank my editor David McBride at Oxford University Press for encouraging me to break beyond the disciplinary-focused writing style of political science to write a book for a broader audience. Thanks to Alexandra Dauler and Leslie Johnson for shepherding the book through the production process at Oxford. Special thanks to Chrystal Gray and Tania Belan-Gaubert for assisting me in locating images for the book. I also thank Princeton University Press for allowing portions of my previously published essay, "Entering the Promised Land" in *Religion and Democracy in the United States*, which was edited by Alan Wolfe and Ira Katznelson, to appear.

This would have been a far different book without the encouragement, support, humor, and friendship of two-thirds of the Musketeers, Carl Hart and Valarie Purdie-Vaughns. They allowed me to barge in their offices at will whenever I had an idea to explore, and they always gave me honest feedback regarding many of the ideas presented here. They have truly made intellectual life at Columbia a fulfilling experience. And lastly, I would like to thank my son Nigel Ellington Harris, whose bright eyes, laughter, and curiosity makes it all worth the effort.

Fredrick C. Harris
New York, New York
February 8, 2012

THE PRICE OF THE TICKET

1

Clash of Ideas

ON JANUARY 25, 1972, Congresswoman Shirley Chisholm mounted the podium at Concord Baptist Church's school auditorium in Brooklyn and declared herself a candidate for the presidency of the United States. Her small frame barely visible behind the podium, the candidate, who stood five feet tall and weighed barely one hundred pounds, was a heavyweight in the rough-and-tumble politics of central Brooklyn and a rising political star on the national stage. As the first black woman elected to Congress, Chisholm declared her candidacy for the presidency on her own terms: "I am not the candidate of black America, although I am black and proud," Chisholm told the crowd of five hundred mostly black women. "I am not the candidate of the women's movement of this country," she continued, "although I am a woman, and I am equally proud of that." Chisholm proclaimed: "I am a candidate of the people, and my presence before you now symbolizes a new era in American political history."[1] Chisholm's announcement stands as the symbolic beginning of the long, winding, and complicated trek that led to the election of Barack Obama as the nation's first black president.

The actual path leading to the election of a black president started a few years earlier, in the mid-1960s, on the eve of the passage of the 1965 Voting Rights Act. It was then that black leaders began discussing strategies blacks should pursue to obtain greater influence at the ballot box. Should black voters organize separately among themselves to gain political power or should they work with other racial minorities and "fair-minded" whites to press for change? These two viewpoints on black electoral politics—the desire to build a cohesive, independent bloc of black voters who push for a black agenda versus the practicality of supporting the Democratic Party as a part of a larger coalition in the pursuit of progressive policies that benefit all Americans—have been at odds for decades.

In 1964, Malcolm X's fiery speech the "ballot or the bullet" offered black voters a framework to understand how they should use their votes effectively. Malcolm X questioned blacks' wholesale support of the Democratic Party, especially since white southern Democrats had a stranglehold on civil rights legislation in Congress. Distrustful of white politicians and black politicians who were dependent on white party support, Malcolm X believed that "the black man should control the politics and the politicians in his own community." This independent perspective on black electoral politics viewed the black vote as leverage to advance the interests of black communities, as well as a means to hold politicians accountable if they ignored the interests of black communities.

Malcolm X believed that the 1964 presidential election offered an opportunity for blacks to exercise their political independence, and he declared that the year posed the choice of either the "ballot or the bullet"—a veiled warning that if blacks did not receive their rights as citizens, they would turn to violence to express their discontent. The Black Nationalist leader urged blacks to use their unity at the ballot box to "determine who will go to the White House and who will stay in the dog house." When Malcolm X broke with the Nation of Islam and founded the Organization of Afro-American Unity—created to defend and promote the interests of black Americans—the development of an independent, black political force was a central mission of the organization. They planned to "organize the Afro-American community block by block to make the community aware of its power and potential." Voter registration drives would be undertaken "to make every unregistered voter in the Afro-American community an independent voter," Malcolm X proclaimed. Only "independent candidates for office" and elected officials who "answer to and [are] responsible to the Afro-American community" would receive support from his organization. Though Malcolm X did not live to see how electoral politics would come to dominate black politics (he was murdered in 1965), his viewpoints on independent black politics would shape perspectives on black political life for decades.[2]

In what became a manifesto for independent black politics, Black Power activist Stokely Carmichael and political scientist Charles V. Hamilton wrote a widely acclaimed book, *Black Power: The Politics of Liberation*, first published in 1967. The book, apparently inspired by the principles articulated in Malcolm X's "ballot or bullet" speech and his plans for the Organization of Afro-American Unity, would be used as a blueprint for black politics. Carmichael and Hamilton advocated black self-determination— "Black Power"—at the ballot box and, like Malcolm X, argued that blacks should control the politics in their communities. Electing blacks to public office did not automatically lead to the representation of black interests. Black Power was "not merely putting black faces into office," Carmichael and Hamilton reasoned, because "black visibility is not black power." Their stand for independent black politics, which called for racial solidarity and asked blacks to remain skeptical of casting their lot with one political party, clashed with the vision of a progressive, multiracial coalition of progressive Democrats.

The architect of the coalition school was civil rights activist Bayard Rustin, who wrote a widely influential essay, "From Protest to Politics: The Future of the Civil Rights Movement," two years after Malcolm X's précis on black politics. In contrast to the independent strategy of black politics, the coalition strategy, as articulated by Rustin, laid out a strategic vision that called for transforming foot soldiers of the movement into dependable voters for the Democratic Party. Rustin believed that the future of black political struggle "depends on whether the contradictions of this society can be resolved by a coalition of progressive forces which becomes the effective political majority in the United States." This coalition, the one formed to press for passage of the civil rights reforms of the mid-1960s, was composed of "Negroes, trade unionists, liberals, and religious groups," the same coalition that laid the basis for Democrat Lyndon Johnson's landslide election in 1964. Eschewing calls for the black vote as the swing vote in elections, Rustin believed that black voters needed allies and that coalitions were inescapable in the real world of politics. "Independence," Rustin reasoned, "is not a value itself . . . The difference between expediency and morality in politics is the difference between selling out a principle and making smaller concessions to win larger ones." Rustin proclaimed: "The leader who shrinks from this task reveals not his purity but his lack of political sense."[3]

This old ideological battle between independent black politics and coalition politics is slowly fading, but its imprint on contemporary black political life still survives. While political pundits and journalists describe black political life today as the "new black politics" (a proclamation that occurs every fifteen years or so as blacks pass political milestones) that represents a generational rift between old-guard leaders who exploit blacks' grievances and "pragmatic" young leaders who wish to reach beyond race to solve problems, the current state of black politics is far more complex.

To understand that complexity is to journey back into time to explore the ideological tensions that existed between the two schools of black politics. Civil rights leaders, Black Power activists, and black politicians felt that 1972 was the year when a black man should run for president. Blacks were winning highly visible public offices as mayors in Cleveland, Ohio; Gary, Indiana; and Newark, New Jersey, and recent additions to the House of Representatives had produced a critical mass of black House members who vowed to flex their political muscle through the recently formed

Congressional Black Caucus. This was really the era of the "new black politics." Like the trope of the "New Negro" that emerged in the late nineteenth century and reemerged during critical moments of black progress in the first half of the twentieth century, proclamations of the new black politics emerged and reemerged during the later part of the twentieth century and into the twenty-first. In a 1972 essay titled "Emerging New Black Politics," St. Louis Congressman William Clay proclaimed: "Today the old politics of accommodation has been replaced by the new politics of confrontation . . . Those leading the politics of the new, the articulate, the dedicated—those who possess a deep sense of personal commitment to the concept of justice and equality at any cost."

Comparing the vanguard of black politicians from that era with today's cadre of new black political leaders produces a topsy-turvy picture of ideological opposites. While today's so-called postracial politics—a repackaged version of the coalition school—focuses on politics and policies benefiting all Americans, the new black politics of 1972 advocated an approach to politics and policy that focused on the concerns of blacks and other minorities.

> There is a new breed of blacks in politics who are demanding a reevaluation of the old concept that "what is good for the nation is good for minorities." We now couch our thinking in the fundamental concept that "what's good for minorities is good for the nation." This position necessitates the development of a new political philosophy. Black politics must start with the premise that we have no permanent friends, no permanent enemies, just permanent interests. We must learn and use the art of retaliatory politics—reward our friends and punish our enemies.[4]

A factor that spurred the idea to run a black candidate for president in 1972 emerged from the Democratic Party's efforts to increase the diversity of the party. After the contentious 1968 Democratic National Convention, the party mandated that more blacks, women, and youth be delegates at the party's 1972 convention in Miami Beach. The mandates created the possibility for the emergence of a candidate who could build a multiracial coalition of blacks, other minorities, feminists, youth, and the poor. The mandate also influenced the independent school of black politics, which believed that greater participation of blacks within the nominating process could be used as leverage to bargain for policy priorities and black political appointments. In a May 1971 meeting to plot a strategy for a black presidential run, a group of black leaders gathered in Chicago (a second and larger, secret meeting would take place in the city the following November) to discuss whether blacks should seek "audacious power" by running one of their own for president. Cleveland Mayor Carl Stokes, who was considered a possible candidate, believed that a black candidate could only be successful if he built a multiracial coalition. "We must get Black, brown, Chicano, poor whites and marginal persons involved in the politics of coalitions," Stokes told the gathering. Manhattan Borough President Percy Sutton, who was one of several masterminds behind the idea of a black presidential candidacy in 1972, believed that black leadership could provide presidential leadership because black leaders were the ones truly concerned with the "problems of racism, war, and poverty"—the "triple evils" that Martin Luther King, Jr., fought against. Foreshadowing the language that Obama— and his supporters—would use to justify his run for the presidency in 2008, Sutton told a *Jet* magazine reporter covering the meeting: "I believe in America. America is a democratic society and why shouldn't there be a black candidate for president? I believe white people will vote for a black man for president. This is audacious thinking and we must get white people to believe this."[5]

Throughout the summer of 1971, *Jet* magazine asked its readers to fill out a mail-in survey listing ten potential black presidential candidates. Readers were asked to check off whether they believed a black person should run for president and if so, who among the ten would be their choice. The list included Percy Sutton, Carl Stokes, three members of the Congressional Black Caucus—Detroit

Congressman John Conyers, Shirley Chisholm, and Detroit Congressman Charles Diggs—Massachusetts Senator Edward Brooke, Supreme Court Justice Thurgood Marshall, former United Nations Representative Ralph Bunche, Georgia State Representative Julian Bond, and Arthur Fletcher, a Republican and a Nixon appointee at the Department of Labor.

Shirley Chisholm was the only woman listed in the poll.

Though the results were an unscientific portrait of black America—indeed of *Jet* readers—the results, nonetheless, uncovered problems Shirley Chisholm faced in convincing black voters to support her candidacy. The poll showed nearly unanimous support for the idea of a black presidential candidacy: 98 percent. But Chisholm polled poorly, mustering only 5 percent of support from readers. Two politicians captured nearly 60 percent of readers' interest—Julian Bond, who polled 30 percent, and Carl Stokes, who followed with 27 percent. Bond, who would turn thirty-two in 1972, was not qualified to run because he could not meet the constitutionally required age of thirty-five to be president. Carl Stokes had no interest in running although he was interested in the black vote being leveraged to gain concessions from the Democratic Party. Blacks "do not have to continue to be the unrewarded servants of either major political party," Stokes insisted.

Jesse Jackson, who was managing the Southern Christian Leadership Conference's "Operation Bread Basket" program in Chicago, believed that a national strategy to run a black candidate for president would deliver to black people "one-fifth of the spoils—jobs and authority—of the Democratic Party" because black people represented 20 percent of the party's base.[6] Percy Sutton wanted to leverage the black vote for "real power." He saw that power in political appointments, a "black being named Secretary of the Treasury or chairing the Securities Exchange Commission, the Federal Trade Commission, and the Federal Reserve Bank and other such nonblack positions in America's power structure."[7]

Black politicians could not agree on what was the best way for blacks to exert their influence in the 1972 presidential election. In a series of closed-door meetings from the summer to the fall of 1971, several strategies were put forward. One was that blacks could unify behind a prominent white candidate and hope that the candidate would win. A proposal offered by Julian Bond suggested running local black politicians as "native son and daughter" candidates; a strategy that would build local power bases, as well as bring a bloc of delegates that could be used as leverage at the convention. Others thought that blacks should run as uncommitted delegates in their communities—a strategy that would also produce a bloc of black delegates at the convention. Another strategy proposed running a black presidential candidate, which would produce the benefit of a more coordinated national strategy and would also draw a bloc of delegates to the convention.

The group could not agree on a strategy or a candidate. Chisholm, who did not attend any of the strategy sessions, tossed her hat into the race. Chisholm did not believe she could win the nomination but saw her campaign as a "catalyst for change"; that is, a means to place issues on the agenda that were important to groups on the margins. She was a strong believer in blacks joining coalitions with Chicanos, women, the poor, and labor—clearly a politician from the coalition school. However, her strategy switched when she arrived at the convention. Chisholm tried unsuccessfully to mobilize and leverage black delegates to gain concessions. Though Chisholm received the support of Percy Sutton and commitments were made to start an advisory group of black politicians that would help guide her campaign, there were bad feelings. Participants in the strategy sessions disliked Chisholm's unilateral decision to jump into the race. It forced many to reluctantly lend support to her candidacy. Percy Sutton said it succinctly: "She put a number of us on the spot . . . I found I could not go around the country committed to a black Presidential candidate concept and not support Shirley." Although, he reasoned, "If I joined her, she is accountable to me."

For the sake of unity, a deal was struck between Chisholm and politicians active in the strategy discussions. But the deal merely reflected the multiple and conflicting strategies that were still on

FIGURE 1.1 Shirley Chisholm announces run for president (*Source*: Getty Images).

the table. During a round of secret and complex negotiations, Chisholm agreed not to run in the District of Columbia, where Walter Fauntroy was running as a native-son candidate. She also agreed not to run in Ohio, where Mayor Carl Stokes and his brother Congressman Louis Stokes pursued the strategy of supporting uncommitted delegates in Cleveland. (They would later support George McGovern, the party's presumptive nominee at the convention.) These deals would deny Chisholm the opportunity to amass as many delegates potentially available to her. Sutton made it clear that support for Chisholm was consistent with national black political strategy and hoped that the campaign would "make it extremely difficult for anyone claiming to be black to support a white candidate."[8] Chisholm performed poorly in the primary contests she chose to compete in, receiving on average 5 percent of the black vote. Hubert Humphrey, the Democratic Party's nominee, who was defeated by Nixon in 1968, received a majority of the black vote during the primaries, averaging 70 percent. Humphrey's long-standing civil rights record attracted the majority of black primary voters to his second bid for the nomination.[9]

Chisholm arrived at Miami Beach with twenty-eight delegates. This was far short of the number of delegates needed for the nomination and not enough to make a dint in demanding concessions from the party's presumptive nominee, South Dakota Senator George McGovern. Disappointed that she had not fared well in the primary contests, Chisholm was determined to leverage some influence at the convention. She and her supporters believed that McGovern had no incentive to address the concerns of minorities because the candidate had the nomination wrapped up; he did not receive strong support from black voters or many endorsements from prominent black leaders. What did he really owe the black community? The only option at this point, the Chisholm forces reasoned, was to deny McGovern the nomination on the first ballot.

Hubert Humphrey's and Edwin Muskie's withdrawals from the race provided an opportunity. Both Humphrey and Muskie agreed to release their black delegates; a move that provided an opening for Chisholm to build a larger delegate base to challenge McGovern. Chisholm began to lobby black delegates who were—or had been—committed to other candidates. She calculated that if she could persuade the convention's four hundred black delegates to vote for her on the first ballot, she could then deny McGovern the nomination on the first ballot. This would force McGovern to broker a deal. There were issues that McGovern forces had pushed off the party's agenda. The Chisholm forces were disappointed that the McGovern delegates did not support a plank calling for an annual $6,500 guaranteed income for poor families. A few feminist delegates came to Chisholm because they were disappointed by McGovern's lack of enthusiasm for a pro-choice abortion plank.

What undermined the strategy was the brokering that other black politicians pursued at the convention. Julian Bond, who became a McGovern supporter, questioned whether Chisholm was trying to become the "chief broker" for blacks. "We said to McGovern we'll go with you if you go with us . . . We'll support you if you deliver goods and services to blacks . . . Now that it's clear he will win," Bond said with a not-too-subtle jibe at Chisholm, "a lot of people want to get in on it . . . Why should I let you come in late and take it?" Walter Fauntroy caused a stir two weeks before the convention when he announced that he had gathered enough committed black delegates to put McGovern over the top on the first ballot. When pressed for names of the delegates, Fauntroy demurred. The delegates never materialized.[10]

Willie Brown, then an assemblyman in the California legislature and a rising star in black political circles, also served a broker role: not for black interests but for McGovern. The California delegation was challenged for its winner-take-all rule that delivered all the 271 delegates to McGovern, the candidate with the plurality. McGovern, who chaired the party's reform commission whose report recommended that winner-take-all primaries be eliminated, received 41 percent of the vote and all the state's delegates, enough for him to win the nomination on the first ballot. Humphrey placed a close second, at 38 percent; and Chisholm placed a distant fourth, behind segregationist George Wallace, with 4 percent of the vote. Humphrey and his supporters labeled McGovern a hypocrite for recommending that winner-take-all primaries be abolished while claiming victory from a close contest in delegate-rich California.[11]

McGovern argued that he played by the existing regulations and that his opponents were trying to change the rules in the middle of the game. The party's Credentials Committee awarded only part of the delegates to McGovern and distributed the rest to the other candidates based on the portion of votes received. McGovern and his supporters contested the decision. What became known as the "California challenge" was brought up for a vote before the convention's delegates. The convention's Black Delegate Caucus— an informal group pledged to various candidates or committed to none—was at the center of the battle to influence the outcome of the nomination. On the one hand, they were asked to cast their votes to stop McGovern on the first ballot and, on the other hand, to vote to overturn the Credentials Committee's decision on the California challenge. As one black party leader noted in the spirit of independent politics, "The watchword for this delegation [of black delegates] is independence, in the sense that you don't owe anybody anything."[12]

The multiracial coalition Chisholm had hoped to attract during her campaign was different from the all-black coalition of delegates she tried to forge at the convention. Her politics at the convention was built on the premise of independent black politics. Although individual feminists supported Chisholm at the convention, feminist groups did not rally to her cause nor did youth delegates flock to her campaign. Nor did she target them. The woman candidate "who happened to be black" went hunting where the ducks were. She shouted to members of the Black Delegate Caucus in a speech before the group:

> Brothers and sisters! Think! You didn't come here to be delivered! Don't play yourselves cheap. You paid your own way here, and you worked hard to do it. A black boss is as bad as a white boss, and some black leaders are willing to advance their own political fortunes at the expense of the masses. Please! Think for yourselves . . . Go with me on the first ballot. And if you can't go with me, go uncommitted! Black people all over the country are watching what we do here![13]

Both McGovern and Humphrey appealed for support before the caucus as well, though Chisholm's speech received the most enthusiastic applause. Willie Brown addressed the caucus in his crusade to release all of the California delegates to McGovern. Brown rousingly asked the caucus to overturn the California challenge. "Give me back my delegation," Brown shouted to the gathering, turning the decision to deny all of the California delegates to McGovern into a personal affront. (Brown later gave another rousing "Give me back my delegation" speech that convinced a majority of the convention delegates to overturn the California challenge.) Neither Chisholm nor Brown could persuade the caucus to endorse their efforts; it was too divided to be swayed either way.

Black Power activist Imamu Baraka's worst fears were being realized. What remained of a unified strategy to support a candidate who best represented the interests of blacks was collapsing before his eyes. Baraka had hoped that the Black Delegate Caucus would unite around the candidate who, point by point, agreed to support the greatest number of issues that were hammered out in March at the National Black Political Convention in Gary, Indiana. But brokers, he thought, derailed the hopes of unity. In the end, McGovern received the nomination on the first ballot and made no solid commitments to blacks. The Democratic ticket would lose to Nixon in one of the most lopsided landslides in modern American history. What transpired in Miami Beach was a crabs-in-the-barrel free-for-all among competing brokers (some negotiating to enhance their own personal benefit) that, in the end, led to no concessions and less influence for blacks in the party. Brokering would be—and still is—a tactic that can either be a blessing or a curse for independent black politics. It can be an effective tool for gaining concessions; it can also undermine efforts to gain concessions by brokers "selling out" the community's interests for personal benefit.

Shirley Chisholm faced obstacles by being the first black and first woman to run for president in the Democratic Party that Jesse Jackson, Hillary Clinton, and Barack Obama did not have to confront. Chisholm and Obama were the same age (forty-six) when they ran for president, but no one ever noted Chisholm's youthful age as a political asset. (Jesse Jackson was even younger when he first ran in 1984, at the age of forty-three.) Some black candidates and public officials currently complain of the subtle racism they face in the media and some women candidates complain of gender bias, but few black or women candidates today encounter the type of bias Chisholm tackled in 1972.

One white male reporter's *Heart of Darkness* description of Chisholm's physical characteristics is so disturbingly racist and sexist that no serious journalist today would dare depict a candidate with such condescension. Stephan Lesher of the *New York Times* wrote:

> Though her quickness and animation leave an impression of
> bright femininity, she is not beautiful . . . Her face is bony and
> angular, her nose flat and wide, her neck and limbs scrawny. Her
> protruding teeth probably accounts in part for her noticeable
> lisp. Still, in her autobiography, *Unbought and Unbossed*, she
> describes herself in a much more favorable light.[14]

White male liberals running in the Democratic primary wanted
her to drop out of the race because they feared she would take
away black voters from their campaigns. Black male politicians
accused her of "castrating" the political fortunes of black men by
deciding to run for president. "In this first serious effort of blacks
for high political office, it would be better if it was a man," an anonymous black male politician told a reporter from the *Washington
Post*.[15] Two members of the Congressional Black Caucus openly
expressed their disdain for Chisholm's candidacy. Cleveland
Congressman Louis Stokes shrugged his shoulders and laughed
when asked by a reporter whether he planned to support Chisholm,
while St. Louis Congressman William Clay sarcastically replied,
"Who's Shirley Chisholm?"[16] Others feared that Chisholm's potential success would be hijacked by white women to the detriment of
the black community. "The specter of white women bargaining in
the Democratic Convention with white men in behalf of the black
community [is] a frightening thing," an anonymous black male
politician declared in the *New York Times*.[17]

The criticism became so heated that Chisholm felt she had to
address the "woman thing" head on. Just before speaking at Chicago's Black Expo, a forum on women and politics in November of
1971, the congresswoman overheard a comment from a black male
politician that infuriated her. "There she is, that little black matri-
arch who goes around messing things up," Chisholm recalled
hearing the man say in a loud voice. When it came for her turn to
speak, she told black men who resented her running for president
to "get off my back." Chisholm spoke openly about the twin obstacles she faced—sexism and racism. If black women were interested

in politics, she warned, they have to overcome those barriers. "I had far more discrimination because I am a woman than because I am black," she told the audience. Chisholm answered critics who argued that raising the issue of gender discrimination divided the black community by saying that ignoring the plight of black women held back the entire community. "Black women are not here to compete or fight with you brothers," she told the audience. "If we have hang-ups about being male or female, we're not going to be able to use our talents to liberate all our Black people."[18]

Chisholm never shied away from speaking her mind. She thought that most black politicians had a limited vision of what a black presidential candidate should do. "I was not out to become only the black candidate," Chisholm recalled. She believed that had she received the full support from the (mostly male) group that was considering running a black candidate for president, "I would have been locked into a false and limiting role." Taking the mantle as the black candidate—rather than the candidate that happens to be black—would have prevented her from building a broader coalition of voters who felt excluded in the political process. As Chisholm explained, "My potential support went beyond the black community. It could come from the women's movement, from young voters, and even from a growing number of older white voters who had reached the end of their patience with the programs and candidates of the two major parties." Arguing that no other black politician had the ability to bring together such a diverse coalition, Chisholm believed, "I was far and away the strongest black candidate because, paradoxically, I was not solely a black candidate." Chisholm described the coalition she tried to form as the "union of the disenfranchised," a campaign slogan Jesse Jackson would pick up in his bid for the presidency a decade later.

Though many believed that the Chisholm campaign was a colossal failure, it set the stage for subsequent efforts. "The next time a women of whatever color, or a dark-skinned person of whatever sex aspires to be President, the way should be a little smoother because I helped pave it," she wrote in her 1973 memoir. Though no substantive benefits were gained in this largely symbolic effort, the importance of Chisholm's largely forgotten campaign would reverberate for decades. "Perhaps some black or Spanish-speaking child already dreams of running for the Presidency someday, because a black woman has dared to," the defeated candidate believed. "That child's dream would be more than enough for me to accomplish, would it not? And is not that kind of dream a great gain for American society?"[19]

Three presidential campaign cycles elapsed before a black candidate would again run for president in the Democratic Party. In 1984, when Jesse Jackson decided to run, blacks had become a bloc of loyal voters for the Democratic Party in local, state, and national elections; yet their participation was not adequately reflected in the policy priorities of the party or its leadership. Like Chisholm, Jackson's goal was to build a multiracial coalition— what the candidate characterized as a "Rainbow Coalition" of the "disenfranchised," the "disaffected," and the "locked out"—that would pressure the party to address black concerns. But Jackson's campaign theme of "Our Time Has Come" would be aimed primarily at blacks, who were becoming increasingly impatient with the Democratic Party's "lack of respect" for black voters. In particular, black politicians were disappointed in the party's lukewarm response to Ronald Reagan's conservative agenda and the defection of white Democrats in Harold Washington's successful 1983 bid to become Chicago's first black mayor.[20]

Like the gear-up to the 1972 presidential contest, a series of black unity conferences were held to plot a strategy for 1984. Many of the same players from 1972 joined discussions in 1983: Walter Fauntroy, Jesse Jackson, Julian Bond, and Richard Hatcher, and others. But there were also new participants in the mix. The inclusion of a new class of political leadership reflected the progress that blacks had made in electoral politics since 1972. These new leaders included Philadelphia Congressman William Gray, Houston Congressman Micky Leland, and Atlanta Mayor Andrew Young, among others. Several prominent leaders were opposed to the idea of a black running for president altogether—particularly Detroit Mayor Coleman Young, NAACP President Benjamin Hooks, and National Urban League President John Jacob. Their view was that blacks should get behind the best liberal candidate who stood for labor and civil rights.

A position paper produced by the Washington-based black think tank the Joint Center for Political Studies weighed the costs and benefits of a black presidential candidacy. On the positive side, a black running for president could highlight issues important to black voters, stimulate black voter registration, produce a large number of cohesive black delegates at the party's convention, and serve as a "trial run for a future black candidacy." On the negative side, a black candidacy could take black voters and delegates away from desirable white candidates, brand the Democratic Party's nominee a captive of "black special interests"—a charge that could hurt the party's chances with southern whites and white working-class voters—intensify racial polarization in the electorate, and divide rather than unite black leaders. Though the group came to a consensus that the benefits of a black presidential run outweighed the potential costs, the group could not come to a consensus on a candidate.[21]

Jackson decided to run. Adopting rhetoric from the Chisholm campaign and the philosophy of independent black politics, Jackson declared that his campaign would represent a "Rainbow Coalition" of "rejected groups." Jackson said during his campaign's formal announcement:

> I offer myself and my service as a vehicle to give voice to the voiceless, representation to the unrepresented, and hope to the downtrodden . . . Lest there be confusion, let the word go forth from this occasion that this candidacy is not for blacks only. This is a national campaign growing out of the black experience and seen through the eyes of the black experience—which is the experience and perspective of the rejected . . . Thus, our perspective encompasses and

includes more of the American people and their interests than does most other experiences.[22]

The campaign was organized around the theme of blacks—and other disaffected groups—gaining their fair share of power within the Democratic Party. An equally important goal was using the campaign to place a black agenda at the top of the Democratic Party's issue agenda. Democrats, Jackson argued, were not challenging the Reagan administration's attacks on civil rights policies, affirmative action, and social welfare programs. Reagan was attacking poor people, calling them Cadillac-driving "welfare queens" and "strapping young bucks" unwilling to work—racially coded phrases used to justify cuts in social services. Reagan was so disliked by blacks that a 1985 poll by ABC News and the *Washington Post* revealed that 77 percent of blacks believed that Reagan was prejudiced against black people and a poll by the Joint Center for Political Studies found that over half of blacks—56 percent—were convinced that Reagan was a racist.[23]

Black leaders behind Walter Mondale—the party's leading candidate who was also backed by labor—believed that the Minnesota senator's progressive record on civil rights and social welfare programs made him acceptable. Besides, they reasoned, Mondale would have a better chance of defeating Reagan than Jackson. Despite widespread support for Mondale among prominent black leaders—including Harlem Congressman Charlie Rangel, Coretta Scott King, Los Angeles Mayor Thomas Bradley, Birmingham Mayor Richard Arrington, Georgia State Senator Julian Bond, and Detroit Mayor Coleman Young—black voters overwhelmingly backed Jackson. What made Jackson's campaign a break from the past was that black voters did not follow civil rights leaders or prominent black politicians. Jackson appealed directly to black voters, and they responded. In the Alabama and Georgia primary contests, the first two primaries with large numbers of black voters, Jackson split the black vote with Mondale. But after Jackson's strong showing in his home state of Illinois, where he received 79 percent of the black vote, Jackson received, thereafter, on average, 80 percent of the black vote. Relying on a large, but tightly knit, network of black ministers and churches, Jackson was able to mobilize black voters without the mainstream media and a large campaign chest. Jackson raised $3.4 million, a sum considerably greater than the $95,000 the Chisholm campaign raised but considerably less than most of Jackson's white rivals. Jackson raised most of his campaign funds through grass-roots sources, by passing the collection plate at black churches and by collecting donations at political rallies and benefit concerts.[24]

Not only did the Jackson campaign increase black voter registration and turnout, but it also brought unregistered black voters into the political process. In some southern states, 20 percent of black voters in the primaries voted for the first time. The campaign also had a small coattail effect: the wave of black voter participation encouraged southern black voters to run for lower-level offices.

In the end, the Rainbow Coalition was mostly a black affair. Jackson received less than 10 percent of the white vote and about one-third of the Latino vote, which came mostly from Puerto Rican voters in New York, who were already part of a larger black-brown coalition in the city. Jackson's 1984 campaign adopted an independent strategy to attain concessions. This could be done by leveraging the bloc of delegates Jackson acquired during the campaign. Using delegates to empower blacks in the party is a strategy that goes back as far as the 1964 Democratic Convention in Atlantic City, where civil rights activists contested the seating of the all-white Mississippi delegation before the party's Credentials Committee. As a compromise, Fannie Lou Hamer and the Mississippi Freedom Democratic Party were given two seats at the convention. Most of the Freedom Democrats considered the offer tokenism, specifically Hamer, who famously said, "We didn't come all this way for two seats when all of us are tired." The battle to seat the Freedom Democrats set the stage for subsequent struggles for inclusion and "respect" for blacks in the Democratic Party.

The Jackson forces received little at the party's convention in San Francisco. In their fight to add four minority planks to the party's platform, the Jackson forces lost two (denouncing "first use" nuclear strikes by the United States and a commitment to reducing military spending); compromised on one, an affirmative action plank; and lost one, on the elimination of second primaries. Oddly, for a campaign directed toward the "dispossessed" only two of the four platforms dealt with issues that could be construed as "black interests": the elimination of run-off primaries, an electoral rule that was thought to disadvantage black candidates in the South; and support for stronger affirmative action policies. None of the platform fights directly addressed economic issues or promoted social policies focused on the poor.

The Jackson forces agreed to drop the word "quotas" that was embedded in the minority plank's language and settled on "verifiable measures," a phase that toned down efforts to assess the progress of affirmative action goals. But the Jackson forces insisted that the party support the run-off primary minority plank. They believed that in instances when black candidates received a plurality—but not the majority—of votes in the first primary, black candidates were more likely to lose in the second primary. (If no candidate received more than half the vote, the two largest vote getters were required to compete in a second primary election.) The Jackson forces argued that black candidates were more likely to lose because white voters often worked to defeat the black candidate in the second primary by giving all their votes to the white candidate. In the spirit of "fairness," the Jackson forces argued, the party should work to end the practice.

Mondale disagreed and refused to compromise. He deployed Atlanta Mayor Andrew Young to oppose the primary plank, sparking further outrage from Jackson supporters. Jackson delegates saw this move as Young "selling out" and felt that the former civil rights leader was being used by Mondale to put Jackson delegates in their place. Though the skirmishes among black politicians and activists at the 1972 Democratic Convention were contentious and fierce, and in 2008 tensions often ran high between black Clinton and black Obama supporters, nothing in the history of black convention politics compared to the battle that erupted among black delegates at the San Francisco convention.

In a speech given before the convention in defense of Mondale's position on the second primary, Andrew Young was met with boos and hisses by Jackson delegates. As Ethel Payne, the grande dame of black newspaper reporters, described it to her readers in the Baltimore *Afro-American*: "It was a pathetic spectacle of a once proud black symbol of courage and integrity who had been the close confidant of Martin Luther King Jr. now reduced to a Charley McCarthy wooden puppet mouthing the instructions of his handlers." The minority plank was soundly defeated, by a two to one margin. The Jackson delegates were furious. In a meeting before the Black Delegate Caucus the next day, Coretta Scott King chastised Jackson delegates for mistreating Young. Already in a frosty mood after hearing remarks by Mondale and his running mate, Geraldine Ferraro, that offered no consolation for the perceived betrayal, Mrs. King added fuel to the fire: "I'm here to support my mayor, Andrew Young . . . Those of you who wronged Andy Young need to say, 'I'm sorry,'" she lectured.

Catcalls, boos, and hisses erupted from the floor. When Mrs. King mentioned her long involvement in the civil rights movement, a heckler shouted, "What about today?" When she stated that everyone was entitled to free expression, another heckler quipped, "It don't justify prostitution." It was an empress-has-no-clothes moment for Mrs. King, who, as the widower of the martyred civil rights leader, was not accustomed to receiving public criticism. A tearful Mrs. King left the podium, stunned at the hostility she faced at the hands of Jackson supporters. As a ploy to calm passions, Jackson did his own chastising. "When I think about the roads I've walked with Andy and the leadership of Mrs. King," Jackson told the now-subdued audience, "she deserves to be heard." Jackson continued that it is "a source of embarrassment for me, for those of you who respect my leadership for you to boo or hiss any black leaders." In a move to redirect the delegates' discontent, Jackson stated: "Most of us are not mad because of what Andy did or Mrs. King did. That ain't the issue. Y'all mad because you came out here and the woman got the vice presidency, the south got Burt Lance, New York had the keynote speech [from Mario Cuomo] and [Charles] Manatt got the DNC, and you ain't got nothing."[25]

The Jackson forces still held out hope that concessions from Mondale would be forthcoming after the convention. Jackson still had one last card in his deck—the ability to influence black voter turnout in the November general election. He could either enthusiastically support the ticket or coolly signal to blacks that they should stay at home. Few blacks supported the idea that blacks should form their own political party (an option that has always been on the table by practitioners of independent black politics); only 13 percent of blacks supported the idea in 1984. But a majority—57 percent—reported in one poll that they would vote for Jackson if he decided to run as an independent candidate that November.[26]

Many Jackson supporters—and, increasingly, black Mondale supporters—were irritated with the Mondale camp's dismissive attitude toward black demands. Black interests were still not seriously considered, they complained. One source of irritation was that black Democrats—Jackson as well as Mondale supporters— were not being brought into the Mondale campaign. Even Andrew Young, who had stuck his neck out for Mondale on the second primary plank, expressed dismay, complaining that Mondale's advisors were all "smart-ass white boys who think they know it all." In a closed two-hour meeting of disgruntled black Democrats held that September, Mondale was grilled. Former Manhattan Borough President Percy Sutton and former Atlanta Mayor Maynard Jackson were the main questioners—Why wasn't the candidate committed to a black agenda?

Both inquisitors also demanded to know why Mondale was reluctant to support special job-creation programs for poor communities given the astronomically high levels of black unemployment. Mondale responded that fiscal restraint required that no

FIGURE 1.2 Jesse Jackson delegates at the Democratic National Convention (*Source*: Corbis).

such commitments could be made. He had pledged to cut the federal deficit by two-thirds, he told the group, and austerity measures required to stimulate the economy would have a "rising tide lifts all boats" effect, raising employment for everyone, including blacks. Then what ideas did Mondale have to curb black unemployment? Mondale agreed that if elected he would require greater minority employment participation in federally financed projects. Despite reservations, the group, dubbed the Black Leadership Family, unanimously endorsed Mondale. Afterward, Maynard Jackson and Detroit Mayor Coleman Young were appointed to high-level campaign positions, a move designed to quell doubts about the nominee's commitment to inclusion.[27]

Even if Mondale had agreed to all of Jackson's policy demands, the success of the independent strategy would have met the fate of the Reagan landslide. Reagan defeated Mondale in the second-worst electoral rout in modern American history. Reagan won forty-nine states. Mondale won his home state of Minnesota—by only 3,700 votes—and the majority-black District of Columbia. (McGovern fared worse in 1972 only because South Dakota had fewer electoral votes than Mondale's home state of Minnesota. Like Reagan, Nixon had also carried forty-nine states.)

Jackson ran again four years later, and this time he was prepared. With the support of prominent black politicians and civil rights leaders, and a better financed campaign, Jackson's Rainbow Coalition campaign was far more successful in 1988. Jackson's strong showing from black voters four years earlier put many black politicians and civil rights leaders on the spot; they found it difficult to explain to their black constituents and followers why they did not endorse Jackson's campaign. Relying less on passing the church collection plate to raise funds and more on conventional campaign techniques, such as direct-mail solicitation, Jackson was able to penetrate previously untapped sources of financial support from black business people and black professionals.

Jackson's campaign emphasis on social justice in 1984 gave way to a universal theme of combating "economic violence" against American workers in 1988. Jackson focused on expanding his coalition to include distressed white factory workers and family farmers, both of whom were marginalized by the economic policies of the Reagan administration. He opened his exploratory campaign office in Greenfield, Iowa, an agricultural hamlet of 2,200 people, nearly all white, just fifty miles from Des Moines. "There is something very wrong with an economy where Wall Street's profits soar while working people scramble; where the government talks about excellence, but cuts back on education, pays more attention to guns in Central America than jobs for Middle America," Jackson told a crowd in Greenfield.[28] Jackson marched with striking meat-packers in Dakota City, Nebraska, and rallied with displaced autoworkers in Kenosha, Wisconsin. The switch in strategy paid off. Jackson expanded his base and became a stronger contender. Even though Jackson made efforts to reach out to white voters, he never camouflaged his support for black issues or subsumed all the ills of black America under an umbrella of universalism. In all, Jackson received 29 percent of the total primary vote and earned 30 percent of convention delegates—a vast improvement from 1984— which put him in the range of winning the nomination.

For a moment it appeared that Jackson had a realistic chance of capturing the nomination. Jackson stunned political pundits— and himself—on March 26, 1988, when he handily defeated the frontrunner—Massachusetts Governor Michael Dukakis—in the Michigan Caucus, 54 to 29 percent. Though Jackson had a slight lead in popular votes over Dukakis before the victory in Michigan, because of party rules in the allocation of delegates, Jackson trailed Dukakis in the delegate count. After the win in Michigan, Jackson came within seven delegates of surpassing Dukakis. Jackson was gaining momentum, and the focus on universal issues and cross-racial coalition building was starting to pay off. Ann Lewis, a Jackson advisor (who later became a senior campaign advisor in Hillary Clinton's 2008 campaign), declared that Jackson's decisive victory in Michigan represented a "new political world."

Indeed, Jackson's victory shepherded in more of a new political world than Lewis and pundits may have realized. Though Jackson's victory in Michigan depended on a heavy turnout in two predominantly black congressional districts in Detroit, Jackson's success in Michigan demonstrated the inroads the candidate had accomplished in his pursuit of white voters. Besides winning Detroit, Jackson also carried the predominantly white cities of Grand Rapids, Kalamazoo, Lansing, and Saginaw. Analysts estimated that Jackson received somewhere between one-quarter to one-third of the white vote. This moment was a breakthrough not only for the Jackson campaign but also for black candidates in general. If a polarizing figure like Jesse Jackson could appeal to a significant number of white voters in 1988 by emphasizing universal issues, just think what a black candidate without racial baggage could do. The lessons learned from Jackson's success in that one contest reverberated for decades.[29]

However, Jackson's status as frontrunner was short-lived. Illinois Senator Paul Simon and Missouri Representative Richard Gephardt dropped out of the race after the Michigan Caucus, leaving Dukakis, Jackson, and Al Gore, who trailed last in a five-man field, to compete in the upcoming contests. In an effort to slow down Jackson's momentum, there appeared to be a "Stop Jesse" movement afoot. New York Governor Mario Cuomo began to be touted as a possible draft candidate. "A lot more Democrats are thinking more seriously about Mario Cuomo now," California Senator Alan Cranston declared after Jackson's win in Michigan. There was speculation that Gore decided to remain in the race—despite his anemic 2 percent performance in the Michigan Caucus—so that the white vote would split between him and Dukakis in the New York primary, a contest rich in delegates. Splitting the white vote, some thought, would ensure a Jackson victory and therefore ignite a draft-Cuomo campaign.[30]

Jackson performed poorly in two primaries before the New York contest. He placed a distant second to Dukakis in the Connecticut and Wisconsin primaries, which slowed Jackson's momentum. Though party leaders assured Jackson that there were no efforts underway to sabotage his campaign, Al Gore's attacks appeared to encourage a draft-Cuomo movement. Gore did not directly attack Jackson but attacked Dukakis, accusing the Massachusetts governor of "subtle racism" for handling Jackson with kid gloves. "If the country is going to mature to the point where we are color-blind and see candidates in terms of their ability and leadership," Gore proclaimed, "then we must be prepared to engage in the rough and tumble of politics."[31]

Dukakis's decision to not criticize Jackson because he was black, Gore surmised, gave Jackson a free pass—he held him to a "different standard" because of his race. Gore reminded Jewish voters of Jackson's "Hymietown" comment in 1984—an ethnic slur on Jews—and Gore received the endorsement of New York City Mayor Ed Koch, who appeared to be on a one-man crusade to end Jackson's campaign. (Koch stated that Jewish voters would be "crazy" to vote for Jackson and declared that if Jackson became president the country would go bankrupt in two weeks.) Dukakis defeated Jackson in New York—48 percent to 28 percent—and went on to capture the party's nomination. Gore received only 10 percent of the vote, far from the strong showing needed to throw the race for the nomination into a state of chaos. After another huge defeat, Gore finally decided to suspend his campaign.[32]

In the end, Jackson came in second behind Dukakis, winning eleven primary contests and garnering nearly seven million votes. Jackson captured 1,075 "earned" delegates, an impressive performance from a candidate who had relatively fewer resources and who many thought could not move beyond his black base. Dukakis received 1,790, and, with the backing of the party's superdelegates, he was assured the nomination. Jackson's strong second-place finish made him the frontrunner in the 1992 election (if Dukakis lost). As one political scientist estimated, "Simple extrapolation of geometric values of increase through 1992 would have made Jesse Jackson the 1992 Democratic Party nominee, with 47 percent of the primary vote and 75 percent of the convention delegates."[33] While the success of a Jackson nomination in 1992 would have been highly improbable given Jackson's consistently high negatives among white voters, a Jackson candidacy that year would have certainly hindered Bill Clinton's nomination—a victory that depended on the solid support of black voters.

The political dividends from Jackson's 1988 campaign yielded greater black inclusion in the Democratic Party. As Jackson told *Ebony* magazine readers in an October 1988 essay titled "What We Must Do," the tangible reward that the campaign netted for black America was greater influence within the Democratic Party. Nearly one-quarter of the delegates were black and 20 percent of all members who served on policymaking committees at the convention were black. (This level of convention participation by blacks would not be replicated until the 2008 Democratic Convention.) The success of the Jackson campaign "meant that for the first time in the history of American Politics Blacks had substantial impact on the proceedings, including the drafting of the policy platform." The progress that was made from the campaign, Jackson predicted, "will have a significant impact on the politics of the 21st century," planting political seeds that would ultimately "bear fruit."[34]

The Jackson campaign's surprise performance elevated Ron Brown—a long-time party activist and Jesse Jackson's advisor, and convention manager in 1988—to the chairmanship of the Democratic Party in 1989. Jackson's campaigns nurtured the careers of hundreds, if not thousands, of black party activists on the local, state, and national levels. Donna Brazile, who at the age of twenty-four was Jesse Jackson's campaign field director in 1984, became an operative in the 1984 Mondale campaign, served as Richard Gephardt's deputy campaign manager in the 1988 primary, and worked for Dukakis in the 1988 general election. In 2000, Brazile was Al Gore's campaign manager in the razor-thin loss to George W. Bush for president. That was the first time that either a woman or a black person managed the campaign of one of the two major parties' presidential nominee. Jackson "made it possible not just for blacks to sit at the black desk," Brazile observed years later, "but to sit at every desk in American politics."[35]

The infusion of black activists in the Democratic Party was not the only political dividend the Jackson campaigns produced. The campaigns ignited black registration and turnout, bringing in millions of new registered voters for the Democratic Party. These voters had an impact beyond the 1984 and 1988 elections. Heightened black voter participation helped the Democrats take back the Senate in 1986, which the Republicans had captured in the Reagan landslide in 1980. The power of the black vote was especially felt in the South where four white Democrats were elected to the Senate. In at least two cases—for Alabama conservative Richard Shelby and Louisiana moderate John Breaux—Democratic Senate candidates won with overwhelming black support but with less than a majority of the white vote. Returning the Senate back to the Democrats in 1986 helped defeat the Reagan administration's ultraconservative Supreme Court nominee Judge Robert Bork, who was anathema to civil rights groups and feminist organizations. The wave of black voter participation also created the conditions for David Dinkins's successful mayoral campaign in New York and L. Douglas Wilder's victory in the Virginia governor's race, both in 1989. These two victories were considered breakthroughs that ushered in yet another era of the "new black politics."

In 1988, Jackson built a multiracial coalition of the disaffected that included displaced factory workers and distressed family farmers. It was a campaign that reflected the politics that Bayard Rustin called for: building multiracial coalitions rather than Malcolm X's "ballot or the bullet" option on black political independence. Even though the Rainbow Coalition expanded its coalition in 1988, receiving over 90 percent of the black vote, one-third of the Latino vote, and one-fifth of the white vote, Jackson still made little headway in influencing the party's policy agenda. But exercising the strength of the impressive number of delegates he accumulated— an overwhelming majority of whom were black—Jackson was able to leverage change within the Democratic Party.

Indeed, Jackson's greatest contribution to Barack Obama's ascendency to the White House is an obscure rule change Jackson negotiated in 1988. Jackson had been complaining since the 1984 election that delegates were unfairly allocated. Candidates who did not meet a threshold of 20 percent of the vote in a congressional district were not allocated delegates, a rule that gave frontrunners an advantage in accumulating delegates. In addition to the threshold rule, there were other schemes that disadvantaged second-tier candidates. "Bonus" delegate provisions automatically awarded one delegate from each congressional district to the candidate who gained the most votes in the state (not the district), and "loophole" provisions circumvented party rules against winner-take-all contests by allowing voters to select delegates by voting for individuals running as a candidate's delegate rather than by delegates being distributed to the candidate based on the candidate's performance in a primary race. In some states, winner-take-all provisions were allowed on the district level. If a candidate received a majority of the popular vote, he or she received 100 percent of the delegates in a congressional district. And as former Colorado Senator Gary Hart discovered in 1984, superdelegates, the unelected delegates reserved for party leaders, disadvantaged "outside" candidates. Superdelegates can, if they wish, decide to throw their support behind the party's preferred candidate, a move that may—or may not—reflect the preferences of primary voters and elected delegates.

In 1988 Jackson demanded greater proportional representation and set out to change the rules. Jackson deployed Harold M. Ickes—a high-flying New York lawyer who would later serve as Deputy White House Chief of Staff for Bill Clinton—to head the negotiation team. Jackson prevailed. The Rules Committee agreed to fewer superdelegates; they were to be reduced by one-third, from 15 percent of all convention delegates to 10 percent by 1992. Winner-take-all, winner-take-more, and bonus delegates were thrown out. No longer could states like California, Illinois, Pennsylvania, and New Jersey unfairly allocate delegates to candidates who amassed the greatest number of votes in a primary. (The Jackson forces got the party to reduce the threshold provision from 20 percent to 15 percent before the 1988 contest. They eventually lost on superdelegate reform. Ron Brown, who was part of the Jackson team that negotiated fewer superdelegates, reinstated them after he became chair of the DNC in 1989.)

Twenty years later the outcome over the battle for fair allocation of delegates would be crucial to Obama's victory. Though Obama lost to Clinton in several big states, such as California, Pennsylvania, and New Jersey, winner-take-all primaries and other schemes that unfairly distributed delegates could have jeopardized Obama's nomination. Despite his second-place showing in delegate-rich states like Pennsylvania, Obama received his fair share of the delegates because of the "Jackson rule" that mandated greater proportional representation. Had these reforms not been successfully pushed by Jackson—only about half of 1 percent of the popular vote separated Clinton and Obama—Hillary Clinton would have most likely become the Democratic Party's nominee in 2008. It was the leveraging of black delegate power—in the spirit of independent black politics—that made it possible for a viable black candidate, whose politics is informed by the coalition school, to receive the Democratic nomination for president.

Current assessments of Jackson have focused on his moral lapses, questionable financial dealings, and the civil rights leader's anachronistic political rhetoric. When, in 2007, Jackson raised questions about why the Democratic primary contenders (with the exception of John Edwards) were not addressing issues of importance to minorities and the poor, Jackson was shot down in a newspaper editorial—"Dad, you're wrong"—penned by his own son, Jesse Jackson, Jr. It seems that Jackson's critics silenced legitimate questions—questions that Jackson had consistently posed to Democratic presidential candidates throughout his activist career—by silencing the messenger.

Jackson would be better remembered in 2008 not for his political contributions but for his off-the-camera remark on Fox News. Jackson whispered to a guest at the studio that Obama should have his "nuts cut off" for "talking down to black people." It is unclear if the tears Jackson shed before the world at Chicago's Grant Park after Obama clinched the presidency were tears of joy or regret. But a focus on Jackson the man misses the point. The Jackson campaigns did what could not have happened without the force of independent black politics: the incorporation of black political elites into the leadership structure of the national Democratic Party. The Jackson campaigns cultivated a cadre of black campaign activists in local and national politics—strategists, pollsters, office coordinators, fundraisers, and speechwriters—and altered party rules that made the presidential nomination process fairer for all candidates. These contributions are not trivial. They created the conditions that contribute to the mainstreaming of black political life today, as blacks enter another "new" phase of politics.

Projecting into the future, Baltimore Congressman Parren Mitchell asked the following question in 1984 when black delegates hissed and booed Andrew Young and Coretta Scott King when they fell out of favor: "If ten years from now, Jesse is still on the scene and he takes an unpopular position, will he be booed after all he's done?" It would take more than ten years, twenty-four to be exact, before Jackson's comedy of errors made him an unpopular character in an unfolding drama. The passions that erupted when a more viable black candidate ran for president would further push this former presidential contender into a state of irrelevancy. But the independent movement he led for change in the Democratic Party would have long-lasting effects that even Jackson, himself, might not have foreseen. In 2008, it helped pave the road to victory.[36]

However, the struggles in national black politics reveal only part of the story about how black politics cleared the path for Obama's election. What converged with efforts on the national level was the rise in local black politics, particularly in Chicago, where blacks fought against and, for a short period, defeated the city's Democratic Party machine. Those local battles in Chicago helped to propel Obama onto the national political scene.

2

Chicago: The Political Capital of Black America

ON THE WEEKEND of September 24, 1971, a group of black politicians and civil rights activists gathered at what was supposed to be an undisclosed location in Northlake, Illinois, a town a few miles north of Chicago's O'Hare Airport. The meeting's out-of-the-way location was chosen to keep who was attending a secret. Luminaries in the world of black politics were there in full force—Mayor Richard Hatcher of Gary, Indiana; Manhattan Borough President Percy Sutton; Georgia State Representative Julian Bond; Texas State Senator Barbara Jordan; Black Power activist Imamu Amiri Baraka; and civil rights activists Jesse Jackson, Vernon Jordan, and Coretta Scott King among many others. Though the attendees traveled near and far, they converged near Chicago—the place that had long been the center of black electoral politics.

Dodging reporters, who had caught wind of the meeting, attendees refused to give statements to the press on their arrival at the hotel. Roy Innis, head of the Congress of Racial Equality, offered the only public statement to reporters prior to the proceedings, before ducking into an elevator: "This must be the biggest secret since the atomic bomb." To ensure that intruders would not disrupt the deliberations, guards were posted at the hotel entrance, as well as at the bottom of a spiral staircase, which led to the meeting room. There, in an unusual display of unity of purpose, a cross-section of black leaders faced off on the question of whether a black person should run for president in 1972. The Northlake summit was the second of three meetings held in the Chicago area that year. The regular meetings in the city signaled Chicago's designation as the mecca of black politics.[1]

Some thirty-five years later on February 3, 2007, Chicago's influence in the world of national black politics was again at play. Emil Jones, the influential president of the Illinois State Senate and Barack Obama's "political Godfather," caused a stir during a closed-door meeting of black Democrats in Washington, DC. Speaking before a divided group of the party faithful—some supporting Obama, others supporting Hillary Clinton, and many undecided—Jones took hold of a microphone and began to browbeat party activists committed to candidates other than Obama. "How long do we have to owe before we have an opportunity to support our son?" Jones asked the approximately one hundred black party activists.

Jones questioned blacks' loyalty to the former president and his wife by telling the group that they didn't "owe" anything to anybody—a thinly veiled reference to the Clintons. He admonished the crowd against acting like "crabs in a barrel" by diminishing Obama's prospects of rising as the Democratic Party's first black nominee for president. "How long, how long" was a refrain heard throughout the corridors of the Washington Hilton that weekend, as party activists jokingly—but with a hint of seriousness—pondered the decision to back a viable black candidate for president or support the spouse of a former president who commanded enormous popularity in black America.[2]

Chicago has been at the epicenter of black politics for generations—long before it hosted secret meetings that plotted strategies to elect a black president or produced a powerful politician who would propel the political career of the nation's first black president. The South Side of Chicago's status as the citadel of black political life has a lengthy and deep history. Illinois' First Congressional District, which has been anchored for generations in Bronzeville—historically the cultural, social, and economic hub of black Chicago—has continuously elected a black person to Congress for over eighty years.

In 1928 Oscar De Priest was elected as a Republican from the South Side, becoming the first black member of Congress since North Carolina's George White departed in 1901. De Priest's election signaled the South Side's growing political influence. The sprawling area's rising power was generated by the massive migration of southern blacks to the city during the first decades of the twentieth century. As the first black congressman in the new century, De Priest was not only a representative from Chicago's South Side, he was also a national voice—a lone surrogate in Congress—for blacks across the country. Indeed, De Priest's slim victory in 1928 made him a national symbol: "Admired by Negroes and feared by many whites," wrote University of Chicago political scientist Harold F. Gosnell in the 1935 landmark book *Negro Politicians: The Rise of Negro Politics in Chicago*. As one black newspaper in Washington, DC, reported at the time, De Priest was "easily the outstanding man of the race," becoming "the National idol, inspiring, and to some extent uniting the race." His election, the newspaper asserted, had given blacks across the country "new hope, new courage, new inspiration."[3]

Indeed for many black Americans, De Priest's role as the "race man" in Congress—that is, a black man challenging racism in the interest of black progress—gave some legitimacy to the claim that black people had a stake in the political system. Though De Priest provided little substantive representation for his constituents—he offered few bills, amendments, or speeches on the House floor—his election stood for black progress. "His seat in Congress represented a symbol of Negro achievement," Gosnell wrote of the meaning the South Side seat held in black America. "It stood for the recapturing of a banished hope. It meant that the Negro was part of the national government."[4]

FIGURE 2.1 Oscar De Priest, a black congressman from Chicago, campaigning (*Source*: Getty Images).

Conventional wisdom has it that Harlem was, and still remains, the center of black political life. Adam Clayton Powell, Jr., and a host of other black politicians working within—and at times against—Tammany Hall amassed political influence. During the 1960s Powell rose as a national spokesman for civil rights in Congress and used his political influence to push for progressive social policies. But Harlem lagged behind Chicago in achieving political milestones. New York didn't elect its first black member to Congress until 1944, when Powell joined Chicago's William Dawson, who was elected two years earlier. By the time Powell reached Washington, Dawson was Chicago's third black congressman elected from the city's South Side (following Arthur Mitchell, the first black Democrat elected to Congress). For sixteen straight years Chicago's First Congressional District was the only seat in Congress represented by an African American.

Chicago also had a black mayor before New York. Elected in 1983, Harold Washington became mayor of Chicago six years before David Dinkins became mayor of New York. And Chicago reelected Washington while Dinkins lost his bid for a second term. Though Harlem has elected politicians to statewide offices, such as secretary of state and state comptroller (and an African American elevated from lieutenant governor to governor to fill a vacancy), the South Side has produced three United States senators (including one who was appointed). The three South Siders in the United States Senate—Carol Moseley Braun, Barack Obama, and Roland Burris—account for half of the six blacks ever to serve in the chamber. (The South Side also produced Massachusetts Governor Deval Patrick who along with Douglass Wilder of Virginia are the only blacks to serve as governors since the Reconstruction era.)

The South Side is also home to Jesse Jackson, Sr., the Democratic Party's first serious black presidential contender, as well as to Carol Moseley Braun, who ran a short-lived campaign for president in 2004. The South Side's record of achievement in black politics is unsurpassed by any other black community in the nation. (Reverend Al Sharpton—whose National Action Network is in Harlem—is the only black New Yorker to run for president in the Democratic Party primary. Sharpton's presidential hopes were abandoned after he placed third in the South Carolina primary in 2008.) It seemed that when the country was ready to elect a black president, he or she, in all probability, would rise from the South Side of Chicago.

Black Chicago's legacy is no mere coincidence. It is the result of paradoxical forces—not necessarily of the black community's own making. The geographic concentration of the city's black population—a direct consequence of Chicago's shameful history of racially segregated housing—is one reason for the South Side's reputation as a power base. The contiguous black neighborhoods on the city's South Side and West Side have a high concentration of black voters who have propelled black politicians to citywide, countywide, and statewide offices. The other explanation for black Chicago's reputation has to do with blacks' complicated relationship to the city's powerful Democratic "machine." For many years Chicago's blacks were junior partners in the one-party organization that dominated politics throughout the city.

During the heyday of Richard J. Daley's reign as mayor, a black submachine—presided over by Congressman William "Boss" Dawson and later by his successor Congressman Ralph Metcalf—produced an army of black precinct captains, ward committeemen, and elected officials that oiled the wheels of the machine on the city's South Side. Historically, blacks in New York faced a far different set of circumstances. The dispersal of the city's black population in five boroughs undermined the ability of black New Yorkers to mobilize the type of political solidarity that developed in Chicago. Each borough has its own brand of "club house" party politics, a situation that further divided black politicians and voters where the black population was already separated by geography.

Thus it should be no surprise that of all the places Obama could have started his political career, he chose the South Side of Chicago. He first moved there in 1985 to work as a community organizer and left in 1989 to start law school at Harvard University. He returned after graduating in 1992, settling in Hyde Park, in the vicinity of one of the most politically active black communities in the country. "If you are interested not only in politics in general but interested in the future of the African-American community," Obama told a reporter in 1996 when he first ran for public office, then "Chicago in many ways is the capital of the African-American community in the country."[5]

South Siders favor their native sons and daughters over politicians they perceive as interlopers. Even political aspirants from the city's West Side find it difficult to crack the South Side's dominance in black Chicago's civic life. For those not born or raised in the city—"We don't know nobody nobody sent" Chicago pols say of suspicious up-and-comers—the unfamiliar must earn their stripes. Either by battling rivals inside the machine or fighting to topple the machine, black politicians in Chicago try to prove their worth as representatives of "the people." For Obama, his career as a South Side politician quickly paid dividends, despite being relatively new to the scene. Within just twelve years, Obama won three Illinois State Senate contests, lost a congressional House race, was elected to the United States Senate, and became president of the United States. This is a remarkable accomplishment for any politician, let alone one who did not come up through the traditional ranks of Chicago politics.

Black politics in Chicago has traditionally produced two types of political independents. One group works in coalition with Hyde Park reformers—mostly upper-middle-class whites living in the neighborhood anchored by the University of Chicago. These black independents are interested in progressive politics and government reform. The other group of black political independents operates separately from white reformers and has traditionally been influenced by the ideas of Black Nationalism. They are primarily committed to using the electoral process as a vehicle to challenge racial inequality and less concerned about making government more efficient. Past state senators Richard Newhouse, Alice Palmer, Barack Obama, and Cook County Board President Toni Preckwinke represent the Hyde Park black independents. They rely on a biracial coalition of voters to elect them to office. (Obama's willingness to cooperate with machine politicians to get things done in Springfield made him less of a purist than Palmer, Newhouse, or Preckwinke.)

The late political activist Lu Palmer, former Second Congressional District Congressman Gus Savage, and First Congressional District Congressman Bobby Rush represent the Black Nationalist independents. Adopting the rhetoric of Black Power, these independents instruct blacks to free themselves from the grip of the machine's "plantation politics" so that blacks can amass true political power in the city. Both groups of black independents work within the Democratic Party. However, Black Nationalist–inspired independents believe in developing political empowerment among blacks before building coalitions with other groups.

These black independents occasionally formed third-party alternatives to the Democrats, which helped to unhinge the machine's near-unanimous support from black voters.

Nonetheless, it was difficult for both types of black independents to successfully challenge the machine. Not only did the black submachine dispense city jobs and personal favors to supporters, it also produced skilled politicians who were able to leverage benefits for their communities. As long as machine loyalists brought in the votes for the party's candidates and avoided raising racial issues, the party rewarded them. "The machine honored the minor political quid pro quo in dealing with black voters, exchanging small favors for votes," political scientist William Grimshaw explains, "but the machine did very little to ameliorate the racial segregation and discrimination which devastated the black community . . . The machine played a leading role in confining blacks to second-class levels of citizenship." Thus, fighting racial inequality in Chicago became paramount to fighting the machine.[6]

The machine not only produced black politicians who extracted favors for their constituents, it also produced renegades: machine loyalists who ended up abandoning the party and working toward its demise. By the late 1960s and early 1970s, blacks were growing increasingly impatient with the machine's silence—if not complicity—on issues like police brutality, housing segregation, and crowded public schools. Joining forces with community activists and black independents of both stripes, machine renegades sowed seeds of change during the 1970s.

Lu Palmer was an activist's activist. If there is one individual who single-handedly built the organization that led to Washington's election as mayor, it's Lu Palmer. Fed up with the racism he faced as an op-ed columnist for the *Chicago Daily News*, Palmer quit his job at the paper in 1972 and thereafter worked as a full-time community activist and an independent journalist. Palmer wrote for black newspapers, including one he started on his own, and became a talk show host on WVON, a black-owned radio station in the city. By the late 1970s, Palmer was rising as a popular voice of dissent in black Chicago. Not only did he raise issues about how blacks were treated in the city, Palmer began to do something about it. He started by organizing informally. In 1980 he brought together a small group of black activists and intellectuals that regularly met in his basement for two years, discussing issues that affected blacks in the city. Those talks led to discussions about the need to run a black candidate for mayor in 1983.

Palmer and his group founded Chicago Black United Communities (CBCU). Holding sessions in a coach house behind his South Side home, Palmer and CBCU members taught classes on activism to hundreds who fanned out across the South Side and West Side registering blacks to vote. The training was taken so seriously that a graduation ceremony was held for each class completing the course. In 1982 Palmer co-founded the Task Force for Black Political Empowerment, which served as an umbrella group for grass-roots organizations supporting Washington's candidacy.

Ideologically rigid with an abrasive manner, Palmer was the type of community activist who naturally rises from communities under siege. People such as Palmer view themselves not as political organizers—as Obama described his foray into activism on the South Side—but as political activists. Though the terms activist and organizer are used interchangeably, there is a subtle but important difference between the two. Political activists are from the communities they serve. Organizers, on the other hand, are usually outsiders who go into communities to serve. They are recruited—and often paid—by advocacy organizations to mobilize community activists and institutions that are indigenous to the communities.[7]

In the mid-1980s, Obama was hired as a political organizer to bring together black and white workers facing steel-plant closings on the city's far South Side. As an organizer Obama targeted black churches to get residents involved in the campaign. Nearly a decade later, Obama was part of a legal team working to ensure fair minority representation in city council wards and state legislative districts

after boundaries were redrawn. He then managed a voter registration campaign targeting black voters. A few years later, Obama left
the world of activism and started his career as a politician.

Political organizers like Obama often engage in short-term campaigns to mobilize communities. The goals of community organizers are usually narrowly confined to specific issues, such as housing,
employment, the environment, or voter registration. Political activists, on the other hand, confront multiple issues at once and are
engaged in the life of their communities for the long haul. They
are deeply committed to changing the conditions of their communities because they have deep roots in the communities they serve.
Activists are compelled to challenge injustice not because of an
abstract principle—"to change the world"—but because of a desire
to address the immediate needs that their communities face.

This organic form of black activism is what sociologist Charles
M. Payne calls the *organizing tradition*. Though the organizing
tradition may be confused with what community organizers do, it
really encompasses what political activists do. The tradition entails
a bottom-up, nonhierarchical form of activism where the day-to-day
grunt work of organizing for change is par for the course. This tradition also entails teaching others about activism: the idea of "each
one teach one." Activists engaged in this sort of organizing realize
that episodic campaigns or charismatic leaders cannot sustain
movements for change. Activism centered on intermittent campaigns or which relies on charismatic figures reinforces the idea—
and practices—that oppressed communities need a messiah to save
them. Though civil rights activists like Ella Baker and Septima
Clark harnessed the organizing tradition during the 1950s and
1960s, remnants of that tradition could be found decades later on
the eve of Washington's successful mayoral election in 1983.[8]

In his efforts to mobilize support behind the election of a black
mayor, Lu Palmer became a jack-of-all-trades. In addition to his
responsibilities as a talk show host, Palmer trained organizers,
managed strategy meetings, hosted political rallies, and staged
protest demonstrations through working with the CBCU and the

Task Force for Black Political Empowerment. Bridging scholarly research and activism, Palmer along with other activists organized the conference "Toward a Black Mayor" at Malcolm X Community College in 1981. The conference brought together academics and community activists to discuss the prospects of electing a black mayor of Chicago. The conference added gravity to existing grass-roots efforts to oust Mayor Jane Byrne and elect a black mayor. Byrne, who in 1979 ran as a reform candidate with the support of black voters, had become anathema to blacks during her stint as mayor. Once she became mayor, Byrne carried on the old-style machine tactics of her predecessors. She allowed discrimination to persist in the allocation of city jobs and neighborhood services. Byrne also reneged on promises to appoint blacks to her adminis-tration. Far from a break from the past, the problems of police brutality, education, and housing for blacks continued—and in some cases worsened—under Byrne's administration.

To ensure that the search for a black mayoral candidate reflected the sentiments of the community, CBCU developed a survey that asked blacks across the city to select the candidate they favored most for mayor. This was independent black politics in action. Palmer saw the need to build solidarity in the black community before establish-ing coalitions with whites and other groups. Mailed to over thirty-five thousand black households, the results were used to democratically choose the community's preferred candidate. CBCU's survey showed—along with a couple of other surveys gauging black opinion—that Harold Washington was the leading favorite to challenge Mayor Byrne. CBCU hosted a plebiscite—led by Palmer—to determine who would be the community's candidate. It was attended by hundreds of leaders of grass-roots organizations across the city. Washington was unanimously endorsed by the plebiscite.

Despite widespread support for his candidacy, Washington was reluctant. Washington had successfully run for Congress in the First Congressional District, handily defeating the machine-backed incumbent Bennett Stewart in 1980. Washington politically strad-dled the fence between Black Nationalist–inspired independent politics and good-government reformers. He started out as a machine politician but became a machine renegade after his defeat in the special Democratic primary election for mayor in 1977. Michael Bilandic, the machine-backed candidate, who was hand-picked by white aldermen to replace Richard J. Daley after his death on December 20, 1976, won easily. Black alderman Wilson Frost, who served as president pro tem of the city council and was next in line to replace Daley, was bypassed by the machine. Over-looking Frost added to the growing black dissatisfaction with the party. "I'm going to do which maybe I should have done 10 or 12 years ago," Washington declared after his defeat. "I'm going to stay outside the damn Democratic Party and give it hell."[9]

In the run-up to the 1983 primary, Washington agreed to be a candidate on one condition—that fifty thousand blacks be placed to the voting rolls. When that goal was reached, Washington upped the ante, demanding fifty thousand more. In total, over one hundred thousand new registrants were placed on the rolls. Washington agreed to run. Five years after placing fourth in the 1977 Demo-cratic primary race for mayor, Washington was victorious in the primary. The push to defeat Byrne—a movement that was simul-taneously about accountability and black political empowerment —was accomplished by building solidarity within Chicago's ideo-logically and economically diverse black communities. That coali-tion brought together black voters from the South Side and West Side, middle class and poor, machine and independent, Black Nationalists and coalitionists. It energized black communities in Chicago like never before.

As Abdul Akalimat and Doug Gills, two scholar-activists involved in the campaign, recalled a few years later, the movement to elect Washington was something never seen before among Chicago blacks, or since:

> There were many Lazarus-like winos and street people in the campaign who put on ties, picked up notebooks, pens, and pencils—not merely to vote, but to advocate that others do

so also . . . Women's groups united under the Women's Network in Support of Harold Washington, where middle-class highbrows joined hands with welfare recipients. Youth joined together with senior citizens who had passed the baton of active struggle to those younger. The elderly, many of whom had been trapped in their highrises for years in fear, walked in defiance (of the gangs) to "punch 9" and await the unfolding of their wildest dreams—a black mayor in their lifetimes.[10]

The coalition that coalesced around Washington's candidacy in 1983 was one of the most spectacular insurgent movements in the history of urban politics.

Though Washington's success as a candidate is celebrated today as a model for coalition politics and stands as a testament to the virtues of race-neutral politics, Washington's victory in 1983 and later in 1987 were hardly kumbaya moments. Unlike black candidates today in high-stakes elections who run in predominantly white districts, Washington did not avoid raising questions about racial inequality. "We have given the white candidates our vote for years and years and years," Washington told a majority black audience two days before he declared his candidacy. "Now it's our turn, it's our turn, it's our turn."[11]

Washington acknowledged the racist legacy of Chicago politics and did not hold his tongue. When asked, for instance, whether he had the "good qualities" of past Chicago mayors, Washington let loose:

There are no good qualities of [past] mayors to be had. None. None. None. None. I did not mourn at the bier of the late mayor. I regret anyone dying. I have no regrets about him leaving. He was a racist from the core, head to toe, hip to hip. There's no doubt about it. And he spewed and fought and oppressed black people to the point that some thought that that's the way they suppose to live. Just like some slaves on the plantation thought that was the way they suppose to live.[12]

Mentioning Richard J. Daley's legacy, no doubt, recalled past atrocities meted out against Chicago blacks over the years. Those atrocities became part of the collective memory of black Chicago— Daley's shoot-to-kill orders during riots that were triggered by Martin Luther King's assassination in 1968; the Chicago police's planned night-raid that murdered Black Panthers Mark Clark and Fred Hampton in 1969; and the death of Dr. Daniel Claiborne, a seventy-year-old dentist who suffered a stroke while driving and died in police custody without medical attention in 1972.

Washington linked this legacy to the son of the late mayor, Richard J. Daley. The son of the former mayor was at the time Cook County's state's attorney and a candidate for mayor in the 1983 Democratic primary. Washington accused Daley of riding on his dead father's coattails. "I give no hosannas to a racist, nor do I appreciate or respect his son," Washington declared to an audience during a campaign speech. "If his name were anything else but Daley, his campaign would be a joke. He has nothing to offer anybody but a bit-of-a-tin-can smile, no background, and he runs on the legacy of his name, an insult to common sense and decency."[13] Washington was no less direct in his assessment of the incumbent mayor, Jane Byrne. During a televised debate, Washington told the audience: "There are those who believe I should avoid the race issue but I will not avoid it because it permeates our entire city and has devastating implications . . . I'm running to end Jane Byrne's four-year effort to further institutionalized racial discrimination in this great city."[14]

On February 22, 1983, Washington won the mayoral Democratic primary in a stunning upset. With 80 percent of the black vote, Washington barely squeaked by Byrne and Daley, receiving 36 percent of the total vote. Byrne and Daley—splitting the white vote—received 34 percent and 30 percent, respectively. As a result of the massive black voter registration campaign, blacks surpassed whites in voter registration, 87 percent to 82 percent, and equaled whites' voter-turnout rate of 64 percent. Latinos—whose voter registration and turnout were considerably lower than blacks and whites—distributed their votes among the three candidates, giving a plurality to Byrne (45 percent), nearly one-third to Daley (30 percent), and one-quarter to Washington (25 percent).[15]

The candidate who wins the Democratic primary in Chicago normally coasts to victory in the general election—but Chicago's white Democrats abandoned their party's nominee, instead choosing Barnard Epton, the Republican nominee, who until then was a little-known former state representative. Epton emerged as the "Great White Hope" candidate in a city that had not elected a Republican mayor since 1927. Epton's strategy was to exploit the racial fears of white voters. The Republican candidate ran a campaign commercial that asked (white) voters to get behind his candidacy "before it's too late." Nevertheless, Washington prevailed, garnering 52 percent of the total vote, receiving a minuscule 12 percent of the white vote and an astonishing 99 percent of the black vote. What put Washington over the top was the support he received from Latino voters, who stuck with the Democratic Party's nominee by giving Washington 82 percent of their vote. When the votes were all counted, the racial composition of Washington's electoral coalition only slightly changed. Blacks comprised 80 percent of Washington's vote tally, while Latino voters and white voters contributed 7 percent and 13 percent, respectively.[16]

Years and decades later, political analysts and reporters celebrated Washington as a coalition builder. But a truly broad-based multiracial coalition never transpired in 1983 or in 1987 when Washington ran for reelection. Though as mayor Washington promised—and executed—fairness in the distribution of resources to neighborhoods across the city, he still could not muster a plurality of the white vote when he ran for reelection. The mayor assured whites that his administration would be "fairer than fair," a stance that alienated some of his supporters—particularly Lu Palmer—who thought that since the black community had been neglected for so long by former mayors Daley, Bilandic, and Byrne, Washington should direct more resources to the black community. To further demonstrate his commitment to fairness, Washington assembled a racially diverse team of department heads and advisors in his administration. Because of the deep divisions between pro-Washington and anti-Washington forces on the city council—a battle known as the "Council Wars"—Washington accomplished little in his first term.

David Axelrod, who in 2008 was one of Obama's chief campaign strategists, helped to keep the mayor's winning coalition intact in 1987, as Washington's media advisor. Washington won 53 percent of the vote in a head-to-head primary contest against former mayor Jane Byrne. With black and Latino voters solidly backing his ree-lection, Washington spent 60 to 70 percent of his time campaign-ing in predominantly white neighborhoods. Axelrod remembered, years later, Washington's disappointment in capturing only 20 percent of the white vote. While Washington's advisors celebrated the increased support from white voters—almost double the 1983

FIGURE 2.2 Mayoral candidate Harold Washington gives the victory sign (*Source*: Corbis).

percentage—Washington could not contain his disappointment. "Ain't it a bitch to be a black man in the land of the free and the home of the brave," Axelrod recalled Washington saying. Having to grin and bear the news of the weak support he received from white voters, Washington, Axelrod related, gave a "joyous and rollicking" press conference the morning after the primary.[17]

But the election was still not over for the incumbent mayor. Washington's nemesis in the city council, Alderman Edward "Fast Eddie" Vrdolyak, who led the twenty-nine white aldermen who opposed Washington's initiatives in the council, was Washington's opponent in the general election. Vrdolyak ran as the candidate on the "Solidarity Party" ticket even though he held the chairmanship of the Cook County Democratic Central Committee. Thus as the head of the Democratic Party, Vrdolyak ran against his own party's nominee for mayor. Washington won with 54 percent of the vote, a 1 percent improvement over his performance in the Democratic primary.

Though Washington is used to fit the script of Barack Obama's ascendancy in Chicago politics, Obama is more of an inheritor of Washington's legacy rather than an extension of Washington's politics and the movement that put him in office. In a political environment as racially charged as Chicago was then, the race-neutral politics that Obama adopted for his political career would not have worked for Washington. On Thanksgiving eve, November 25, 1987, six months after his reelection, Washington died of a heart attack. The electoral coalition he forged unraveled. (Alderman Eugene Sawyer, a black machine-loyalist who received the support of Vrdolyak and his henchmen to serve as acting mayor until a special election, was defeated by Daley in the 1989 Democratic primary.) It would take years before a black politician could successfully build on the coalition that Washington assembled.

Though the coalition fell apart, Washington's winning formula in the 1983 primary survived. The formula was simple. One viable black candidate running with solid black support against multiple white candidates splitting the white vote had a more than even chance of winning in a citywide, statewide, or countrywide contest.

Nine years after Washington's 1983 victory, the Washington formula elected Carol Moseley Braun to the United States Senate. Braun, who at the time was Cook County's recorder of deeds, tossed her hat into the race. Her opponents were the incumbent Alan Dixon and Al Hofeld, a millionaire lawyer with no prior political experience. Braun won the primary by a margin of 3 percentage points, edging out Dixon 38 percent to 35 percent. Hofeld, who spent his own money running negative television commercials against Dixon, received 27 percent of the vote.

These results mirrored Washington's three-candidate primary race in 1983. But in 1992 Braun went beyond what Washington accomplished. With the solid support of black voters—Obama directed a voter registration campaign that put over one hundred thousand blacks on the roll—Braun was able to build on the Washington formula beyond the boundaries of the City of Chicago. In the "collar counties," the ring of mostly white suburban counties surrounding Cook County, Braun ran neck in neck with Hofeld, and outpaced Dixon. Most of her support from the collar counties came from women, many outraged by Dixon's vote to confirm Clarence Thomas to the Supreme Court, whose nomination hearings were marred by accusations of sexual harassment. Braun received 60 percent of the votes cast by women.[18]

The only part of the state where Braun trailed her two opponents was in the conservative downstate counties. Richard Williamson, the Republican nominee for the U.S. Senate seat, tried to link Braun to Jesse Jackson and Harold Washington in television ads to undermine Braun's support from white voters. But to no avail. In Williamson's estimation he was losing because voting for "a non-threatening African American makes many people feel good." The Democratic nominee would go on that November to handily defeat Williamson with 53 percent of the vote. "We have made history," Braun declared to a cheering crowd at her victory party. She told supporters her winning represented a triumph over old divisions that separated Americans. "You are showing the way for our entire country in the future," Braun asserted. "You have shown what we can do when we come together, when we stop dividing us along race lines and gender lines."[19] Obama would make a similar point about the need to bridge racial and partisan divisions more than a decade later during his campaign for the presidency.

Braun's 1992 breakthrough was not the only election that year that had implications for Obama's political future. A congressional contest on the far South Side, in the Second Congressional District, foreshadowed Obama's challenge to Congressman Bobby Rush in 2000. The Second Congressional District contest pitted Mel Reynolds, a Rhodes scholar, community activist, foundation executive, and Roosevelt University college professor, against five-term incumbent Gus Savage. Savage, a pugnacious and controversial Black Nationalist independent, finally lost to Reynolds, after two previous challenges by Reynolds. The Reynolds-Savage race was marked as much by generational differences—Reynolds was forty when he defeated the sixty-seven-year-old Savage—as by ideological fissures. Savage had been a firebrand political independent even before the rise of the Daley machine in the mid-1950s, and he served as Harold Washington's campaign manager during Washington's bid for mayor in 1977. Savage was also a longtime community activist. During the 1940s he was part of a group of Roosevelt University students who desegregated restaurants in downtown Chicago.

Like the aura that surrounded Obama's political climb in the "City of Big Shoulders," Mel Reynolds—the Rhodes scholar—had at his disposal the support of the mainstream media, national Democratic Party officials, and wealthy contributors bankrolling his campaign. Moving into the district just two years before he first challenged Savage, Reynolds became active in several community organizations. He worked with an all-black environmental group that fought the development of more landfills on the city's southeast side. He also became an active member of the South Side branch of the NAACP, winning a position on the branch's board in 1989. Reynolds later established a foundation—with the financial backing of the Irving Harris Foundation—that supported a student role-model program.

Reynolds's political ambitions far exceeded a congressional seat. This Rhodes scholar wanted to be president. In his quest, Reynolds appeared unwilling to consider any office below Congress—a stance that even surprised some of his supporters. As one activist who supported Reynolds recalled, "We asked [Reynolds] to run for alderman in one of the south-side wards and he brushed us off, saying 'I am not starting at that level. I'm going to be president.'"[20]

The campaign generated support beyond the Second Congressional District. While Obama attracted attention for being the first black editor of the *Harvard Law Review*, Reynolds gained establishment credentials by being the first black in Illinois to become a Rhodes scholar. As Obama would do years later, Reynolds befriended members of the Kennedy family. Reynolds once sailed the coast of Cape Cod with Ted Kennedy and Bobby Shriver, Kennedy's nephew, whom Reynolds met during a brief stint at Yale. He worked on Ted Kennedy's presidential election in 1980, serving as a campaign coordinator in Illinois; he also campaigned for Jesse Jackson in 1984. During his work in national Democratic Party politics Reynolds met Ron Brown, who, in 1989, as mentioned, became the first black to lead the national party.

In the *Chicago Reader*, the city's liberal independent weekly, Reynolds was described as a breath of fresh air: "He speaks softly, clearly, with an earnestness that can be off-putting," the puff-piece read. Clearly, in the estimation of the *Chicago Reader*'s reporter Reynolds was a politician to watch in the future. One could infer from the article that the candidate's education, demeanor, and "moderate" beliefs about race were (and are) the attributes that make for a black presidential candidate:

> There is in Reynolds's seriousness, puritanism, and piety an ambition so overarching that it is a little bit frightening. This is a man so determined to overcome those early days of poverty and discrimination that he can say to someone, quite seriously, "I'm going to be president." Yet he is a highly educated man who is immensely proud of the moderation his education has taught him.[21]

In 1990 it looked as though Reynolds was going to unseat Savage. Reynolds received endorsements from the city's two major newspapers, the *Chicago Tribune* and the *Chicago Sun-Times*. The conservative business daily *Crain's Chicago* did not endorse Reynolds but enthusiastically reported that the candidate "prefers to downplay race as a factor in politics." And as one Reynolds supporter explained, Reynolds "can do what Gus can't. He can make coalitions. Harold Washington had the same broad support—whites and Hispanics—and he wasn't branded as a racist or accused of being the white man's candidate."[22]

To neutralize criticism that he was not a man of the people, Reynolds deployed an up-from-poverty story to connect with residents in the district. "I'm not an establishment guy," Reynolds told *Crain's Chicago*. "I have establishment credentials, but I'm a poor kid from a poor background."[23] Yet, Reynolds's story of overcoming poverty while growing up on the city's West Side did not convince some critics, who continued to believe that the challenger was being used as a tool of powerful whites. And Reynolds's accomplishment as a Rhodes scholar only fueled suspicions. Some wondered whether a black man with a degree from Oxford could relate to residents on the South Side. The anti-intellectual tenor of the campaign so bothered one Reynolds supporter that he thought the criticism was sending the wrong message to black youth in the district. "Some people are saying he's an 'Oxfordian' and make it a negative . . . The message they're giving is don't go out and try a Rhodes scholarship because then the community don't accept you. That's insanity."[24]

Illinois State Senator Howard Brookins, who lost to Savage in 1988 and decided against running again, felt outgunned by Reynolds. Reynolds was an unknown who had never been elected to public office, and Brookins wondered how Reynolds was able to amass so much money and media attention. "White politicians have bought and paid for a novice who wasn't even a block captain, or a community leader, even a member of a recognized church," Brookins grumbled. "There's something wrong. His whole staff comes out of City Hall. And that tells you they're being supplied to him to get rid of Savage."[25]

Despite the funding, endorsements, campaign workers, and positive media coverage, Reynolds still fell short in 1990. Savage won the race with 51 percent of the vote. Reynolds received 43 percent, an improvement from 1988 when Reynolds placed a distant third with 14 percent of the vote.

But by 1992 Savage was imploding. His behavior had become even more bizarre than usual. When the congressman was confronted at O'Hare Airport by a reporter who questioned Savage about sexual harassment charges filed against him by a Peace Corps worker in Zaire, Savage told the reporter to "get the fuck out of my face." As news cameras rolled, Savage called the reporter a "faggot" and deflected his questions by asking: "Are you still messing with little boys?" and "Are you still wearing your wife's underwear?"[26] The congressman had generated so much ill will that a brigade of reporters, politicians, Democratic Party activists, and campaign contributors were mobilized to ensure his defeat. Though Savage had one of the most liberal voting records in Congress, receiving near-perfect ratings from the AFL-CIO and the liberal organization Americans for Democratic Action (ADA), the congressman's fiery rhetoric, anti-Jewish statements, fierce opposition to pro-Israel legislation, and investigations into his alleged ethics violations generated a legion of political enemies.[27]

Even conservative *Washington Post* columnist George Will joined the crusade to oust Savage. Will gave Reynolds a glowing endorsement, citing his accomplishments as "Illinois' first black Rhodes scholar" as an indication of his acceptability as a member of Congress. "What a luxury it is to have someone of Reynolds' caliber at hand," Will told his readers, "when replacing Savage with even a stalk of celery would elevate the intellectual and moral tone of Congress."[28]

Savage's own party led the charge against him. This time around Reynolds had at his disposal "a SWAT team of the Democratic

Party's top guns," as one newspaper columnist described the party's efforts to dump Savage. Ron Brown, who by then had become chairman of the Democratic National Committee, lent support to ensure Savage's defeat. Brown provided Reynolds with political operatives and cut off party campaign funds to Savage, an unusual move by a national party chairman. Savage, in turn, ridiculed Brown by questioning his blackness. In speeches Savage called Brown an "Oreo" and referred to him as "Ron Beige."[29]

Reynolds's operatives included individuals with serious expertise in winning congressional races. One political consultant had worked with then House majority leader Richard Gephardt. Another had worked for John Lewis in Lewis's surprise 1990 victory over Julian Bond in a particularly nasty congressional contest in Atlanta. And yet another operative—Rahm Emanuel—had a bare-knuckles reputation as the field director for the Democratic Congressional Campaign Committee. Emanuel, who went on to win a seat in Congress, to serve as Obama's White House chief of staff, and to be elected mayor of Chicago, was deployed by the Democratic Party to conduct "opposition research" for Reynolds. Yet another advantage Reynolds had over Savage was his ability to connect to wealthy contributors. J. B. Pritzker, one of the heirs to the Hyatt Hotel fortune, solicited funds in behalf of the Reynolds campaign.[30] (J. B.'s younger sister, Penny Pritzker, would become the national finance chair for Obama's 2008 and 2012 presidential campaigns.)

On March 17, 1992, Reynolds defeated Savage by a wide margin, 63 percent to 37 percent. Though the tide of opposition led to Savage's defeat, Reynolds benefited from a newly drawn district that enhanced his chances of winning. Redistricting changed the boundaries of the old district, adding more suburban voters, which weakened Savage's reliable base of voters in black poor and working-class neighborhoods in the city. When Reynolds arrived on Capitol Hill he was treated like a rising star. He was granted a coveted seat on the powerful Ways and Means Committee, an unusual—but ideal—assignment for a freshman congressman with higher political aspirations. At that time no other freshman congressman had been assigned to the committee in fourteen years. But as time passed, Reynolds's rising star began to fall, and his dream of becoming the first black president was dashed. The mild-mannered Rhodes scholar with the puritan demeanor was indicted for having sex with an underage campaign worker. He resigned from his seat in 1995.

Reynolds was, in essence, the Barack Obama that almost was.

In 1992 Obama asked veteran political activist Lu Palmer to support his "Project Vote" registration drive. Palmer had encountered his kind before and was not impressed. Palmer, as he remembered it, sent the Harvard Law School–trained community organizer on his way. He thought Obama was a little bit too arrogant. In 1995 Palmer encountered Obama again. This time Palmer had a request. He wanted Obama to withdraw his name as a candidate for the Illinois State Senate seat anchored in Hyde Park. Alice Palmer (no relation to Lu) placed third in the special election to replace Mel Reynolds. After losing the race to Jesse Jackson, Jr., Palmer decided she wanted to return to the state capitol. Obama refused to bow out of the race. Whatever Obama said in response to Lu Palmer's request got the political activist thinking. "Man, you sound like Mel Reynolds," Palmer told Obama. After having Alice Palmer's name knocked off the ballot for invalid signatures, Obama coasted to victory. Obama was sworn in as a state senator in 1997, and his career as a politician began.

When, in 2000, Obama decided to run for Congress in the First Congressional District against Bobby Rush, he miscalculated, badly. Bobby Rush decided to challenge Richard M. Daley for mayor in 1999 and was soundly defeated, garnering only 28 percent of the citywide vote. Rush barely won a majority of the black vote and lost in the Second Ward where he was the Democratic Party committeeman. Opponents smelled blood. Two contenders jumped into the race—Barack Obama and Donne Trotter, who also served in the State Senate. Rush's deep political ties in the city made him a formidable candidate. He was a founding member of the Illinois Black

Panther Party, serving as the party's minister of defense. And he was first elected as an alderman in the Second Ward during Harold Washington's mayoral campaign in 1983.[31]

More than a decade passed when a "new generation" of black politicians was being celebrated as descendants of Washington's legacy by the mainstream press. "A dozen years after the death of Harold Washington, there is a generational shift in the leadership of the black community," *Chicago Sun-Times* columnist Steve Neal proclaimed in the fall of 1999, on the eve of the 2000 congressional primary races. "The most promising of these future leaders have shown, like Mayor Washington, extraordinary skill at coalition building." Obama was named as one of the new black leaders in Chicago. Though framed as a generational battle between an "old school" civil rights veteran and a "new school" politician, the rhetoric during the campaign reflected an old ideological divide in black electoral politics, between independent and coalition politics.[32]

Obama criticized Rush for using outdated approaches to solving problems and for having a narrow vision of politics. "Congressman Rush exemplifies a politics that is reactive, that waits for crises to happen then holds a press conference, and hasn't been particularly effective at building broad-based coalitions," Obama asserted. "It may give us psychic satisfaction to curse out people outside our community and blame them for our plight," Obama charged, "but the truth is, if you can't be able to get things accomplished politically, you've got to work with them."[33]

Obama also believed that protest politics has its limits, a claim that rattled the former Black Panther. "We have never been able to progress as a people based on relying solely on the legislative process," Rush told listeners tuned in to WVON during a candidate debate. "And I think that we would be in real critical shape when we start in anyway diminishing the role of protest . . . Protest has got us where we are today," Rush asserted.

Obama's challenge to Rush was a replay of the Reynolds-Savage race a decade before. Like the "Rhodes scholar" versus the "street fighter" monikers that framed the Reynolds-Savage contest, the Obama-Rush contest was viewed as a race between a Harvard Law School graduate and a legendary member of the Black Panther Party. Questions were raised about whether Obama was authentic enough to represent the predominantly black and mostly working-class district. For Rush, being editor of the *Harvard Law Review* was not an impressive credential to have for a candidate in his district. "He went to Harvard and became an educated fool," Rush told a reporter. "We are not impressed with these people with these eastern elite degrees." Donne Trotter—the other challenger and Obama's fellow legislator in Springfield—was equally suspicious. "Barack is viewed in part to be the white man in blackface in our community," Trotter told a reporter. "You have to look at his supporters. Who pushed him to get where he is so fast? It's these individuals in Hyde Park, who don't always have the best interests of the community in mind."[34]

Suspicions about black people with elite educations are nothing new among black Americans. While the criticism can be easily dismissed as anti-intellectualism, it reflects a distrust of white institutions and black people who represent those institutions. When the historian Carter G. Woodson wrote the classic *Mis-Education of the Negro* in 1933 (the book has gone through more than ten printings), he argued that the educated elite in black America were not contributing to the black community's development. "The large majority of the Negroes who have put on the finishing touches of our best colleges are all but worthless in the development of their people," Woodson wrote. "The so-called school, then, becomes a questionable factor in the life of this despised people."[35]

Just like Lu Palmer and others distrusted Rhodes scholar Mel Reynolds, many were suspicious of Obama, particularly his connections to Harvard and the University of Chicago, whose relationship with surrounding black communities has been historically contentious, to say the least. "If you get hung up into these elite institutions, and if you so impress white folks at these elite institutions and if they name you head of these elite institutions, the *Harvard Law Review*, that makes one suspect," Palmer complained.

But Bobby Rush was no Gus Savage. Though Rush and Savage shared a commitment to independent black politics, Rush was a far savvier politician than Savage. As an incumbent with strong ties to the state and national Democratic Party, Rush was able to raise money; receive endorsements from prominent Democrats, including President Clinton; and boasted of bringing federally financed projects to the district. Rush also received an outpouring of public sympathy after his twenty-nine-year-old son was shot to death five days before the election. The congressman began to take up the cause of gun control—a position that showed just how far his politics had moved since his days as the minister of defense for the Illinois Black Panther Party. (The Panthers advocated using guns for self-defense as a way of protecting the black community from police abuse.)

What made matters worse for Obama's campaign is that he missed a key vote on gun control. During a special session in the Illinois General Assembly, Obama was stuck in Hawaii over the Christmas holiday, tending to his sick daughter, Malia. But his missed vote on the legislation—which failed to pass by five votes in the Illinois Senate—became a campaign issue. Obama found it difficult to explain his missed vote on an issue that was of critical importance in the district. In the end, Obama received a "spanking," as the candidate would later describe his defeat. Rush garnered 61 percent of the vote and Obama received 30 percent. Obama's strongest support came from Hyde Park and the predominantly white areas of the district on the city's southwest side. His ability to capture the support of white voters in this race would prove important in future contests to come.

Obama's political career headed south, to Springfield. His return there would, in the end, set the course for his political ascendancy.

Before Emil Jones took the helm as president of the Illinois Senate in 2002, Obama was languishing as a legislator in Springfield. He entered the Senate in 1997 as a Democrat in a chamber ruled by the Republican majority. Several black colleagues—who didn't like the new senator's move to disqualify Alice Palmer—greeted Obama with scorn. The freshman senator started off with the spirit of a Jimmy Stewart–like character, becoming the state of Illinois' proverbial "Mr. Smith goes to Springfield." With the prestige of a Harvard Law degree and his professorship at the University of Chicago's law school, Obama developed a reputation as a hard worker with a brainy disposition.

When Obama arrived in Springfield he expressed to Emil Jones—then the Senate's minority leader—a willingness to work on "tough assignments." Jones assigned Obama to a committee on ethics reform, an unpopular measure among legislators that was initiated by then retired U.S. Senator Paul Simon. Obama was able to work with reluctant Democrats and Republicans to craft a bill that could pass the floor. During the ordeal Obama built support for the measure—and other legislation—by getting to know his colleagues. He played rounds of golf, showed up at cocktail parties, and joined poker games. The reform bill passed and was signed into law, putting in force tougher regulations on the use and disclosure of campaign funds. But Obama's personal charisma and his ability to schmooze in a variety of social and political settings could only take him so far. Obama needed to link himself to someone with the political power to make things happen for him.[36]

Obama found that link in Emil Jones, who became president of the Illinois Senate in 2002. Though much has been made of Obama's connections to better-known national figures, little has been made of Jones's impact on Obama's political ascendancy. Jones, a chain-smoker whose gravelly voice and gruff demeanor conjures up the caricature of an old-style backroom politician, became one of the most powerful politicians—and, by default, the most powerful black politician—in Illinois. After state legislative district lines were redrawn in 2001, the Illinois Democrats won enough seats to regain power. Jones was elevated to Senate president, giving him the power to set the legislative agenda in the state capitol. (In the spirit of full disclosure, I was hired by Jones's office as an expert advising the party's redistricting plan for the State Senate. I testified before the Senate's bipartisan redistricting committee in support of the Democrat's plan.)

Jones's roots run deep in machine politics. His father was a precinct captain and Jones worked the streets for John F. Kennedy's presidential campaign in 1960, in a razor-thin victory for Kennedy that was settled when "Boss Daley" delivered enough votes to swing Illinois Kennedy's way. For thirty years Jones was on the City of Chicago's payroll, spending many of those years receiving a salary as a sewer inspector. Like most black machine politicians, Jones did not endorse Harold Washington in 1983, a decision that landed him in hot water with his constituents. In *Dreams From My Father*, Obama referred to an "old ward heeler" pushing himself on stage at an event Obama planned for Mayor Washington. Though Obama did not mention the name of the politician, that "ward heeler" was Emil Jones. (Jones endorsed Washington for reelection in 1987.) In 1997 Jones and a group of other public officials were under investigation for a "ghost payroll" scheme of receiving salaries for no-show city jobs. Jones was never charged in the investigation, though the accusations did not help shake his reputation as a corrupt machine politician.[37]

Before becoming president of the Illinois Senate, Jones had higher ambitions. He twice ran for Congress in the Second Congressional District, coming in third place against Gus Savage in 1988. Jones ran again in 1995 in the special election to replace Mel Reynolds. In his second bid for Congress, Jones ran a distant second to Jesse Jackson, Jr., who, with the support of his father and endorsements from luminaries in the national Democratic Party, won the primary with 50 percent of the vote in a five-candidate field. But Jones's loss turned out to be Obama's gain. Had Jones been successful at his second attempt at being elected to Congress—or even his first—Obama's path to the United States Senate, and indeed to the White House, would have taken longer to achieve, or might not have happened at all. With a Democratic governor and both chambers controlled by the Democrats, Jones had a chance to push through a legislative agenda targeted to poor and minority concerns.

Obama asked Jones to use his power to make him a United States Senator, and Jones obliged. Jones became Obama's political godfather. Jones's reputation as a political godfather in Springfield had so much cachet that Jones's cell phone ringtone played the theme from the movie *The Godfather*. Because Jones saw Obama being effective in making connections with Republican lawmakers, the Senate president handed the baton to Obama, who led the charge of major legislative initiatives while Jones worked behind the scenes to leverage his influence to build support for Obama's run for the United States Senate. As Obama climbed up the political ladder, he would credit his work in the Illinois Senate as mostly his own initiative rather than acknowledge Jones for leveraging his political muscle to get things done.

Jones's mark on history is assured, but, interestingly enough, he was not the first African American president of the Illinois Senate. He was the second. Had Obama been a senator from Hyde Park in the 1970s, he would have encountered a different type of black leadership in power. In 1971, Cecil Partee, another machine politician from the South Side, became Senate president through the maneuvering of State Senator Richard Newhouse, a black Hyde Park–based reformer who threatened to vote absent on all roll-call votes if Democrats refused to elect a black Senate president. By the early 1970s, the Illinois Senate was evenly divided between Democrats and Republicans. Paul Simon, then the Democratic lieutenant governor, was the constitutionally mandated tie-breaker. This gave Democrats a slight majority and the ability to elect one of their own as Senate president. If Newhouse voted absent it would have given Republicans a voting majority.

The threat worked. Newhouse's strategic move was black political power at its most forceful. By using the legislative process to benefit the interests of black communities, Newhouse demonstrated how black solidarity in the legislature could propel blacks into powerful leadership positions. Partee was elected Illinois

Senate president, not only becoming the first black person in the state to do so, but also the first black to lead any state legislative body since the Reconstruction era. Though Partee and Newhouse stood on opposite sides in the Democratic Party, the two South Side senators were united in their efforts to ensure that a black (or for Partee ensure that he) would become senate president. Though Partee became a tarnished symbol of black pride in Chicago, many blacks questioned whether Partee's new status would bring any substantive benefits to the black community. A Daley loyalist, Partee's legislative agenda was dictated by the machine. In Newhouse's estimation, the new Senate president was even less supportive of reform and a progressive agenda than previous, white Democratic Party leaders.[38]

Thus, Newhouse soon regretted his decision to support Partee, and it gnawed at him for decades. "Worst mistake I ever made," Newhouse mused. For Newhouse, Partee's tenure as president "was the old days all over again—worse I think, because a black can do more damage to a people and their hopes than a white can." Harold Washington didn't think much of Partee, either. When Washington ran for mayor in 1977, challenging the machine-backed candidate, Michael Bilandic, Partee threw his support behind Bilandic. A bewildered Washington denounced Partee as "the biggest Uncle Tom on God's green earth."[39]

Newhouse was a warrior for black interests locally and nationally, but his political career did not go far. He was the moving force in the development of a national organization of black state legislators—a network that became a model for the Congressional Black Caucus—and he served as a delegate at the 1972 National Black Political Convention in Gary, Indiana. In 1975, Newhouse was the first black candidate for mayor in Chicago, running as a reformer against Richard Daley in the Democratic primary—when running against the Daley machine was akin to political suicide. But despite the inroads Newhouse made, he spent the rest of his career in obscurity as a state senator. While Obama would launch his political career as a coalition builder from the same seat five years after Newshouse's retirement, Newhouse spent his years as a state senator building the independent black political networks that helped clear the path for Obama's election as president. (Newhouse's choice of a white spouse did not help his political career either. He was derided by the Black Nationalist independents for "talking black but sleeping white."[40]) Newhouse retired in 1991, after serving twenty-four years in the legislature.

Over the span of his thirty-three years in public life, Partee remained a machine loyalist, who was respected but feared by machine loyalists and reformers alike. After leaving his position as Senate president (some say to make room for Richard M. Daley to take the reins as Senate president), Partee's political career thrived. With the support of black voters and "white ethnic" voters committed to the machine, Partee was elected city treasurer of Chicago. He was appointed Cook County state attorney after Richard M. Daley resigned from the post to run for mayor in 1990. (Partee retired from public life after losing the Cook County state attorney's race in 1990.) As Newhouse's stalled political career shows, there were consequences to being a fiercely reform-oriented, independent black politician in a city where go-along-to-get-along politics had—and some would say still has—its privileges. Newhouse's steady commitment to challenging the powers that be would not be the path that Barack Obama would take.

Unlike Cecil Partee, Emil Jones was his own man among the regular Democrats, and Obama was fortunate that Jones had a different philosophy and leadership style than Partee. That Emil Jones decided to hand off an ambitious legislative agenda to a relative newcomer to the Senate—who did not come up through the machine—says a great deal about Jones's commitment to promoting the future generation of black leaders. After all, by the time Jones became Senate president he had spent nearly thirty years in the General Assembly—ten as a member of the House and twenty as a senator. Obama had only served in the chamber seven years when Jones was elected Senate president. That's less than one-quarter of the time Jones put in Springfield.

As a 2005 profile of Jones in *Ebony* magazine highlighted, the Senate president was celebrated for surrounding himself with "a relatively young staff of business, legal, and political professionals from top schools." Jones believed that part of his goal as a leader was to prepare the next generation. "I not only have to serve now, but to prepare others to take the baton in the future." If anything, Jones's upbringing could have bred resentment toward Obama rather than confidence. "You have to understand, I was a poor, dark child with no real opportunities," Jones told *Ebony* about his experience growing up on the South Side. "Everything was designed for you to fail. There were not real heroes for us to look up to." Jones could have sized up Obama and concluded that the Harvard Law School graduate had not struggled as much as he had and was thus undeserving of his political largess. He could have passed the baton to other members with greater legislative experience, handing over his legislative agenda to black senators like Ricky Hendon or Donne Trotter. But Hendon and Trotter could not do what Obama could—build bridges with white senators to support Jones's legislative agenda.

A great deal was accomplished during Jones's stint as Senate president. Jones increased the funding for public education by nearly $400 million, increased the minimum wage, passed legislation mandating pay equity for women, and expanded opportunities for minority-owned businesses. He also required that revenues from a new gaming license be used to fund inner-city Chicago State University on the South Side rather than the better endowed University of Illinois in downstate Champaign-Urbana. As chair of the Health and Human Services Committee, Obama authored legislation that expanded health care coverage for the poor, cemented a 5 percent earned-income tax credit for low-income working families, and commissioned a study on ways to implement universal health care in the state. Obama steered important legislation on criminal justice issues into law. He got the so-called driving-while-black bill passed, which monitors racial profiling by requiring police departments to collect data on the race of drivers

stopped for minor traffic violations.[41] Obama was also instrumental in passing legislation on death-penalty reform. While Obama
adopted these legislative accomplishments during his campaign
for the United States Senate, Jones operated behind the scenes as
power broker, flexing his muscles to convince Democratic officials,
labor unions, and businesspeople to get behind Obama's candidacy.

Building on the success of Carol Moseley Braun in her surprise
primary victory for the United States Senate in 1992, Obama not
only performed well among Chicago voters and "collar county"
voters, he also did well among rural downstate voters. With a
crowded field of seven candidates, Obama received 53 percent of
the vote. Obama's victory demonstrated that a black candidate—
or at least this black candidate—no longer needed to mainly
depend on Washington's formula of splitting the white vote to
ensure that the black candidate would win the Democratic primary race. Obama's Republican opponent—the ultraconservative
Alan Keyes, who is black—was "bussed-in" from the state of
Maryland to run against Obama after the Republican nominee
Paul Ryan pulled out of the race. (Ryan withdrew after divorce
records revealed that the ostensibly straitlaced Republican allegedly forced his former wife to have public sex with him at sex
clubs. Obama coasted to victory with 70 percent of the vote.)

The day after Obama's victory, the senator-to-be held a press
conference at his campaign headquarters in downtown Chicago.
Obama seemed uncomfortable with becoming a national rising
star and was especially concerned about whether his status as the
only black member of the Senate would place too many demands
on his family and his political obligations in Washington. "It's
going to be important for me to say 'no,' when it just comes to
appearances, wanting to be the keynote speaker at every NAACP
Freedom Fund dinner across the country," Obama confessed. In
those early days, before Obama would grow uneasy about speaking
out on racial issues, the future president viewed his ascendancy to
the Senate as the lone black member as a chance for blacks to
have a collective voice in the chamber.

Much like Oscar De Priest's choice to speak up for black interests as the only black member of Congress during the first decades of the twentieth century and Carol Moseley Braun's voice of representation for blacks—and women—in the United States Senate just over a decade before, Obama expressed similar desires the day after his election to the Senate. "When it comes to *speaking out* on issues that are of particular importance to the African-American community," Obama told reporters, "I don't think that's a conflict with my role as an effective legislator for the people of Illinois."[42]

The newly elected senator's commitment would be short-lived. The senator-to-be who then saw himself as a national voice for black interests in the Senate would, a couple of years later, abdicate that role when he rose as a viable presidential candidate. On the road to the White House, speaking out on special issues affecting blacks was heard less and less as Obama's electoral prospects grew stronger and brighter. Obama would ask to be treated like any other candidate—like any other president—who "just happens to be black."

Entering the Land of Milk and Honey

ON SUNDAY EVENING, April 13, 2003, some twenty-five days after the United States invaded Iraq, the Reverend Jeremiah Wright took to the pulpit of the Trinity United Church of Christ on Chicago's South Side to deliver a sermon titled "Confusing God and Government." The sermon was like many others preached by Reverend Wright, who is a widely known minister within black religious circles for his theatrical style of preaching and his ability to tie in lessons from the Bible to current events that relate to the black condition. In 1993 *Ebony* magazine named Reverend Wright one of the fifteen top preachers in America, placing him alongside stewards such as Gardner C. Taylor of the Concord Baptist Church in Brooklyn, Samuel Dewitt Proctor of the Abyssinian Baptist Church in Harlem, and civil rights activists Jesse Jackson and Joseph Lowery. On that Sunday evening, during the typical low-key church service, Reverend Wright took his message from the shortest verse in the Bible, "Jesus wept." The simple scripture served as the basis of Reverend Wright's long—and at times rambling—sermon about how people can easily fall prey to believing whatever their government tells them.[1]

Reverend Wright told the congregation that Jesus cried for his people because they were blinded by "being in the spot where they desired—deeply desired—revenge, and they could not see things that make for peace." Using the language of war to describe the events leading to the crucifixion of Christ, Reverend Wright told the congregation "it was the Italian army who led Jesus out to Calvary on Friday morning. It was the occupying military brigade who forced Simon of Cyrene to carry the cross for Jesus . . . These people were tired of their oppression and they wanted the enemy up out of their land," he insisted. "They also wanted revenge."

Alluding to the war in Iraq and the United States' justification for invading the country, Reverend Wright informed the congregation that a foreign military presence in a nation does not make for peace, even in the absence of armed resistance against the occupying force. "War only makes for escalating violence and a mindset to payback by any means necessary." Only God can grant peace, Reverend Wright declared, not a military force. "The things that make for peace only God can give . . . Y'all looking to government for that which only God can give," Wright pronounced in earthy language that was his trademark. "No wonder he wept, he had good cause to cry. The people under oppression were confusing God and government."

Wright continued the sermon by highlighting how Christianity had been used to sanction the immoral actions of governments, which included the United States confiscating land from Native Americans and justifying inequality in wealth. "We believe that God approves six percent of the people on the face of the earth controlling all of the resources on the face of this earth while the other ninety-four percent live in poverty and squalor, while we give trillions of dollars of tax breaks to the white rich." He went on to preach that governments deliberately tell lies to the people to cover up its crimes. A former marine, Reverend Wright stated: "Our money says 'In God We Trust,' and our military says we will kill under the orders of our Commander-in-Chief if you dare to believe otherwise." And then Reverend Wright listed the offenses that the United States government had committed against black Americans over the centuries. "She put them in chains," he starts. "The government put them in slave quarters, put them on auction blocks, put them in cotton fields, put them in inferior schools, put them in substandard housing, put them in scientific experiments, put them in the lowest paying jobs," he recounted in rapid-fire succession. The government "put them outside the equal protection of the law, kept them out of the racist bastion of higher education and locked them into positions of hopelessness and helplessness," he continued. "The government gives them the drugs, builds bigger prisons, passes a three-strikes law, and then wants us to sing 'God Bless America.' No, no, no. Not God Bless America, God Damn America!" Those last three words spoken by Reverend Wright nearly derailed the presidential aspirations of Trinity United Church of Christ's most celebrated congregant, Barack Obama.

Though cable news networks would replay Reverend Wright's phrase—"God Bless America. No, no. no. Not God Bless America. God Damn America"—over and over again as evidence that Obama's pastor—and presumably Obama himself—harbored anti-white and unpatriotic attitudes about the United States, few journalists took the time to hear what Wright actually said before and after his denunciation of the United States. Reverend Wright went on to tell the congregation that the word damn was written often in the Bible and America should be indeed damned for "killing innocent people" and "treating her citizens less than human."

The speech had been delivered five years earlier, but because Barack Obama was running for president and Obama was a member of the church, Reverend Wright's image and words of damnation would be continuously rotated on cable news. In an era of heightened patriotism after the 9/11 terrorist attacks on the United States, Reverend Wright, in words of condemnation that reflect the style and the substance of prophetic tradition in black religion, criticized the United States for its militarism and foreign policy. His message declared that the United States was being "damned" by God for its military pursuits throughout the world and for its treatment of powerless people at home and abroad.[2]

For those unfamiliar with the prophetic tradition in Afro-Christianity, Reverend Wright's comments were shocking. Many asked how a candidate who transcended race could affiliate with a minister who promoted hatred against America. But those with a deep familiarity of black religious culture could recognize the historical foundations of Reverend Wright's prophetic message of damnation against the nation. In 1829, the abolitionist David Walker would write an appeal—titled "To the Coloured Citizens of the World, But Particular, and Very Expressly, to Those of the United States of America"—that threatened America with the wrath of God. Walker decried the sins perpetrated against African slaves in the United States and proclaimed condemnation against America. "They forget that God rules in the armies of the heaven and among inhabitants of the earth," Walker wrote. "And being a just and holy Being will at one day appear fully in behalf of the oppressed, and arrest the progress of the avaricious oppressors." Though the destruction Walker foresees might not come directly from the slaves themselves, he predicted that "Lord our God will bring other destructions upon them." As if foretelling the Civil War thirty years into the future, Walker believed God would "cause them to rise up one against another, to be split and divided, and to oppress each other, and sometimes to open hostilities with sword in hand."[3]

The abolitionist Frederick Douglass, in language just as bombastic as Reverend Wright's, decried the hypocrisy of the United States for holding lofty beliefs in justice and equality while maintaining slavery. In a speech given in Rochester, New York, in 1852 in celebration of the Fourth of July, Douglass called the nation's day of rejoicing its freedom a "sham." In language that would surely make him an enemy of the state today, Douglass proclaimed to those gathered:

There is not a nation of the earth guilty of practices more shocking and bloody than are the people of the United States at this very hour. Go where you may, search where you will, roam through all the monarchies and depositions of the Old World, travel through South America, search out . . . every abuse and when you have found the last, lay your facts by the side of the everyday practices of this nation, and you will say with me that, for revolting barbarity and shameless hypocrisy, America reigns without rival.[4]

Malcolm X would also proclaim destruction on America for its treatment of black people more than a century after Walker and Douglass. Referring to the United States as a "modern house of bondage," Malcolm X declared, "white America is doomed." In a speech given on December 4, 1963, two weeks after the assassination of John F. Kennedy, Malcolm X told a meeting of Muslims to "search even the history of other nations that sat in the same positions of wealth, power, and authority that these white Americans now hold and see what God did to them." Like David Walker, Malcolm X declared that God would condemn America for its past sins of slavery. "If God's unchanging laws of justice caught up with everyone of the slave empires of the past, how dare you think white America can escape the harvest of unjust seeds planted by her white forefathers against our black forefathers here in the land of slavery," Malcolm X thundered. When asked about President Kennedy's assassination after the speech, Malcolm X responded that the violence Kennedy had failed to stop against blacks had led to Kennedy's death. It was a case of "chickens coming home to roost."[5]

As a minister who adheres to the teachings of black liberation theology and as a church that practices the social gospel tradition of assisting the poor through a variety of church-sponsored services, Reverend Wright and Trinity United Church of Christ came under attack for upholding tradition. Not only was Reverend Wright assailed by Senator Hillary Clinton's campaign, the media, and political conservatives, he also was criticized by many black ministers for having an outdated and impractical theological worldview. It was a view that no longer, some thought, addressed the immediate needs of black communities. The undercurrent of the controversy about Reverend Wright and his theological commitment to black liberation theology shined light on a debate about what the priorities of black churches should be in the twenty-first century. To proponents of the progressive side of the black church—a perspective steeped in the social gospel and liberation theology traditions—this debate is intertwined with questions about the rise of the prosperity gospel.

While historically activist black churches developed both social and political strategies to combat poverty and discrimination, the growing influence of the prosperity gospel presents a challenge to what has been described as the "civic traditions of black churches."[6] They are steeped in these traditions, with a long history of engaging in electoral politics and economic development efforts in their communities. Ministers have long provided spiritual and political guidance to their congregants, encouraging them to use their talents and skills to foster social change in their communities. This activist tradition may have met its strongest ideological challenge in many decades. Indeed, theologian and Morehouse College President Robert M. Franklin describes the prosperity gospel as "the single greatest threat to the historical legacy and core values of the contemporary black church tradition." As a religious doctrine that supports a worldview which according to Franklin "permits and rewards extraordinary inequalities of wealth and power," critics claim that the theology neglects the concerns of the poor and the pursuit of social justice. Though elements of the prosperity gospel in Afro-Christianity are not new, evidence suggests that its contemporary incarnation is more mainstream than marginal. Prosperity churches attract predominantly middle-class and working-class blacks to arena-sized churches where the virtues of living an "abundant life" of wealth, good health, and positive relationships are preached.[7]

The prosperity gospel is not only popular among African Americans but has strong appeal among white evangelicals and "un-churched" Christians in general who have recommitted themselves to their faith, which they now see as having more relevance to and practicality for their lives than the churches they grew up in. With the help of popular preachers, such as best-selling author Joel Osteen who has one of the largest congregations in the country and attracts millions of people to his ministry through his special appearances around the country and weekly television program, the theology of prosperity has moved from the margins of Protestant Christianity toward the center. Though some might think that prosperity gospel is on the fringe of American religious life or, conversely, that the social gospel holds little sway today, an opinion poll points to how their tenets undergird the theological tensions that exist among believers. In a 2006 *Time*-CNN poll, respondents expressed positions that reflect the social gospel tradition and the prosperity gospel. About 60 percent of Christians in the survey believed that "God wants people to be financially prosperous," slightly over 20 percent agreed that "material wealth is a sign of "God's blessings," while one-third reported that "if you give away your money to God, God will bless you with more money." Nearly half the respondents agreed that "Jesus was rich and we should follow his example."

On the other hand, responses to some questions indicate support for values associated with the social gospel. Forty-four percent of the respondents rejected the idea of a rich Jesus and 43 percent believed that churches were not doing enough to assist the poor—a response that would indicate support for the values of the social gospel tradition. Only half the respondents were familiar with the prosperity movement, and a mere 17 percent reported that they were followers. However, the responses do indicate that a significant number of American Christians see their faith linked with material success even though less than 20 percent claimed to be part of the prosperity gospel movement.

Anecdotal evidence suggests that blacks are among the strongest followers of the Word of Faith movement in the United States and that black ministers such as Frederick Price and Creflo Dollar are among the leading proselytizers. As such, the idea that the prosperity gospel has a greater influence on Afro-Christians has far more political consequences for them than for white evangelicals, whose religious worldviews reinforce the core American value of individualism. For African Americans, at least historically, the idea of the collective has been more central to their political values than the importance of individualism. In essence, the prosperity gospel represents a clash with core political values in the black church tradition.[8]

The social gospel/liberation theology tradition and the theology of prosperity gospel are at loggerheads. The latter, with its emphasis on transforming individuals into prosperous and healthy Christians, and the prophetic tradition, with its commitment toward transforming poor and marginal communities, has implications for the future of black politics. As political scientist Michael Dawson explains in his theory of linked fate, blacks—rich and poor and of all religious persuasions—evaluate political preferences and policy initiatives based on their perception of how preferences and policies affect blacks as a group. Black churches have been central to nurturing those communalist values that contribute to a sense of linked fate, as well as fostering the political discussions and skills that connect congregants to electoral and community politics. The rich networks and institutions that are embedded in black churches are—alongside the black family, community organizations, and black media—responsible for reinforcing and enhancing a sense of solidarity among blacks by "crystallizing the shared historical experience of African Americans into a sense of collective identity," as Dawson explains.[9]

As the most extensive institutions in African American communities, black churches have the capability to reinforce the political saliency of race-specific political interests. They also provide congregants with information about the status of the race. Thus, the influence of the prosperity gospel, either through the proliferation of Word of Faith churches that draw black adherents or through the adoption of prosperity preaching in more traditional black churches, may have the effect of eroding—or at the very least softening—the sense of linked fate among blacks. Prosperity gospel is more likely to have its followers adopt religious values that emphasize individualism and depoliticize church-based efforts that address racial inequality.

The evolution of black churches in American life has its roots in social and political protest. After blacks were enslaved and uprooted from both their land and their indigenous religious practices, they were Christianized in the New World. They developed a religious worldview that both challenged and provided explanations for their enslavement. These worldviews opposed the ideology and the practices of white-supremacist-infused Christianity that offered biblical justifications for the capture and enslavement of Africans and their descendants. Although black Christians shared the same fundamental views of white Christians about the birth, life, and resurrection of Christ, very early on, black Christians interpreted the Bible and Christ's life in ways that cut against the dominant white society's interpretation of their oppressed conditions.[10]

African American Christians, for instance, have historically placed greater emphasis on the lessons of the Old Testament; the belief in the personal intervention of God in history; biblical perspectives on the suffering and the ultimate triumph of Christ; and the belief in equality and consequent equal treatment of all Christians, no matter their race or economic circumstances.

The importance and interpretation of "freedom" in black religious traditions are distinct from the traditions of white Christians. Involving more than freedom from religious persecution, the themes of freedom that evolved in the black religious experience reflect the social and political struggles that African Americans experienced during slavery, Reconstruction, and the struggle for full citizenship that took place for more than half the twentieth century. The meaning of freedom has evolved over time, but one constant element has been collectively improving the lot of blacks in the United States. As C. Eric Lincoln and Lawrence H. Mamiya explain in *The Black*

Church and the African-American Experience, "During slavery [freedom] meant release from bondage; after emancipation it meant the right to be educated, to be employed, and to move about freely from place to place. In the twentieth century freedom means social, political, and economic justice." In sum, Afro-Christianity has placed less emphasis on individual freedom and more on a collectively oriented sense of freedom that not only liberates African Americans from political, economic, and social persecution in a white-dominated society, but also liberates the nation from its failure to live up to its democratic ideals.[11]

This sense of freedom that developed in both secular and religious institutions, both at the center and the margins of black society, provided the leadership, networks, and language that guided African Americans in their quest for equality. The institutional resources and symbolic power of Afro-Christianity's vision of freedom provided individual blacks with a means to understand their oppression and struggle, regardless of their ideological inclinations at a given historical moment. With the exception of black Marxism, which only during rare moments in history adopted Christian perspectives in efforts to appeal to African Americans, ideological tendencies among African Americans such as black versions of liberalism, nationalism, and conservatism were, and still are, influenced by Afro-Christianity.

The conflict between prosperity gospel and social gospel/liberation theology is, from an ideological perspective, a debate on how best to advance the black community in the twenty-first century. This conversation is as old as Booker T. Washington and W. E. B. DuBois' conflict over social and economic uplift versus civil rights at the turn of the twentieth century and Martin Luther King and Malcolm X's perspectives on integration versus separatism during the 1960s. Today the debate has turned to whether a lack of individual responsibility is the reason for the condition of the black poor or if institutional racism is. This debate has influenced Barack Obama's secular views about the need for greater personal responsibility among blacks.

Thus the conflict between the social gospel/liberation theology wing of Afro-Christianity and its emerging prosperity gospel wing is at its core a theological *and* ideological debate about the best strategy for African Americans to advance in American society. As Michael Dawson reminds us in his discussion about the historical tendencies in African American political thought, "The fact that two African Americans can believe their fate is linked to that of the race does not mean that they agree on how best to advance their own racial interests."[12]

In similar terms, the disagreements between the two theologies are partly over what God truly wants for the "destiny of the race" rather than doctrinal debates about which theology represents the best path to salvation. As the prosperity gospel gains greater currency in Afro-Christianity, through both its Pentecostal roots as well as through its adoption in more traditional black churches, it may challenge the prophetic tradition in the black church movement, a tradition that coincides with both the coalition wing of black politics and the independent wing of black politics. In a so-called postracial America, where race matters less than other identities and political commitments, adherents of the prosperity gospel may reflect more conservative political attitudes. These conservative views might discourage both coalition and independent black politics, and promote instead political conservatism that may have the effect of fostering apolitical views on black activism. By default, the prosperity gospel will likely soften support in black communities for liberal social policies targeted toward the poor.

The theological "civil war" brewing among the ministers and theologians of the prophetic tradition and the gospel of prosperity reflects political tensions within black communities about how government should respond to the plight of poor blacks. Reverend Frederick Haynes III of Dallas's Friendship-West Baptist Church, accuses prosperity ministers of being "co-opted by American capitalism" and for "blaming the poor for their circumstances and praising the pursuit of earthly riches."[13] At the 2006 annual meeting of the National Baptist Convention, the largest black denominational body in the United States, Reverend Haynes accused prosperity ministers of abandoning the poor and deceiving followers for financial gain. "Black communities are suffering," Reverend Haynes proclaimed, "while the prosperity-pimping gospel is emotionally charging people who are watching their communities just literally dissolve."[14]

Prosperity gospel preachers, on the other hand, think that to not teach about the biblical virtues of prosperity is heresy and a barrier to bringing sinners to Christ. Their appeals are based more on biblical reinterpretations rather than on the more explicit ideological and political commitments that are apparent in black liberation theology and the social gospel tradition. Frederick K. C. Price, a black pastor of a megachurch and one of the leading proponents of the prosperity gospel, argues in his book, *Prosperity on God's Terms*:

> It has to be a satanic deception for the Christian to speak against prosperity. Satan very well knows that if we become financially independent of our circumstances, we will no longer control our progress. "Poor-mouthing" Christians are not going to be credible witnesses of the goodness of God, nor will they influence very many people. But more importantly, they are not going to get the Gospel out. They are aiding the enemy—while rejecting the command of God Who told us to promote the gospel—and they don't even know it.[15]

As mentioned, this theological worldview, which emphasizes the virtues of good health and material gain to its adherents, is at odds with the prophetic tradition in Afro-Christianity. While proponents of the social gospel and liberation theology recognize how structural inequalities in American society place barriers before minorities and the poor, adherents of the prosperity gospel see negative spiritual forces preventing the faithful from receiving financial blessings from God. The social gospel commands that Christians transform the communities of the poor and acknowledge the existence of racial inequality. The theology of liberation emphasizes that God sided with the oppressed and that the suffering of black people in particular indicated that God, Himself, is black. A look back at the development of the prophetic tradition in Afro-Christianity and the evolution of the prosperity gospel provides context to how these two theological perspectives support values that may well have diametrically opposed impacts on the future of black politics.

The social gospel, a religious movement that evolved in the late nineteenth and early twentieth centuries, commands that the faithful uplift the poor and transform poor and disenfranchised communities though community uplift and political activism. As the religious arm of the Progressive movement, the social gospel tradition developed a theological worldview that the righteous should not only be concerned about the salvation of sinners—whose sins reflected the social environment in which they lived—but should also be concerned about the plight of the dispossessed here on earth. So in order to save sinners from damnation, the social gospel advocated improving their environment and saving the souls of sinners.

The founders of the movement reflected the sentiments of mainline white, middle-class Protestants and supported the settlement house movement, labor rights, civil rights, and later the peace movement. The tradition has not only included mainline Protestants but also, at least historically, Catholics and Jews. Led by urban black clergy, the social gospel tradition among blacks provided a morally sanctioned framework that justified and legitimized the church's involvement in the civil rights movement. The social gospel tradition within black communities combined the perspectives of the social gospel, whose early supporters often overlooked the prevailing racism in American society, and the ideology of racial uplift, which promoted the idea that black elites and institutions were obligated to uplift the poor.[16]

While uplift ideology and the biblical justification that supported it existed among black elites prior to the Civil War, its influence became dominant in black communities at the turn of the twentieth century, when black communities became marginalized in the wake of the collapse of Reconstruction. Using the biblical story of the Exodus, Afro-Christians saw themselves as an oppressed people, enslaved, liberated, and wandering in the wilderness of America's racist society. This view of Afro-Christians has its origins in slave religion, in which slaves who became Christians adopted the biblical story of the Exodus as a way to understand their bondage and their struggle for freedom.[17] While white Christians saw their conquest of the New World as manifest destiny and America as the land of "milk and honey," converted slaves saw America as Egypt, the land of bondage.[18]

Some traditions within Afro-Christianity, particularly Holiness and Pentecostal churches, primarily hoped for a better situation in the afterlife, but urban churches affiliated with the black "mainline" focused their energies on saving souls and improving the social environment of their congregants by building schools, orphanages, hospitals, and mutual-aid and burial societies. Thus, the work of redeeming the souls of the poor linked both sinners and the righteous in racially segregated communities. During the "great migration" North between the two World Wars, the social gospel of racial uplift helped advance civil rights by influencing secularly based social-uplift organizations such as the Urban League and the National Association for the Advancement of Colored People (NAACP).[19]

One of the first texts, from a theological perspective, to interpret biblical scriptures and symbols in support of the idea that Jesus sided with the oppressed—and by extension African Americans—was Howard Thurman's *Jesus and the Disinherited*, published in 1949. In Thurman's interpretation, the life of Jesus represented all disinherited people and as such the Gospel of Christ and the actions of Christians should reflect that viewpoint. Anticipating Martin Luther King's public theology of social justice, Thurman argued that

the economic predicament with which (Jesus) was identified
in birth placed him initially with the great mass of men on

earth. The masses of people are poor. If we dare take the position that in Jesus there was at work some radical destiny, it would be safe to say that in his poverty he was more truly Son of man than he would have been if the incident of family or birth had made him a rich son of Israel.[20]

Indeed, the theological perspective that God sided with the oppressed was appropriated by King and used as a biblical justification for blacks to actively resist segregation. In his first movement speech, delivered in December of 1955 at the Holt Street Baptist Church in Montgomery, King preached, "We are determined here in Montgomery to work and fight until justice runs down like water and righteousness like a mighty stream," a command that was inspired by the Old Testament prophet Amos. Referencing both Thurman's biblical interpretation of the oppressed and the story of the Exodus, King told the audience that "we, the disinherited of this land, we who have been oppressed so long, are tired of going through the long night of captivity." King would use the story of the Exodus and the idea that Christ sides with the oppressed throughout his many speeches. His very last, delivered in Memphis at a mass meeting for striking garbage workers in 1968, the symbol of the Promised Land in the Exodus story was used to convey to African Americans that their freedom was inevitable, whether he reached the Promised Land with them or not. Like the biblical Moses, who led the Israelites out of Egyptian slavery and received God's commandment on Mt. Sinai, King told the mostly black audience:

But it doesn't matter with me now, because I've been to the mountaintop. And I don't mind. Like anybody, I would like to live a long life. Longevity has its place. But I'm not concerned about that now. I just want to do God's will. And He's allowed me to go up to the mountain. And I've looked over. And I've seen the Promised Land. I may not get there with you. But I want you to know tonight, that we, as a people will get to the Promised Land.

As a revolt against the interracial and nonviolent, turn-the-other-cheek philosophy of King's social gospel, black liberation theology saw the suffering of Christ as a context for the persecution of black people in the United States and argued for a more radical interpretation of the Bible and the life and death of Jesus. In his influential book *Black Messiah*, Detroit minister Albert Cleage argued that not only did God side with the oppressed but that Christ, because of the suffering he endured, was black. As an ideological challenge to the Nation of Islam's criticism of Christianity as the "white man's religion," Cleage justified support for building a separate black nation on the foundations of Christianity, a stance ideologically compatible with Black Nationalism. Reverend Cleage wrote that Christianity promoted communalist values and opposition against the status quo; virtues that he argued have historical links to Afro-Christianity. "Black Americans need to know," Cleage asserted, "that the historic Jesus was a leader who went about among the people of Israel, seeking to root out the individualism and the identification with the oppressor which had corrupted them."[21]

The leading theologian of black liberation theology then and today is James Cone, a professor at Union Theological Seminary in New York. His works have influenced a generation of black seminarians throughout the country who have become ministers at traditional black churches and racially diverse mainline Protestant churches. Adopting the viewpoints of Black Nationalism, Cone in his work has contested the very meaning of Christianity in the United States. Since mainstream white churches were complicit in supporting slavery and racial segregation, Cone argues that a Christian worldview that does not consider the plight of the oppressed is a useless theology. "There can be no Christian theology which is not identified unreservedly with those who are humiliated and abused," Cone argued in 1970. Furthermore,

theology ceases to be a theology of the gospel when it fails to arise out of the community of the oppressed. For it is impossible to speak of God of Israelite history, who is the God who revealed himself in Jesus Christ, without recognizing that he is the God for those who labor and are heavy laden.[22]

Some evidence from opinion surveys suggests that the political significance of black liberation theology may have softened since the activist era of the 1960s and 1970s. The political scientist Allison Calhoun-Brown reports that nearly one-third of African Americans believe in the image of a black Christ, a finding that would indicate support for black liberation theology. She finds that holding an image of a black Christ increases support for the development of a separate black nation, which in turn supports separation from American society—a finding that coincides with Cleage's theology of Christian Black Nationalism. The belief in a black Christ, however, did not enhance feelings of group solidarity, predict voting behavior, or indicate the idea that churches should be involved in politics, behaviors that would be more in line with the prophetic tradition that calls for social change. These findings suggest that the social mission of the black church may be more important for activist churches than the theological viewpoints of black liberation theology.

The growing popularity of the prosperity gospel among African Americans may be partly attributed to the perceived failures of the prophetic tradition in dealing with the persistence of racial inequality in the post–civil rights era. A theological worldview that centers on transforming the lives of blacks as individuals appears to have more appeal than a theology that focuses too much on the past, particularly since a generation of black Americans is less familiar with historic struggles against legalized segregation. As the memory of the civil rights and Black Power movement fades, the story of the Exodus may have less appeal among a new generation of black Christians.

The funeral of Martin Luther King, Jr.'s widow, Coretta Scott King, in February of 2006, symbolically revealed the diminishing influence of the prophetic tradition in black politics. What surfaced in this ritual of remembrance and homage to Mrs. King, who for over thirty years kept the memory and the values of her husband's message of peace and social change in the nation's consciousness, was a nod to the gospel of prosperity, whose theological worldview is antithetical to the prophetic tradition Dr. King embraced. While Dr. King's funeral in 1968 was held at Ebenezer Baptist Church, which is today surrounded by a poor neighborhood east of downtown Atlanta, the final service for Mrs. King was held at New Birth Missionary Baptist Church—a suburban megachurch fifteen miles outside of Atlanta—whose minister, Bishop Eddie Long, is an ardent supporter of a theology that teaches the virtues of material prosperity.

Long had been criticized just months before Mrs. King's death, when a newspaper investigation revealed that he received compensation from the church's charity organization that included a million-dollar-plus salary, a $1.4 million dollar mansion, and a Bentley automobile. When asked by a reporter about the compensation, Bishop Long responded: "We're not just a church, we're an international corporation." Informing the reporter that "Jesus wasn't poor," Bishop Long justified his compensation from the charity, pointing out that "we're not just a bumbling bunch of preachers who can't talk and all we're doing is baptizing babies . . . You've got to put me on a different scale than the little black preacher sitting over there that's supposed to be just getting by because the people are suffering."[23]

The controversy did not end there. When the Interdenominational Theological Center (ITC), a predominantly black Christian seminary in Atlanta, invited Bishop Long to speak at its commencement, students protested, an honorary degree recipient boycotted the ceremony, and a longtime trustee of the seminary expressed outrage. The honorary degree recipient was James Cone, discussed previously, who is considered the "father" of black liberation theology. Cone objected to Long denigrating the prophetic tradition of the black church and distorting the legacy of Dr. King. "King devoted his life to the least of these," Cone remarked. "He could have been just like Bishop Long with all the millions he has, but he chose to die poor . . . He would not use his own message or his own movement to promote himself."[24] ITC trustee Bishop John Hurst Adams of the African Methodist Episcopal Church was more direct in his criticism. Long, Adams argued, "substituted the pursuit of justice for the pursuit of prosperity."[25] (In 2010, Long became embroiled in a scandal in which several young men accused Bishop Long of sexually exploiting them.)

With its roots in Pentecostalism, the prosperity gospel encourages believers to address personal problems—and by extension societal problems—by using faith and positive thinking to improve their health and material prosperity. While most of the black Protestant churches evolved out of protest from the exclusion and discrimination of white Protestants, Pentecostalism evolved as a multiracial religious movement and is heavily influenced by religious practices indigenous to the black American experience. As a religious movement that developed around the same time as the social gospel movement, known colloquially in black communities at that time as "sanctified churches," mainstream black churches considered Pentecostal churches part of a fringe movement, if not a cult. If there ever was a religious tradition that was associated with an otherworldly, pie-in-the-sky orientation, it is the Pentecostal movement; a movement that prepared its adherents for the biblical prophecy of the rapture, an event where the faithful will disappear from Earth and ascend into heaven.[26]

Pentecostalism was inspired by the biblical account of the day of Pentecost, where the followers of Christ spoke in unknown tongues, which followers considered, along with the practices of faith healing and the ability to give and interpret prophesies, "gifts of the spirit." In the United States the spread of Pentecostalism occurred through the Azusa Street Revival, an event where whites, blacks, Asians, and Mexicans, as well as people across social classes, gathered in revival services between 1906 and 1915 in Los Angeles to experience the "gifts of the spirit." Led by William Seymour, a black minister from Texas, whose biblical perspectives on Pentecostalism were taught to him by the white minister Charles Parham of Topeka, Kansas, the Azusa Street Revival was influenced by the charismatic black religious practices that remain a part of the movement today.

Adopting Negro spirituals and the preaching styles of black ministers of the day, the Azusa Street Revival was the first truly racially integrated and cross-class religious movement to develop in the United States. As one historian of the movement explains, the beginnings of Pentecostalism "meant loving in the face of hate—overcoming the hatred of a whole nation by demonstrating that Pentecost is something very different from the success-oriented way of life." Yet the dominant views of racism in society at the turn of the twentieth century disrupted the initial multiracial characteristics of the movement. Its theological founder, Charles Parham, sympathized with the Ku Klux Klan, racially segregated students at his bible school in Topeka, preached against the intermingling of races, and believed that Anglo-Saxons were the master race—all of which ran counter to the Azusa Street experience.[27]

Despite racism dividing the Pentecostal movement, the Assemblies of God, the predominantly white and leading denomination of Pentecostals, acknowledges today the racially diverse origins of the movement. Writing nearly a hundred years after the birth of Pentecostalism in the United States, the Assemblies of God recognizes that "the Azusa Street revival witnessed the breakdown of barriers which normally divide people from one another: race, class, and gender, wealth, language, education, church affiliation and culture . . . The mission had an integrated leadership and congregation—and although it was decades before the civil rights movement, had an amazing lack of discrimination." Indeed, the interracial origins of the Pentecostal movement positioned Pentecostalism to become the most diverse religious movement in the United States today; a fact that came about because of the success of the civil rights movement, in which, ironically, Pentecostals, black or white, had little if any involvement.[28]

Because of the lifting of racial barriers that separated racial and ethnic groups in the post–civil rights era, Pentecostalism has been able to spread its message to a diverse group of Christians without being hindered by the divisions that plagued the movement at its beginnings. But a more racially tolerant society is only part of the story of its success as a national and global religious phenomenon. The growth of neo-Pentecostalism in the 1960s and 1970s was also the result of a more this-worldly Pentecostalism, where less emphasis was placed on behavioral restrictions (conservative dress along with bans on social dancing and women wearing make-up), the virtuousness of forsaking material possessions, and separation from the secular world and its culture. No longer stigmatized as the religion of the oppressed, neo-Pentecostalism is popular among the working- and middle-classes in the United States (but less so in developing countries where it is popular among the poor). These Pentecostals see the embracement of popular culture as complementing their lifestyles and the teachings of the movement as practical guidance to matters of family and work. Consequently, less emphasis is placed on the "by and by" and more on receiving blessings and guidance in the "here and now." The theology of prosperity emphasizes self-actualization, in which individuals can alter the course of their lives by "naming and claiming" health and prosperity for themselves. This worldview operates on a principle of reciprocity between believers and God—the more they give to the ministry and positively confess their desires to God, the more they will be materially and spiritually rewarded with God's blessings. A person's lack of material success is not attributed to societal forces but to his or her lack of spiritual commitment.

While the prophetic tradition is indigenous to the development of Afro-Christianity, the prosperity gospel has its modern origins in white, mid-twentieth-century Pentecostalism. Kenneth Hagin, Sr., who is considered the "spiritual father" of the prosperity gospel, has been distributing religious books and audiotapes on prosperity gospel since the mid-1960s. However, several scholars have noted that Hagin actually appropriated and plagiarized the writings of a little-known early twentieth-century evangelist, E. W. Kenyon, whose perspective on prosperity blended Pentecostalism and New Thought metaphysics. Though on the fringes of Pentecostalism in the 1960s, Hagin popularized the prosperity gospel through his radio broadcast, a magazine (*The Word of Faith*), and his Bible-training schools.[29]

The perspectives on the social gospel and liberation theology have been nurtured mostly in the corridors of seminaries. In contrast, the Word of Faith movement has disseminated its message broadly through a loosely formed network of nondenominational churches, Bible training schools and seminars, revivals, festivals, books, video and audio tapes, and especially through television cable networks such as the Trinity Broadcasting Network and the Word Network. Hagin's writings and sermons have influenced many of the contemporary prosperity gospel ministers, both black and white. Kenneth Copeland, a white minister from Fort Worth, Texas, and Frederick K. C. Price, a black minister from Los Angeles, have taken up Hagin's mantle as leading proselytizers of the doctrine, writing self-help-styled books on prosperity that have mass appeal. With titles such as *The Laws of Prosperity* (first published by Copeland in 1974) and *Name It and Claim It! The Power of Positive Confession* (published by Price in 1992), the Word of Faith movement has developed a cottage industry of Bible-based self-improvement books that provide guiding principles for the "abundant life."

Taking a page from the best-selling book *Rich Dad, Poor Dad*, which provides readers instructions on how to become wealthy, John Avanzini's *Rich God, Poor God* offers a biblical parallel to enhance the riches of the righteous:

As children of God, we have a heavenly father who "owns the cattle on a thousand hills" (Psalm 50:10). The rich God of the Scripture openly declares, "The silver is mine, and the gold is mine, saith the LORD of hosts" (Haggsi 2:8). Everyone knows the real God has limitless assets. However, much too often His Children declare to the world by their diminished lifestyles that He should be classified as a poor god! They are constantly using every possible means to raise funds for their various programs, while they go without the things they need in their personal lives. The thinking folks of this world ask, and rightly so, "How is it possible that a truly rich Father would have so many poor children?"[30]

Just as the social gospel and liberation theology preachers interpret biblical icons and scriptures to argue that Jesus and God side with the oppressed, prosperity gospel preachers also use biblical stories and scriptures to convey to believers that Christians should pursue wealth. Another popular minister of the prosperity gospel, Creflo Dollar, argues that Jesus was born into wealth because "Kings brought Him gold" after his birth and that Jesus had a "treasurer who [kept] up (with his money)," which suggests that the image of Jesus as a liberator by the prophetic tradition is, for proponents of the prosperity gospel, a mischaracterization.[31] Luke 4:18–19, a scripture that has been the cornerstone of prophetic teaching, proclaims: "The Spirit of the Lord is upon me, because he hath anointed me to preach the gospel to the poor; he hath sent me to heal the broken hearted, to teach deliverance to the captives, and the recovering of the blind, to set at liberty them that are bruised, to preach the acceptable day of the Lord." Dollar interprets this passage as a command to teach the poor to change their situation. "Jesus said that the poor will always be with us always," he asserts and that "Jesus takes the poor man who has no control over his life and puts him back in control of his circumstances when he receives this message" (of prosperity).[32]

Kirbyjon H. Caldwell, who preaches the prosperity gospel at the majority black Windsor Village United Methodist Church in Houston, argues that Christians have misinterpreted the well-known biblical scripture that commands that it is more difficult for a rich man to ascend to the kingdom of heaven than for a camel to pass through the eye of a needle. While reading Joshua 1:8, which refers to prosperity for those who keep God's law, Caldwell had an epiphany about the meaning of prosperity for Christians:

'Whoa!' I thought. God wants me to be prosperous and have good success! God did not make provisions—whether it's stocks and bonds, nice cars and nice homes, or peace of mind, joy, and healthy self-esteem—for Satan's kids. God's provisions are for His children, if they're for anybody.[33]

T. D. Jakes, who has been dubbed the next Billy Graham and is one of the most popular preachers in the United States, argues that the tactics of the activist black church of the 1960s hold less importance today. Rather than an emphasis on social justice, Jakes argues, there needs to be a greater focus on helping people obtain the good life:

Jesus said, "I come that you might have life and have it more abundantly" . . . I'm not against marching, but in the '60s the challenge of the black church was to march. And there are times now perhaps that we may need to march. But there's more facing us than social justice. There's personal responsibility,

FIGURE 3.1 Reverend Creflo Dollar signs his new book at Borders (*Source*: Getty Images).

motivating and equipping people to live the best lives that they can really does help them live the scriptures and to bring them to life.[34]

(Bishop Jakes delivered a sermon the morning of Obama's inauguration during a private service for the president-elect at St. John's Episcopal Church. Both Reverend Caldwell and Bishop Jakes have provided spiritual guidance to President Obama.[35])

While the prosperity gospel is growing in popularity among black adherents, aspects of the doctrine are not new in Afro-Christianity. The first half of the twentieth century saw the emergence of "Negro cults" such as Charles Manuel "Sweet Daddy" Grace's United House of Prayer, and Father Divine's Peace Mission. Although these religious leaders were known for their flamboyant lifestyles and were accused of taking advantage of their largely poor followers, both Grace and Divine provided social services for their members that included affordable housing, food pantries, and daycare centers for working parents. Indeed, they were directly involved in politics, which included supporting civil rights causes such as anti-lynching legislation and participating in electoral politics. However, unlike the prosperity ministers and their followers today, Grace's and Divine's ministries were composed of people primarily on the margins.[36]

A more direct line to the prosperity gospel in Afro-Christianity is the ministries of Reverend Frederick Eikerenkoetter (better known as Reverend Ike) of the United Church and Science Institute in New York and Boston, and the Reverend Johnnie Colemon of the Christ Universal Temple in Chicago. Both these ministers were known to teach the importance of prosperity and adopted New Thought metaphysics as part of their religious message, starting back in the 1970s and 1980s. Reverend Ike, who flaunted materialism, preached to his followers that the "lack of money is the root of all evil." The anthropologists Hans A. Baer and Merrill Singer describe this religious perspective in Afro-Christianity as "thaumaturgical sects." These sects "maintain that the most direct way to achieve socially desired ends—such as financial prosperity, prestige, love and health—is by engaging in various magico-religious rituals or acquiring esoteric knowledge that provides individuals with spiritual power over themselves and others."

Thaumaturgical sects undermine followers' participation in social reform and civic activism because they "tend to hold the individual responsible for his or her present condition and stress the need to develop a positive frame of mind while at the same time overcoming negative attitudes . . . Because of their individualistic orientation, such groups are largely apolitical and express little interest in social reform."[37]

Though followers of prosperity gospel do not practice magico-religious rituals that require their adherents to acquire esoteric knowledge, the prosperity gospel does practice positive confession as a way to acquire material prosperity, health, and positive family relationships. What is new about the emergence of the prosperity gospel in the post–civil rights era is that its adherents are not on the margins of society nor is the prosperity gospel viewed as a cult-like religion. Many followers are thought to be from the striving black working class and middle class rather than from poor, inner-city communities.

As a religious worldview that is anchored in individualism, prosperity gospel has the potential to undermine the civic traditions of black churches. One important study on the influence of the prosperity gospel in black churches notes that "instead of advocating protest marches, voting drives, and other forms of activism familiar to black church movements," the prosperity gospel "teach[es] members that poverty is the curse of the devil and the power to transform their oppression resides within the ability to appropriate their faith and take their rightful place in the Kingdom of God." This worldview not only appeals to the growing black middle class, whose class status would have predicted that they would become less religious or join middle-class mainline denominations, it also appeals to "all poverty-stricken minorities stretching for a glimmer of hope."[38]

FIGURE 3.2 Reverend Ike at church service (*Source*: Getty Images).

Though the prosperity gospel is not as explicitly political as the liberal theologies of the social gospel and black liberation, its popularity emerged simultaneously with the rise of political conservatism in the 1980s. Since then, the civil rights community has been under attack for its lack of new ideas for solving the problems of the poor and for continuing to believe that racial discrimination is the primary explanation for why many in the black community have not progressed. Civil rights initiatives, most notably affirmative action, and the social programs of the New Deal and Great Society, have been challenged not only by conservatives but also by liberals, and as a consequence social welfare programs have been gradually dismantled. Part of the appeal of the prosperity gospel is that even if government cannot solve the problems of the poor, followers believe that God can bring about prosperity and good health despite the secular world's systems of poverty and racism.

To adherents of the prosperity gospel, positive thoughts and the practice of planting financial "seeds" through monetary contributions to ministries may do more for social mobility than either antipoverty policies or laws forbidding racial discrimination. There is no analysis of racism or "suffering" in the prosperity gospel, because

> racism is not important because the individual and the desire for money is all that is important. The poor are blamed for their poverty, the poverty itself seen as evidence that they do not fully believe in Christ. With money, all seeming injustices can be corrected. Justice is just another commodity in their theologies.[39]

Indeed the black community is divided on whether the lack of progress in black communities is mostly due to racism or to the individual fault of blacks themselves: a perspective that would complement the individualistic thrust of the prosperity gospel movement among Afro-Christians. In a survey commissioned by Columbia University's Center on African-American Politics and Society (CAAPS) and the ABC News Polling Unit, a plurality of blacks—44 percent—think that the lack of black progress is attributable to insufficient initiative among blacks themselves, while 37 percent believe that the reason blacks have not moved forward is because of racism. Clearly, for a large number of blacks, structural forces in American society have less of an impact on black progress than individual responsibility.[40]

Another explanation for the rise in the prosperity gospel's popularity is one of the very successes of the civil rights movement—the rise of a visible black middle class, the largest in the nation's history. Like their white counterparts, the mainline black Protestant congregations are losing members to fundamentalist and charismatic churches, many of which are nondenominational and promote the gospel of prosperity. While middle-class congregations of the past were rooted in the social gospel tradition, the poor and working-class-oriented Pentecostal congregations were more likely to be apolitical and "otherworldly." No longer considered cults or marginal to the African American religious experience, neo-Pentecostalism has evolved in the post–civil rights era as a religion of respectability that appeals to the black middle class and "strivers" who link their upward mobility to a spiritual worldview that rewards wealth and good health.

Another possible explanation might be the realization that black political empowerment has not been accompanied by black economic success. While the prophetic tradition served as a religious justification for the Black Power movement and helped to facilitate that movement's incorporation into electoral politics by promoting the belief that activist churches have an obligation to support candidacies that represent the interests of oppressed communities, blacks remain, as a group, on the economic margins of American life. Indeed, while the number of black elected officials has climbed in the past forty years, including unprecedented numbers of blacks elected to Congress, to city halls, and to local and state governments, services to the poor have been severely cut. Thus, perhaps for many followers of the prosperity gospel, the ideas and strategies of the social gospel tradition are perceived as no longer capable (at least not solely) of "uplifting" black communities from poverty.[41]

While Barack Obama appears not to embrace the gospel of prosperity, he does believe that greater individual responsibility on the part of blacks is needed if they plan to make it to the land of milk and honey. In a celebrated speech given at a commemoration of the Selma Voting Right March at Brown Chapel AME church on March 4, 2007, Obama talked about the obligations of the "Joshua generation." He told the audience that the Moses generation of the civil rights movement had fought hard for black Americans to receive their rights. Now it was time for the succeeding Joshua generation—as told in the biblical story of the Exodus—to take black America to the Promised Land. Obama reminded the audience—which included members of the Moses generation such as Reverend Joseph Lowery and Congressman John Lewis—not to be blinded by materialism and not to "forget where you came from." The candidate also mentioned that the principles that the previous generation fought for—such as the enforcement of anti-discrimination laws and affirmative action—still have to be vigilantly fought for every day. And the candidate also declared that the Joshua generation should focus on the economic rights of black people that can be solved, partly by closing the disparities in health care and in education.

But Obama, as the emerging leader of the Joshua generation, also told the audience that "government alone can't solve problems." What is needed by the current generation is the "discipline and fortitude that was instilled in all the people who participated" in the civil rights movement. What is missing in the lives of today's generation is personal fortitude and respectability. "Imagine young people, sixteen, seventeen, twenty, twenty-one, backs straight, eyes clear, suit and tie, sitting down at a lunch counter knowing somebody is going to spill milk on you but you have the discipline to understand you are not going to retaliate because in showing the world how *disciplined we were as a people*, we were able to win over the conscience of the nation."

In its sojourn to the Promised Land, the Joshua generation—from Obama's perspective—has lost its way. "We have too many children in poverty in this country and everybody should be ashamed, but don't tell me it doesn't have a little to do with the fact that we got too many daddies not acting like daddies." It is the responsibility of the current generation, Obama informed the audience, to "fight against the oppressor in each of us." The presidential candidate distanced himself from the prophetic tradition of black political culture in the aftermath of the Reverend Wright incident. But Obama also embraced an ideological tradition of racial uplift—what has become known as the politics of respectability—that is just as old in black religion and politics as the prophetic tradition. As a candidate for the presidency of the United States, he did not decry the United States for its unfair treatment of black people in both the past and the present. He instead proclaimed the failure of blacks themselves to hold up their end of the bargain as citizens in a nation full of freedom and opportunity.

4

Respectability as Public Philosophy

ON FEBRUARY 28, 2008, during a speech delivered a few days before the Texas primary, Barack Obama chastised a predominantly black audience in Beaumont for being negligent parents: "I've got to talk about *us* a little," the candidate told the wildly cheering crowd. "We can't keep feeding our children junk all day long, giving them no exercise. They are overweight by the time they are five or four years old, and then we are surprised when they get sick." Launching into a lecture on how bad food choices lead to childhood obesity, Obama proclaimed: "I know how hard it is to get kids to eat properly but I also know that if folks [are] letting our children drink eight sodas a day, which some parents do, or, you know, eat a bag of potato chips for lunch or Popeye's [fried chicken] for breakfast," they are not holding up to their responsibility as parents. Switching to a southern—black—dialect, Obama asks the crowd: "Y'all have Popeye's out in Beaumont? I know some of y'all you got that cold Popeye's out for breakfast. I know. That's why y'all laughing . . . You can't do that. Children have to have proper nutrition. That affects also how they study, how they learn in school."[1]

During Obama's jousting with the audience, the candidate neglected to mention social and economic barriers that may account for parents' allegedly poor decisions—limited food choices in black poor and working-class neighborhoods and the high price of fresh food compared with the cheap cost of fast food. Nor does Obama mention the difficulties of single parents working full time and short on time to prepare meals or the oversaturation and marketing of fast-food restaurants in minority neighborhoods.[2] To Obama, bad eating habits, at least in this speech, are a reflection of personal failings, not societal barriers. These are unusual—and potentially risky—comments for a typical Democratic presidential candidate to make before a predominantly black audience. Democratic primary candidates rely on the support of black voters if they want to win the nomination, and accusing blacks of being neglectful parents is not a smart way to gain black votes, or so conventional wisdom dictates. But, to black America—and indeed for the rest of America—Obama was not a typical candidate. To understand the exchange that took place between Obama and the predominantly black audience in Beaumont is to unravel a long-standing tradition in black politics—a tradition that was hardly noticed by the media but was effectively deployed by Obama and his handlers in 2008.

The shift in the century-old ideology—the politics of respectability—to a public philosophy directed at policing the black poor is one of the most curious transformations occurring in contemporary black politics. It was in 1903 when W. E. B. DuBois called for the Talented Tenth—the one-tenth of black America who possessed an "aristocracy of talent"—to take on the cause of "uplifting" the black masses. "It is the problem of developing the Best of this Race that they may guide the Mass away from the contamination and the death of the Worst, in their own and other races," DuBois declared in the *Souls of Black Folks*. In an era that marked the "nadir" of black life since the emancipation of slavery in 1865, the mission of Uplifters at the turn of the twentieth century encompassed more than improving the educational status of the black masses or leading the cause for civil rights. It also meant civilizing the untalented nine-tenths, that swath of black folk whom black elites declared were in need of rescue and guidance.

Evelyn Brooks Higginbotham notes in her history of turn of the twentieth-century activism among black Baptist women that the politics of respectability involved changing the behavior and habits of the black masses so that blacks as a group could be accepted by white America. Elites engaged in the politics of respectability; they "equated public behavior with individual self-respect and with the advancement of African-Americans as a group," believing "that 'respectable' behavior in public would earn their people a measure of esteem from white America." The strategy of linking blacks' public behavior with whites' recognition of blacks' humanity meant that black elites "strove to win the lower class's psychological allegiance to temperance, industriousness, thrift, refined manners, and Victorian social morals." Guided by the hands of the Talented Tenth, less fortunate blacks could be taught how to be upright people, exemplars in a society dominated by white-supremacist views on the inferiority of black people.[3]

Though conservative leader Booker T. Washington rejected the concept of the Talented Tenth, his vision for black America accepted the fundamental premises of the politics of respectability. Washington's bottom-up approach to black progress through industrial education did not depend on the commitment of Uplifters to guide the masses; it did, however, depend on the idea that changing black people's behavior would set them on a path to equality. As the personal habits of the black community's down-trodden improved—through hard work, thrift, and sobriety—Washington believed that white America would eventually accept blacks as equals worthy of citizenship. Although DuBois and Washington were divided over which strategy would lead to black progress—Should blacks confront discrimination head-on through political agitation or gradually assimilate by building an economic foundation as workers and entrepreneurs?—they were united in their view that the habits of ordinary black folk needed self-correction and supervision in order for the race to progress.

While black elites were well intentioned in their efforts to uplift the black poor, the politics of respectability undermined efforts for blacks to challenge societal barriers that accounted for black subjugation. As historian Kevin Gaines argues, the focus by elites on the behaviors and habits of ordinary black folks—particularly surrounding the failings of black families—amounted to "unconscious internalized racism." Gaines wrote that "the racist and antiracist preoccupation with the status of the patriarchal family among blacks and the notion of self-help among blacks as building and promoting family stability came to displace a broader vision of uplift as group struggle for citizenship and material advancement." The politics of respectability "misplaced equation of race progress with the status of the family" and consequently "blamed black men and women for 'failing' to measure up to the dominant society's bourgeois gender morality." As Gaines further explained, Uplifters "seemed to forget that it was the state and the constant threat of violence, not some innate racial trait, that prevented the realization of black homes and families."[4]

In the early decades of the twenty-first century, the politics of respectability survives not only as an ideology promulgated by the black middle class and directed at blacks economically left behind in an era celebrated as "postracial," it survives also as a public philosophy trumpeted by black elites who have entered the inner sanctums of mainstream American institutions. These select few not only make up today's Talented Tenth, they are also part of the nation's elite. Thus, as black leaders became partners in the nation's dominant institutions—in business, media, entertainment, politics, and academia—the politics of respectability has moved beyond the protected precincts of black America into mainstream American politics.

In the past, usually civil rights leaders, ministers, teachers, family, and community elders circulated the idea of respectability. But today's leading purveyors of the politics of respectability also include black politicians, business people, public intellectuals, entertainers, and journalists. Often camouflaged as "tough love" homilies about the need for greater personal responsibility in the lives of young black people, the poor, and the down-and-out, the rhetoric of the politics of respectability may have far greater consequences in the lives of today's "untalented" black folk than it did in decades past. Today, draconian policies targeted at poor and working-class blacks now receive the public backing of black elites whose influence and status in American society provide cover for racist practices and policies.

The election of Barack Obama and his adoption of this rhetoric during the 2008 presidential campaign raised the prominence of respectability in American politics and society to new heights. The racially transcendent rhetoric of the Obama campaign—whose surrogates constantly repeated the refrain "Obama is not a black man running for president, but a presidential candidate who happens to be black"—made the politics of respectability even more palatable as a public philosophy. Indeed, respectability served dual purposes for the Obama campaign. It was used as a tactical ploy to shore up support among skeptical white voters concerned that an Obama administration would favor minorities. It also functioned as a familiar discourse that reinforced the candidate's connections with black voters under the guise of tough love. In black America, the presidential candidate "who happens to be black" was elevated with ease to the rank of Mr. Respectability-in-Chief, a role that Obama was more than eager to assume on his trek to the White House.

What is different about today's politics of respectability is that it has evolved into a public philosophy that influences policy debates about the *black* poor. The focus on public behavior and the personal habits of poor blacks—especially concerning the breakdown of the nuclear black family and the lack of personal responsibility among black males—has shifted policy discussions toward a near wholesale emphasis on how the individual failings of the black poor have stifled their progress and away from explanations that focus on how social and economic barriers impede the progress of the black poor. Consequently, the politics of respectability as public philosophy has become a social policy solution for dealing with an assortment of concerns facing poor and working-class black communities, most notably entrenched poverty, declining educational achievement, criminality, and single parenthood.

Though the politics of respectability resembles prevailing neoliberal views that privilege the logic of market institutions and private enterprise over the ability of government to solve social problems, the politics of respectability predates neoliberalism. Indeed, when it comes to solving the problems of the black poor, the politics of respectability as a public philosophy accommodates neoliberal perspectives, emphasizing the need for the poor to solve their own problems with minimal or no assistance from government. Respectability as public philosophy also demands little from government to solve the problems of poverty because it blames the black poor for not being "productive citizens." Thus the self-care ethos of neoliberalism is legitimized by black-elite rhetoric on respectability that makes it easier for policymakers to abandon government support for the poor or to not act on the behalf of the poor at all.[5]

What is particularly powerful about the politics of respectability is that its purveyors run the ideological gamut in black politics, joining together black liberals, black conservatives, and Black Nationalists into an army of crusaders, who think the black poor—and blacks who "behave" like them—need special instruction. Rather than seeing the poor as citizens who have the right to advocate policies on their behalf, the proponents of respectability tell poor black people to shape up and deliver homilies stressing that there are "no excuses" for their plight.

Social class distinctions in black America have historically had less to do with differences in occupation, income, and wealth than with how black people publicly conducted themselves as representatives of the race. Speaking before a black women's group in Charleston, South Carolina, in 1898, Margaret Murray Washington, Booker T. Washington's third wife and a founder and future president of the National Association of Colored Women, declared,

"We need, as a race, a good strong public sentiment in favor of a sounder, healthier body, and a cleaner and high toned morality." Noting that black leaders were too quick to emphasize blacks' "strong points"—a practice she felt harmed the race—Margaret Murray Washington believed that blacks could improve their lot if more leaders placed greater emphasis on blacks' "weak points" and their "lack of taking hold of opportunities" before them.[6]

As if anticipating part of DuBois' rationale for cultivating the Talented Tenth, Margaret Murray Washington offered a similar strategy for the moral uplift of the race, five years before DuBois' call for the black middle class to lead the black masses. "No nation or race has ever come up by entirely overlooking its members who are less fortunate, less ambitious, less sound in body and hence in soul, and we can do it," Washington asserted. "The condition of our race, brought about by slavery, the ignorance, the poverty, intemperance, ought to make us women know that in half a century we cannot afford to lose sight of the large majority of the race who have not, as yet, thrown off the badge of the evils which I have just mentioned."

From Washington's perspective, infant mortality, disease, early death, and the disruption of the nuclear family were not the fault of the state or the broader society but mostly the result of flawed choices made by impoverished blacks. She believed that social ills could be avoided if poor blacks would change their personal habits. And it was the duty of black churchwomen to help uplift "our poorer classes and second class folks" by getting them to embrace a "cleaner social morality." Racial progress, Washington argued, entailed the black middle class making informed choices when selecting marriage partners and the black poor purging themselves of immorality, poverty, and ignorance. Citing statistics on black illegitimate birthrates—as high as 25 percent in one city, Washington pointed out—and noting only three requests for marriage licenses by black men in another city, Washington concluded that these behaviors were dragging down the race. "Twelve hundred colored men and women, for whom there is no excuse, living immoral lives, handing down to their offspring disease and crime, and only three living in such a way as to advance the race," Washington thundered. "No spectacle can be more appalling." For Washington, social immorality was also responsible for the disproportionate number of blacks in prisons whose lack of "physical ability" prevented them from resisting crime. Washington believed black criminality resulted more from personal failings and physical weaknesses rather than racist practices, such as the convict-lease system, a semi-slave system of labor that was rampant during the turn of the twentieth century.

Washington also believed that too many black men were not taking care of their families—a claim that would be echoed in the later part of the twentieth century and into the twenty-first. "Go North or South, East or West, and the numbers of dens of abandoned women, of profligate men is too large," Washington surmised. "These are the breeders of disease and the millstone of the race." Washington's remedy for lifting disadvantaged black people out of their circumstances involved black clubwomen teaching blacks the importance of regular hygiene, good eating habits, and sound financial decisions:

> The average colored person dislikes water, and he won't keep himself clean. He bathes, if at all, once a week Saturday night and changes his clothes in the same indifferent way. He seldom uses a tooth brush. He often even neglects to comb his hair, except on Sunday. There is no excuse for this. Bathe at least twice a week, and change the clothes as often, and be sure to clean the teeth at least once a day, and do not forget to comb the hair each day. We eat too little or too poor food. We are ready to buy showy clothing, but we stint our stomachs too often. They call us great eaters. Let us eat more and better food. There is very little vitality in grits and gravy.

Changing the behavior of poor blacks would prove to whites that black people were worthy of acceptance. Despite the legacies of slavery, the onset of legalized racial segregation, and white racist violence against blacks during this era, for Washington the virtues of good behavior trumped societal, economic, and political forces that confined blacks to the bottom of society. "You say there are causes for all these, causes for which we are not responsible," Washington told the clubwomen. "I admit this much, but there are also causes for which we are responsible. And the fact that there are causes ought to make us hopeful, because we have it in our power to remove these causes." With the right attitude and behavior black people could "prove to their enemies that our condition physically and morally is nothing inherent or peculiar to race, but rather the outcome of circumstances over which we can and will become masters." In essence, racism for blacks was something to be managed rather than challenged directly. And it was to be managed by the elites whom Washington instructed should "stoop down now and then and lift up others" in the cause of racial progress.

During the Great Migration in the first decades of the twentieth century, black elites also took up the mission of respectability. This time respectability was a response to southern black migration to northern cities. As purveyors of respectability, northern black elites—who viewed themselves as "Old Settlers"—assumed the cause of instructing black migrants how to conduct themselves in their neighborhoods, at work, and on public transportation. The Old Settlers were committed to the politics of respectability, regardless of social-class standing in the community. In Chicago, a city receiving the greatest number of migrants during the 1910s, the Urban League, the Wabash Avenue YMCA, and the city's leading newspapers—the *Chicago Defender* and the *Chicago Whip*—called attention to what they considered migrants' displeasing habits. "Fearful that the immigrants, with their rural manners, would disrupt the community and embarrass the race," historian James R. Grossman wrote in his classic history of the black migration to Chicago, "middle-class black Chicago tried to protect its respectability by instructing newcomers in acceptable forms of behavior."[7]

The Chicago Urban League greeted migrants with pamphlets and hand cards at train stations with instructions on how to behave and hosted "Strangers Meetings" where migrants were instructed on "cleanliness, sobriety, thrift, efficiency, and respectable, restrained behavior in public places." The *Defender* regularly published a list of do's and don'ts for migrants to follow. While many of the rules gave practical advice on public health, steering children from trouble, and maintaining employment, most rules were designed to police the behavior of migrants. "Don't use vile language in public places," one list began followed by warnings against acting "discourteously to other people in public places," being "drawn into street fights," making "yourself a public nuisance," congregating "in crowds on the streets to the disadvantage of others passing along," using "liberty as a license to do as you please," or encouraging "gamblers, disreputable women or men to ply their business any time or place."

As James Grossman further explains, the Old Settlers were not just horrified by displeasing behavior; they were also horrified by the migrants' southern folk culture. The city's black newspapers often "castigated women who were 'frequently seen in their boudoir caps, house slippers and aprons around the corner in the grocery store.'" Grossman recounts that the black middle class became embarrassed by the sights of "streetside barbecue stands and such icons as watermelon and head rags." The Urban League even asked migrants to sign a pledge that they would not wear "dust caps, bungalow aprons, house clothing and bedroom shoes out of doors." While the reaction to southern black migrants by the northern black elites mirrored the reactions of Jewish-American and Irish-American elites during influxes of poor Jewish and Irish immigrations, the elites of the European immigrants embraced the folk culture of the Old World while the northern black elites rejected the "backwardness" of southern folk culture.[8]

Many criticisms of the black migrants were misdirected. While Old Settlers recognized the societal barriers that the migrants faced in Chicago and other cities, they nonetheless blamed black

HELPFUL HINTS

DON'T carry on loud conversations or use vulgar or obscene language on the street cars, streets, or in public places. Remember that this hurts us as a race.

DON'T go about the streets or on the street car in bungalow aprons, boudoir caps and house slippers. Wear regular street clothes when you go into the streets.

TRY to dress neatly at all times, but don't be a dude or wear flashy clothes. They are as undesirable and as harmful as unclean clothes.

General Disorderly Appearance

DON'T think you can hold your job unless you are on time, industrious, efficient and sober.

DON'T sit in front of your house or around Belle Isle or public places with your shoes off. Don't wear overalls on Sunday.

DON'T stay away from work every time someone gives a picnic or boat ride. Stay on your job. Others do.

DON'T spend all your money for pleasure. Save some of it for extra clothing and fuel for the winter and to take care of your family and yourself when sickness comes.

na II, 276

FIGURE 4.1 Detroit Urban League 1918 pamphlet gives instructions on proper behav to black southern migrants (*Source*: Bentley Historical Library, University of Michiga

DON'T forget that cleanliness and fresh air are necessary to good health. Keep your windows open.

DON'T do your children's hair up into alleys, canals and knots if you don't want other children to make fun of them. Keep them clean.

DON'T keep your children out of school. See that they attend the nearest school to you.

DON'T fail to start a savings account with some good bank or building loan association.

DON'T throw refuse and tin cans in your back or front yards. Keep your surroundings as clean as possible. This makes for good health.

Neatly Clothed and Orderly Appearance

DON'T fool with patent medicines in case of sickness. Send for a good doctor. In case you have no money, go to some of the Board of Health clinics.

DON'T be rude and ugly to people on the streets. Be courteous and polite and thereby keep out of trouble.

DON'T fail to meet the teachers of your children. Keep in touch with them. Every hateful thing that your child says about the teacher is not true.

DON'T fail to become connected with some church as soon as you get in the city.

DON'T make lots of unnecessary noise going to and from baseball games. If the parks are taken away from you it will be partly your own fault.

₣ure 4.1 (*continued*)

migrants for their living conditions. Chastising black women for not taking proper care of their homes, for instance, overlooked the obstacles that working-class black women faced. Unlike middle-class black women, and many European immigrant women, working-class black women were employed outside of the home, a reality that made it difficult for them to live up to middle-class standards of maintaining "respectable" homes. Although the black poor's decrepit housing had more to do with the structural disrepair of buildings and less to do with the "filthiness" of its inhabitants, admonishments easily turned into victim-blaming by elites.[9]

Even during the Great Depression, the politics of respectability perpetuated the idea among many blacks that the most socially and economically disadvantaged blacks had themselves to blame for their misfortunate. Writing in the NAACP's *Crisis* magazine during the height of the Depression, W. E. B. DuBois, in an essay titled "Our Class Struggle," observed in 1933, "the general attitude of the race is one of irritation toward these members of their group who have brought the whole race into disrepute." Though DuBois believed that the real class struggle in America was "not between the colored classes, but rather between colored and white folk," DuBois observed that conformity to respectable behavior was a mark of class distinction among blacks. Whether criminals, the "feeble-minded," or paupers dependent on charity, relatively well-off blacks resented the shortcomings of the "unfortunates of the race" because they failed to "progress as rapidly as a Negro thinks a black man must." As blacks at the very bottom of the untalented nine-tenths, they were "regarded not so much as unfortunate as in some vague way *blame worthy*" for the conditions and situations they found themselves facing.[10]

The civil rights movement—and especially the Black Power movement—brought into question the wisdom of the politics of respectability as a strategy for black progress. A mass movement for social change would require more participants than the Talented Tenth, a concept that DuBois abandoned in 1948.[11] Many of the movement's leaders emerged from the black middle class, but the bulk of the foot soldiers for the movement were ordinary people, many of whom placed their lives on the line for a greater cause. The rhetoric of the movement reflected a moral-centered respectability that asked southern blacks to be willing to suffer the indignities of racial segregation to demonstrate their ability to love in the face of hate. But the call for this type of upright moral behavior was more a strategy to legitimize nonviolent resistance than an appeal to whites to accept blacks on equal terms because of their proven moral worth.

Nonetheless, there were instances when the politics of respectability held sway during the movement. While Rosa Parks is often remembered for her bravery in refusing to give up her seat to a white man on a Montgomery bus on December 5, 1955, at least two other black women were arrested on buses before Parks for violating Alabama's segregation laws on public transportation. One was Claudette Colvin, a teenager who resisted relinquishing her seat to a white woman on March 2, 1955. Colvin was dragged from her seat by two white police officers, kicking and screaming: "It's my constitutional right!" Colvin was charged for violating the state's segregation law, as well as with disturbing the peace and assaulting police officers. Colvin's conviction was used in federal court as the lead case to challenge the state's segregation laws on public transportation, and the teenager served as the star witness in the case, which found Alabama's public transportation laws unconstitutional.

Her arrest, however, did not trigger the call for a boycott by community leaders as Rosa Parks' arrest did months later. One reason is that Colvin's status in the community—she was thought to be from the wrong side of the tracks *within* Montgomery's black community—and her comportment during the confrontation deemed her not respectable enough to be used as a symbol of community resistance. Black leaders and ordinary folks described Colvin as "mouthy," "emotional," and "feisty" while Parks' soft-spoken demeanor and dignified manner made her the perfect model to challenge Montgomery's white power structure. "My mother told me to be quiet about what I did," Colvin recalled decades later. "She said: 'Let Rosa be the one. White people aren't going to bother Rosa—her skin is lighter than yours and they like her.'"[12]

What further isolated Colvin from boycott leaders and Birmingham's black community was that months after her arrest Colvin became pregnant by a married man whom many blacks in Montgomery suspected was white. Though community leaders most likely wanted to protect Colvin from the grief of enduring ridicule by Montgomery's white power structure for being an unmarried pregnant teenager, Colvin wondered why boycott leaders abandoned her after she testified at the federal trial. "I knew they couldn't put me up on stage like the queen of the boycott, but after what I had done, why did they have to turn their backs on me?" Colvin asked decades later. E. D. Nixon, a longtime community activist who recruited King to lead the boycott, made it a point to say to white authorities that the police had "messed with the wrong woman" when Parks was arrested. Colvin recalled later why she felt boycott leaders may have overlooked her case as a catalyst for a boycott:

> I was shunned because I had gotten pregnant. It was made worse because my parents wouldn't let me just explain, "This is what happened and here's who the father is," . . . But because [my son] was light-skinned, and I couldn't name the father, they all assumed the father was white. Socially I had three strikes against me: I was an unmarried teenager with a light-skinned baby. Without school, I had no choice of friends my age, and there was no way any of the women in town would accept me. To them I was a fallen woman.[13]

A second teenager who was arrested before Parks was also deemed unworthy as a symbol since it was rumored that her father was an alcoholic.

By the late 1960s, with the onset of the Black Power movement, the politics of respectability fell out of favor. Black Power's rhetoric offered radical critiques of American society's prevailing norms and culture, and the black middle class was coming under attack for aping white values and culture rather than embracing black—African—culture. And sociologist E. Franklin Frazier's scathing critique of the black middle class in his influential 1957 book, *The Black Bourgeoisie*, also helped to cast aspersions on the black middle class. Frazier argued that the black middle class was obsessed with conspicuous consumption and lived in a "World of Make-believe" because they psychologically and materially were invested in white supremacy, refusing to compete in the "white world."

The anti-elitist rhetoric of the Black Power movement (activists regularly referred to mainstream black leaders as "Uncle Toms" and the black middle class as "House Niggers") temporarily muted the politics of respectability in black politics. The widening ideological gulf between affluent blacks and poor blacks had become so tense that in 1968 the upper-middle class black fraternity Sigma Pi Phi—also known as the Boulé—had to change the location of its Pittsburgh convention. Local members feared that "black militants" would wrongly perceive "luxury-loving elite Negroes coming into one of Pittsburgh's finest hotels" to spend huge sums of money while Pittsburgh's blacks were suffering. A committee created to investigate the tensions in Pittsburgh had concluded, in so many words, that the Talented Tenth was losing its grip on the black masses. "Tragic is the indisputable fact that the underprivileged of our group and their leaders discern no possible collaboration between us—'the reputed talented tenth'—and those who compose their programs and enunciate their aspirations. There is 'irreconcilable polarization between these two forces in the black community,'" the report concluded.[14]

When *Ebony* magazine published a special edition featuring the "new" black middle class in 1973, rhetoric on the politics of respectability was virtually absent. Instead of stories extolling the need of the black middle class to guide blacks left behind in the ghettoes, several articles featured in the special issue cast a critical eye on the black middle class. A one-page editorial on the responsibilities of middle-class blacks asked them to do simple things to help themselves and black communities. It instructed them to ensure that their children accomplish more than their parents, to become educated about black history so that they could maintain their self-respect in the white professional world, and to pay "back debts" to the black community by supporting black institutions and causes. And middle-class blacks were asked not to look down on the black poor. "This means that the black middle-class must know that black people don't live in poverty because they want to live in poverty," *Ebony* informed its readers. "Many live in poverty because no one has made an effort to help them get out of it." In essence, *Ebony* was asking middle-class blacks to link their fates with poor blacks. Though the politics of respectability asked middle-class blacks to teach poor blacks how to improve their behavior so that *all* blacks could be recognized by white society as worthy of first-class citizenship, the new charge for middle-class blacks in the Black Power era was to clasp hands with poor blacks as equals rather than stoop down and lift them up.

By the late 1980s, and certainly by the 1990s, the politics of respectability began to reemerge. Its reemergence was brought about by two similar but separate discourses in the academy and media—the appearance of a so-called urban underclass and the rise of gangsta rap. While structural explanations had been the dominant academic approach to explicate the plight of the black poor since the 1960s, newspaper articles, magazine stories, television documentaries, and academic studies began to report that the values of the black poor were different than the rest of society. The black poor were portrayed as embracing self-destructive values that kept them entrapped in poverty. And in addition to the social isolation that the black poor experience, they—especially poor black youth—were thought to be embracing a destructive culture that promoted antisocial and deviant behavior. Biological explanations for black inferiority that were dominant for much of the twentieth century had given way to cultural explanations about why some blacks were left behind by the turn of the twenty-first century.

A 2007 Pew Research Center survey asked whether the values held by middle-class blacks and the values of poor blacks had become more similar or more different over the past ten years. A majority of blacks—60 percent—believed the values of the black middle class and the black poor had diverged, while nearly one-third of blacks thought the two classes' values had become more similar. But among representatives of today's Talented Tenth the perceived differences in values between the black poor and the black middle class were even greater. Seventy percent of black college graduates reported that the values of poor blacks had become more different compared to 55 percent of black high school graduates and 57 percent of blacks with less than a high school education.

Indeed, the perception that poor blacks and middle-class blacks no longer share similar values has widened over the past two decades. The Washington-based black think tank the Joint Center for Political Studies commissioned a Gallup Poll in 1986 that showed that blacks were roughly split in their belief that the values of poor blacks and middle-class blacks had become more different or more similar over the years. Forty-four percent of blacks believed that the values between the two classes were more different while 40 percent believed that values had become more similar between the groups. Compared with the 2007 findings, the perception of value differences between well-off and less well-off blacks had shifted substantially. In the twenty-one-year period there has been a 17 percentage point increase in all blacks reporting that the values of the two classes had become more different.

Moreover, the greatest shift in the perception of a values gap took place among the most and least educated blacks. Comparing the 1986 and 2007 figures among the Talented Tenth, there has been a 20 percentage point shift in the perception that values have become more different between poor and well-off blacks. For those blacks with less than a high school education the shift in their perceptions is also striking. In 1986 only 42 percent perceived diverging values; by 2007 that jumped to 57 percent, a difference of 15 percentage points. (The perceptions of blacks with a high school education changed less over the same period of time—from 46 to 55 percent—indicating that value perceptions may be more relevant for blacks at the very top and the very bottom of the social class order in black America than in the middle.)[15]

The shifts in the perception of a values gap, particularly among the black middle class, illustrate why the politics of respectability is back in vogue from a variety of voices and in the most unsuspected places. Nation of Islam leader Louis Farrakhan, the organizer of the 1995 Million Man March on Washington, promotes a variant of the classic politics of respectability that asks blacks to change their negative behaviors so that black people can be respected among the nations of the world. For Farrakhan black Americans have to be purged of their immoral behavior by being "concentrated upon" so they can gain self-respect. Interestingly, Farrakhan's description of his social distance from poor blacks is an updated version of late-nineteenth-century descriptions of blacks at the very bottom of the untalented nine-tenths. In a 1991 interview in *Spotlight*, a newspaper of the ultraright Liberty Lobby known for its anti-black and anti-Jewish views, Farrakhan told the following to the editors about how he felt about blacks in the ghettos:

> Not one of you [*Spotlight* editorial staff] would mind, maybe, my living next door to you, because I am a man of a degree and intelligence, of moral character. I am not a wild, partying fellow. I am not a noisemaker. I keep my lawn very nice . . . For some of us who have learned how to act at home and abroad, you might not have problems . . . Drive through the ghettos, and see our people. See how we live. Tell me that you want your son or daughter to marry one of these. No, you don't.[16]

Economist Glenn Loury, a black former conservative turned liberal, promoted the idea of respectability as public philosophy during the conservative phase of his career. One of the few prominent blacks active in the conservative movement during the 1980s, Loury, who was then an economist at Harvard University, argued that middle-class blacks had a special obligation to help poor blacks change their negative behaviors. Teenage pregnancies, unwed mothers, and the arrest and incarceration rates plaguing black America "lie outside the reach of effective government action," Loury believed. Addressing the "values, attitudes, and behaviors of individual blacks" could cure social ills facing poor black communities, not government programs. In Loury's view it was the responsibility of the black middle class to uplift poor blacks because whites might not have an interest—or feel obligated—to assist them. And because the black middle class derived so much political capital from black misery, Loury reasoned, middle-class blacks should repay the race by leading the charge in altering poor blacks' negative habits. "Too much of the political energy, talent, and imagination abounding in the black middle-class is being channeled into a struggle against an 'enemy without' while the 'enemy within' goes relatively unchecked," Loury said.[17]

The idea of an enemy within black America was expressed in 2004 in the highly controversial comments made by comedian Bill Cosby during a dinner in honor of the fiftieth anniversary of the Supreme Court's *Brown* decision. What is interesting about Bill Cosby's attack on the black poor is that the entertainer has a reputation for being politically liberal, having backed an array of causes over the years, including support for jailed black journalist Mumia Abu Jamal, Jesse Jackson's presidential runs, and historically black colleges. But even by the standards of turn of the twentieth-century reformers, Cosby's diatribe on the black poor that evening was beyond the pale. "Ladies and gentleman, the lower economic and lower middle economic people are not holding their end in this deal," Cosby declared. In Cosby's world, the bottom of the untalented nine-tenths is composed of terrible parents condoning irresponsible behavior. Constantly referring to poor blacks as "these people," Cosby rambled on that evening about black high school dropouts, incarcerated blacks, and black single mothers.

"Fifty percent drop-out rate, I'm telling you, and people in jail, and women having children by five, six different men," Cosby surmised. "Under what excuse? I want somebody to love me. And as soon as you have it, you forget to parent. Grandmother, mother, and great-grandmother in the same room, raising children, and the child knows nothing about love or respect of any one of the three of them." Despite the fact that the average welfare recipient has two children—a number that mirrors the average number of children in families that are not on welfare—Cosby perpetuated the myth of the black woman on welfare with too many children and multiple fathers.[18]

Cosby sees all poor blacks deserving the treatment they receive in the criminal justice system. "Looking at the incarcerated, these are not political criminals," Cosby argued. "These people are going around stealing Coca Cola. People getting shot in the back of the head over a piece of pound cake! And then we all run out and are outraged: 'The cops shouldn't have shot him.' What the hell was he doing with the pound cake in his hand?" The comedian wants to return to the "good old days" when unmarried women had to wear a scarlet letter of shame, be banished from the community during the pregnancy, or be rescued by a mother concealing her daughter's pregnancy by claiming the infant as her own.

Like early twentieth-century Uplifters, Cosby thinks that the black poor are "dragging you and me down," but like today's politics of respectability as public philosophy, Cosby stated that government can do little to assist the black poor. To Cosby, taxpayers are wasting their money on poor blacks because "the state, the city, and all these people have to pick up the tab on them because they don't want to accept that they have to study to get an education."[19]

Nowhere is the politics of respectability practiced more forcefully than at historically black colleges that have student-mandated dress codes. Though the twentieth-century Uplifters at black colleges groomed students to be shining examples of racial progress in the fight for citizenship, today the politics of respectability at black colleges is designed to prepare students to become marketable individuals in the corporate world. Indeed, it is at historically black colleges where the practices of respectability and neoliberalism intersect, blending two ideologies that justify the need for administrators to police the behavior of black students.

In 2006, Hampton University's Business School instituted a policy prohibiting male students from wearing particular natural hairstyles. Hampton's business dean views natural hairstyles as cultural expressions that undermine the respectable image the university markets to the corporate community. In a course on business leadership, where students are required to interface with business leaders, male students are prohibited from wearing "braids, dreadlocks, and other unusual hairstyles." Responding to critics who argue that the rules deny students the right to culturally express themselves, Sid Credle, Hampton's business dean, responded that receiving regular haircuts represented the type of good habit black men needed to cultivate if they were going to be successful in business. "Just because a guy cuts his hair every two weeks, it doesn't mean he's not representing African Americans," the dean countered. "Look at people like Dr. Martin Luther King, Jr. and Malcolm X . . . even [hip-hop businessman] Russell Simmons, none of these people had braids."[20]

Beyond natural hairstyles, Hampton also restricts what students wear on campus. The university's student conduct code instructs students in maintaining "acceptable manners and selecting attire appropriate to specific occasions and activities." Adopting such behavior improves student morale and the university's image, the student code states, and acceptable habits and behaviors are "essential areas of development necessary for propelling students toward successful careers." Students are prohibited from wearing do-rags, stocking caps, skullcaps, and bandanas outside of their dorm rooms; and women are specifically prohibited from wearing baseball caps or "hoods" in any building on campus. If students want to wear headgear that expresses religious or cultural practices, they must receive written permission from the university's chaplain. With the guiding hands of faculty and support staff who are obligated to "monitor student behavior applicable to the dress code," Hampton's enforcement of respectability in the early decades of the twenty-first century illustrates the durability of an ideology that is centered on policing the personal behavior of "wayward" blacks. Hampton's most famous graduate, Booker T. Washington, would be proud.[21]

These college dress codes not only police students who stray from so-called appropriate hairstyles and dress, but some rules are designed to regulate students' sexuality. At Bennett College, a college for black women in Greensboro, North Carolina, whose president is the politically progressive economist Julianne Malveaux, part of the student dress code resembles a welfare-to-work directive designed to prepare recipients for the workplace. Other parts read like an updated version of the do's and don'ts rules created during the Great Migration. These twenty-first-century black college women are asked not to wear clothing with "obscene or profane language and lewd pictures," reveal "bare midriffs," or show "visible undergarments when wearer is bending, sitting, or walking." Some rules come with acute detail: "Bottom wear must be the appropriate size of the wearer, with no sagging pants or bagging and must be secure around the waist as not to reveal undergarments or tattoos." At the very end of the list of do's and don'ts, students are told not to forget the motto: "You are never fully dressed without a smile."[22]

At the historically black and all-male Morehouse College, the dress code rules reflect the school's mission of producing "strong black men." Like the dress codes at Bennett College—and other black colleges such as North Carolina Central in Durham and Paul Quinn College in Dallas—Morehouse prohibits students from wearing do-rags, sagging pants, pajamas, and clothing with derogatory or lewd messages. (Indeed, student leaders at North Carolina Central proposed distributing hand cards to new students on campus that would instruct them on the do's and don'ts of appropriate dress.) Morehouse students are also prohibited from wearing "decorative orthodontic appliances" or "grills," "hoods," sunglasses in class or at school events, or walking barefoot in public venues. Finally, the school's dress code forbids students from wearing women's clothing:

"No wearing of clothing usually worn by women," the policy states, particularly "dresses, tops, tunics, purses, pumps."

Though some students questioned the policy and considered it a violation of a student's right to personal expression, administrators and other students thought that men wearing women's clothing on campus was an assault on Morehouse's legacy of upright black manhood. "The image of a strong black man needs to be upheld," a member of the student government told a reporter. And the college's vice president for Student Services reasoned that the specific challenges young black men faced in society justified the school's dress code policy. However, the official conceded "how a student dresses has nothing to do with what is in their head."[23] Given the high attrition rates at historically black colleges—which are mainly due to the financial difficulties of students who come from mostly poor and working-class families—and the colleges' small endowments, the priorities given to policing what students wear on a college campus seem trivial.

Respectability also plays out in the mainstream media, helping to bolster the idea in the American mind that black people require special instruction. Though the dress code policy at Morehouse ignited discussions about student rights, the meaning of personal freedom, and homophobia on the all-men's campus, an exchange on CNN on October 17, 2009, between a black anchor and a black educator illustrates how the politics of respectability functions as public philosophy in mainstream media. Straining to play the devil's advocate, CNN weekend anchor T. J. Holmes asked Dr. Steve Perry, the network's education contributor, to offer some reflections on Morehouse's new dress code policy. The CNN anchor showed no hint of neutrality: "Glad to see this policy put in place," Holmes declared. But for the sake of discussion, Holmes wanted to know from Perry whether critics of the policy were right when they raised questions about students' rights to freely express themselves. "There's no such thing as absolute freedom," Perry asserted while adjusting his necktie. "These young men need to understand freedom does not mean you can do whatever you want to do, it's in the confines of what makes sense."

Growing visually agitated when the anchor asked whether the policy went too far, especially since students pay lots of tuition money to attend Morehouse, Perry responded that some black people have problems handling personal freedom, a problem that justifies the policy. "One of the problems, *especially in our community*," Perry insisted, "is that we have allowed the personal to become public." Referring to Morehouse students as "children," Perry argued that students wearing inappropriate clothing were dragging down the black community: "When we blur the lines and even erase the lines so much so that a child feels comfortable wearing his drawers out, wearing pajama pants and a do-rag on his head out in public, *we as a community* look like fools and look like court jesters." These behaviors, Perry believes, discourage potential employers and graduate school admissions officers from taking Morehouse students seriously.

The anchor then wondered aloud whether the real problem lies in students having the right attitudes. CNN's Holmes asked Perry whether "we need to get into these students' heads" and whether students "need to have a better respect for the campus that they are walking on . . . Where have *we* gotten that [appropriate dress] has to be put into policy at *the* Morehouse College?" a bewildered Holmes questioned Perry. In the timeworn tradition of the politics of respectability, the educational expert proclaimed that errant blacks need to be uplifted, or as Louis Farrakhan put it, "concentrated upon." According to Perry, the black community has failed to prepare wayward black students for the competitive market economy. Answering the "what has happened to black people" question, Perry responded with the fervor of turn-of-the-twentieth-century Uplifter Margaret Murray Washington:

We have gotten to Chicago, Detroit, and Hartford. We have gotten to so many places where this is the beginning of a time in which we need to start taking an *honest look at ourselves as a community*. When our children enter the community like that, they are a true representation of us. They're saying to us as parents and as a community, that we have failed to teach them what they need to know to participate in the public sector.

Holmes ended the segment by letting those tuning in know that the two black men standing before them on CNN were respectable members of the black community. "No matter what we [might] prefer wearing this morning, it was an appropriate way to show up this morning," Holmes chuckled.[24] Though it might not have been their intention, the attitudes expressed during the exchange help fuel the public's assault on all black youth, who are dispro-portionately targeted by police because of the perception that their demeanor and dress pose a threat to society at large.[25]

Black popular culture also has a hand in circulating the idea of respectability, reinforcing the commonsense notion among black people that the black poor are different and ought to rid them-selves of bad behaviors and values. In his 1996 comedy routine "Bring the Pain," comedian Chris Rock declared that a civil war was taking place in black America, pitting regular black people against "niggers." Though Rock is not asking middle-class blacks to be responsible for correcting the behavior of "niggers," the come-dian's routine reflects the sentiments of the politics of respectabil-ity as public philosophy at a time when welfare reform was being debated in Congress. Rock makes a distinction between "good blacks" and "bad blacks," a difference marked less by money than by behavior. For Rock, niggers are criminals, on welfare, avoid responsibility, and have little respect for formal education. Black people, on the other hand, are hardworking, responsible, and honor educational achievement. "I love black people," Rock stated, "but I hate niggers." Riffing on the stereotypical image of the irre-sponsible, trifling black male, Rock chastises black men who brag that they are responsible fathers and have managed to avoid the criminal justice system.

You know the worst thing about niggers? Niggers want credit for shit they suppose to do. A nigger will brag about some shit that a normal man just does. A nigger will say some shit like "I take care of my kids." You suppose to, you dumb motherfucker. What are you bragging about? What kind of ignorant shit is that? "I ain't never been to jail." What do you want, a cookie? You ain't suppose to go to jail, you low expectation-having motherfucker.[26]

Tyler Perry, the black playwright, filmmaker, and television producer, often invokes the politics of respectability in his plays, films, and sitcoms on black life. Though many of Perry's characters—particularly the foul-mouthed, gun-toting grandmother Madea—often mock respectability by poking fun at upper-middle-class speech and conventions, the message that black life has gone awry because of black people's (alleged) moral failings is a constant theme in Perry's works. In one scene from the 2006 film *Madea's Family Reunion*, a family gathers on the site of their ancestor's homestead, a place connected to their slave past. While reminding relatives of the sacrifices of past generations and thanking God for bringing the family thus far, Myrtle, an elder of the family (played by Cicely Tyson), speaks of the failings of the present generation, whose displeasing behavior shames the memory of and the sacrifices made by their predecessors:

As we marched up the road this afternoon, what we saw were young men gambling, fighting, cussing. Women with no clothes on gyrating all over on this land. Do you see this shack? The man and woman who were born here gave birth to this generation. They were slaves. They worked this ground, but they bought it from the widow of the slave owner and that's the kind of blood we have running though our veins. That's the stock we are made of. What happened to us? What happened to us? Who are you? Do you know who you are? What happened to the pride and the dignity and the love and respect that we had for one another?[27]

While the politics of respectability circulates as commonsense in black popular culture, respectability in black politics is often presented as "tough love" speeches. Politicians use rhetoric about the need for blacks to become personally responsible to shield inaction on targeted policies for poor and working-class blacks or to justify draconian policies aimed toward the most economically vulnerable. Indeed, the use of the politics of respectability in presidential politics did not begin with Barack Obama, who gave several so-called tough love speeches before majority-black audiences as a presidential candidate in 2008, but with Bill Clinton. In a celebrated speech on November 13, 1993, in Memphis, Tennessee, Clinton asked blacks to change their criminal behavior and strengthen the nuclear black family through the imagined thoughts of Martin Luther King, Jr. Clinton spoke from the pulpit where King gave his "I've been to the mountain top" speech the night before his assassination on April 4, 1968. Clinton engaged in the politics of respectability before the annual convocation of the predominantly black and theologically conservative Church of God in Christ (COGIC), the nation's oldest organized Pentecostal assembly.

Clinton asked the audience of "Saints," a name used by COGIC members to describe the moral purity of fellow travelers, to imagine what King would say that day about black progress if he reappeared. The president surmised that King would be impressed by the number of people of color elected to public office, the freedom of black people to live and go as they pleased, and by the existence of a large black middle class. But King, Clinton believed, would be disappointed to see "the American family destroyed," and by implication, the black family destroyed. "I did not live and die to see thirteen-year-old boys get automatic weapons and gun down nine-year-olds just for the kick of it," Clinton imagined King saying, or "to see people destroy their own lives with drugs and build drug fortunes destroying the lives of others." Clinton then spoke as if King would think that today's black poor were not prepared for freedom: "I fought for freedom . . . but not for the freedom of people to kill each other with reckless abandon . . . Not the freedom of children to impregnate each other with babies and then abandon them, nor the freedom of adult fathers of children to walk away from the children they created and abandon them, as if they didn't amount to anything."

To cure these social ills plaguing black America, Clinton argued that people had a "moral duty" to help change the plight of deviant blacks by working from the "inside out." "Sometimes answers have to come from the values and the love and the stirrings and the voices that speak from us from within," Clinton insisted as a chorus of "amens" emerged from the congregation. Like the economist Glenn Loury, who asked the black middle class to help fight the "enemy within" a decade before, Clinton, the nation's first symbolically black president, asked blacks with means to work on poor blacks from the "inside out." Though Clinton noted that there were some things that government could do to improve the conditions of poor communities—such as improving educational standards and supporting community policing—government policies aimed at the poor were in vain if poor people refused to change their behavior.[28] Clinton's "inside-out" advice to blacks would be needed in years to come as two of his policies—the 1994 federal "three-strikes" law that helped fuel the rise in the life sentences of black men caught in the criminal justice system, and the 1996 welfare-reform law that moved welfare recipients to the ranks of the poorest of the working poor and the homeless—would alter the fate of black people on the margins for decades.

Respectability as public philosophy reached greater heights during the 2008 presidential campaign. As a presidential candidate who claimed a black identity and who is, by default, a member of the black upper class, Obama felt at liberty to lecture black people about personal responsibility using his own voice rather than through the imaginary words of a martyred civil rights leader. Obama's widely acclaimed Father's Day speech on June 15, 2008, at the Apostolic Church of Christ on the South Side of Chicago, illustrates the dual purposes of the politics of respectability as public philosophy during the campaign. Delivered during the final days of the Democratic Party primary season, when Hillary Clinton's decisive wins in Kentucky and West Virginia were raising questions about whether Obama "could close the deal" without the support of white working-class voters, the speech railed against black men's lack of responsibility as fathers. As Democratic Party pollsters discovered decades ago, the more Democratic Party candidates talk about personal responsibility and government's limited role in addressing poverty and the plight of minorities, the more supportive white working-class voters are of Democratic presidential candidates.

Echoing the rhetoric of Louis Farrakhan at the Million Man March, Obama told the audience of Pentecostal churchgoers that most black men have abandoned their responsibilities as fathers: "acting like boys instead of men." This view was not always the predominant one for Obama. After attending the Million Man March on October 16, 1995, Obama returned to Chicago and praised the event as a "powerful demonstration of an impulse and need for African-American men to come together to recognize each other to affirm our rightful place in society." But Obama believed that the message from the march conveyed a narrow understanding of the plight of black men, especially black youth. Structural barriers in society—rather than bad behaviors—placed the greatest limits on the ability of black youth to move forward in society: "Exhorting youth to have pride in their race, give up drugs and crime," Obama told a reporter, "is not going to do it if we can't find jobs and futures for the 50 percent of black youth who are unemployed, underemployed, and full of bitterness and rage."[29]

Those sentiments evaporated once Obama decided to run for president, and the crisis of black men in America was used as fodder for the campaign's strategy to woo moderate and conservative white voters to the Obama camp. The Father's Day speech focused mostly on black men's failings as fathers, without hardly any explanation of the social barriers those men faced in society. According to Obama, the absence of black men in families caused havoc in black communities—gun violence, truancy, imprisonment, poverty,

violence, and drug addiction. The criminal justice system; the educational system; the persistence of barriers to poor and working-
class black men's participation in the labor force ("a white man
with a high school degree and felony conviction has a far better
chance of getting a job than a black man with a high school degree
without a criminal record"[30]); and the legacies of welfare policies
on the nuclear black family figure less prominently to Obama than
black men's personal shortcomings. "We can't simply write off
[black men's irresponsibility as fathers] to past injustices," Obama
told the churchgoers. "Past injustices are real, there's a reason
why our families are in disrepair."[31]

Although Obama conceded that the absence of fathers in children's lives "has to do with our tragic past" and the failure of
government to meet the needs of the poor, Obama informed the
audience that black people could not keep using previous injustices and ill-conceived government policies as excuses for the
current state of black families. In the speech, Obama mentioned
public policies that could address issues facing black poor and
working-class communities—stricter gun laws, more police on the
streets, increased funding for education, and jobs and job training.
However, Obama stressed that those efforts would be useless
unless irresponsible black men modified their negative behavior.
Echoing Bill Clinton's Memphis speech on the need to work on the
black poor "from the inside out," Obama told the audience: "The
change we need is not just going to come from government. It's not
just going to come from the president. It's going to come from each
and every one of us." Obama then departed from his prepared
speech and offered a sanitized version of Chris Rock's joke lam-
basting "niggers" for bragging about what they are expected to do
as responsible men: "Chris Rock had a routine. He said some—too
many of our men, they're proud, they brag about doing things
they're supposed to do. They say, 'Well, I . . . I'm not in jail.' Well,
you're not supposed to be in jail!"

Once Obama secured the nomination, the candidate ratcheted
up the rhetoric of respectability as public philosophy. During a

July 6, 2008, speech at the General Conference of the historically black and the relatively progressive African Methodist Episcopal (AME) Church, Obama continued his message on the limits of government to address problems of racial inequality. "I'm not interested in us adopting the posture of victims," Obama notified the audience. Although he acknowledged that there were black men who took care of their family responsibilities under difficult economic circumstances, and he recognized social and educational barriers that limited their job opportunities, Obama concluded that black people can't use injustice and poverty as excuses for not moving beyond the social ills that plague black communities. "There are things under our control that we got to attend to," he told the cheering crowd.

Moving from the confines of church audiences to the NAACP, Obama addressed the civil rights organization on July 15, 2008, carrying the same message of personal responsibility. The candidate discussed health care, the economy, and modest proposals on tax credits for poor families and job training for ex-felons. The candidate noted that leaders in Washington and on Wall Street needed to be more responsible to citizens and their concerns. But the focus on the irresponsibility of politicians and corporations ended there and turned to blacks: "But we need to demand more from *ourselves*," he told the crowd of civil rights activists. "Now, I know there are some who say I have been too tough talking about responsibility," the nominee defiantly declared as the audience cheered him on. "NAACP, I'm here to report we are not going to stop talking about it." Sermonizing as if black people had broken the social contract between government and individual citizens, Obama advised the audience that black America needed to "seize more responsibility" in their own lives.

In Obama's estimation, some black people are not honoring the sacrifices of civil rights martyrs because they neglect their responsibilities as parents. At this point in the speech, Obama's views are not far from the sentiments of Myrtle, the character in Tyler Perry's movie *Madea's Family Reunion*, who chastises the younger generation for dishonoring the memory of their ancestors. Nor are they much different from Bill Cosby's diatribe against poor blacks' parenting during his speech at the fiftieth anniversary celebration of the *Brown* decision. Obama asserted that some black people were derelict in their duty as parents and, as a consequence, dishonored the memory of those who fought in the past for black progress:

> I know that Thurgood Marshall did not argue *Brown v. Board of Education* so that some of us would stop doing our jobs as parents. That wasn't the deal. I know nine little children did not walk through a schoolhouse door in Little Rock so that we could stand by and let our children drop out of school and turn to gangs for support they are not getting elsewhere in the community. That's not the freedom we fought to achieve. That's not the America that our leadership sought to build. That's not the dream they had for our children. So we are se-rious about reclaiming that dream. We got to do more in our own lives. There's nothing wrong with saying that.

Though Obama acknowledged that the problems of personal respon-sibility were not unique to black people, he, nonetheless, instructed the audience that blacks can "lead by example as we did during the civil rights movement."[32]

On November 3, 2008, a day before the general election, Obama told a news reporter for MTV that he did not think that ordinances banning sagging pants were necessary (like the one in Flint, Mich-igan, see figure 4.2), but he believed that "brothers should pull up their pants . . . There are *some issues that we* face that you don't have to pass a law [against], but that doesn't mean folks can't have some sense and some respect for other people," Obama quipped.[33] No other group in American politics gets lectured about personal responsibility as much as black Americans. It is not sur-prising, then, that a public philosophy has been crafted to police the behavior of poor blacks and blacks that are thought to "behave" like them.

Crackdown on indecency

It's a crime to wear saggy pants in Flint. Here's the price you could pay:

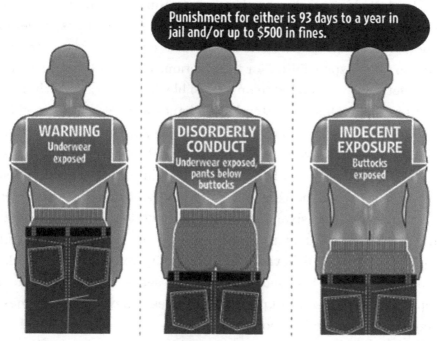

Punishment for either is 93 days to a year in jail and/or up to $500 in fines.

WARNING
Underwear
exposed

DISORDERLY
CONDUCT
Underwear exposed,
pants below
buttocks

INDECENT
EXPOSURE
Buttocks
exposed

FIGURE 4.2 Crackdown on Indecency: Consequences for wearing sagging pants in Flint, Michigan (*Source:* Detroit Free Press).

How might we imagine the reception of other groups to the rhetoric of respectability by a candidate seeking their support? What would be the Latino community's reaction, for instance, if Obama lectured Latinas to have fewer children to decrease the number of children born to undocumented immigrants?—a modification in behavior that would help solve the nation's growing number of undocumented immigrants. Or how would the gay and lesbian community react if Obama asked them to disband Gay Pride parades because the antics of revelers made it more difficult to convince the American public to support gay marriage and the right of gay and lesbian soldiers to openly serve in the military? To most Americans these proposals would be considered ridiculous, and rightly so. So why were Obama's messages of personal responsibility received so well among blacks? And to whom were the so-called tough love messages really intended for?

The ABC News-Columbia University Survey on Race, Politics, and Policy, conducted in September of 2008, asked respondents whether they thought Obama's speeches "calling on black Americans to take responsibility for their actions and pull themselves up in society" were intended to appeal to blacks, whites, or both. Perceptions about Obama's intended audience were clearly shaped by race. While a slight majority of blacks—53 percent—thought that Obama's speeches were intended to appeal exclusively to blacks, 25 percent believed that both blacks and whites were the intended audience. Only 12 percent of blacks thought that the messages were intended exclusively for whites. But whites were nearly split in their assessment of the intent of the messages—37 percent reported that they believed the messages were directed at blacks while 34 percent believed that the messages were intended to appeal to whites. Only 14 percent of whites believed that the messages were intended for both groups.

However, a look at responses by whites' self-reported political ideology suggests that the Obama campaign may have benefited from the perception among some whites that tough love messages were intended for blacks. One would suspect that respondents who believed that the messages were targeted only to whites were also likely to believe that the messages were a strategy for the Obama campaign to win over skeptical white voters. While 31 percent of white liberals and 39 percent of white conservatives believed that the speeches were intended to appeal to whites, a plurality of white moderates—42 percent—believed that the messages were exclusively targeted to blacks. Thus, white moderates—who were key swing voters for Obama—were less likely than either white liberals or white conservatives to be conscious of the idea that Obama was using "tough love" speeches to score points with whites.

Despite the long tradition of the politics of respectability, blacks were particularly receptive to Obama's message for at least one important reason—blacks were more likely to believe that the communities they lived in lacked moral values. When the ABC News-Columbia University survey asked whether "the lack of high moral and ethical standards" was a problem in the respondent's community, 44 percent of blacks answered that the problem was either "extremely" or "very" serious. This belief among blacks was twice that compared with whites (21 percent); it was also greater than Latinos (31 percent). Either a significant number of blacks have internalized stereotypes about blacks lacking moral values or moral failings have become a self-fulfilling prophecy in the lives of many black people.[34]

What is different about the twenty-first-century adaptation of the politics of respectability is that black politicians—particularly Barack Obama—have joined community leaders as the guardians of respectability and have cultivated the politics of respectability as a public philosophy aimed at managing and governing the black poor. The black poor are told they should demonstrate greater personal responsibility in their lives and that they lack the moral standing necessary to deserve public benefits. From city ordinances banning sagging pants, to New York City Mayor Michael Bloomberg's request to deny food-stamp recipients the right to purchase sodas, to DC delegate Eleanor Holmes Norton's one-women crusade to restore the sanctity of marriage to black families, these policy initiatives have the blessings of middle-class blacks who believe that black poor people need to be policed by black elites *and* by the state.

As an ideology that took root over a century ago, the politics of respectability has established considerable staying power. With little fanfare, it has morphed into being part of mainstream discourse when the subject of poverty or racial inequality is at the center of debate. Its assumptions and admonitions emerge in the most unusual circumstances and places (like laws that dictate the proper way to wear pants). It is taken as gospel in black America.

In the aftermath of the euphoria over Obama's victory on November 4, 2008, e-mails circulated among black people that celebrated the victory by poking fun at the prospects of a black family moving into the White House. Telling ethnic jokes is a common activity enjoyed by most every racial or ethnic group, but for one guardian of the Talented Tenth the jokes about Obama were out of bounds, unbefitting the occasion of the election of the nation's first black president. To ensure that the Talented Tenth maintained its decorum, the national president of a public service black sorority sent out a mass e-mail reprimanding blacks for making a "mockery" of the president-elect. The e-mail chastised other blacks for sending e-mails and text messages about "free BBQ on the White House lawn" and "fried chicken, basketball, and red Kool-Aid and pimped-out Presidential vehicles in the White House." The sorority leader declared:

> We are in the midst of one of the most significant events in our nation's history, and how WE carry ourselves is more important than ever before. We cannot allow our President-elect to be made a mockery of, especially by his own people. Not only does he represent everything that is great about our nation; Barack Obama literally personifies how awesome we are as a people. His wisdom, his poise, his eloquence, his fortitude, even his swagger . . . illustrate the greatness of a people who have been dismissed, discarded, discouraged, and disregarded by not only "the majority," but also by our own.[35]

And so, over one hundred years later, at the turn of the twenty-first century, it remains true: to Black America, the politics of respectability works in mysterious ways.

5

Wink, Nod, Vote

THE SPEAKER'S VOICE booms like a Baptist preacher as he stands behind the podium, delivering a speech before a large crowd of black churchgoers, who sit attentively in a college gymnasium. He relates a story about a "miracle baby" that stands as a parable for the plight of the black poor in the United States. As the story goes, a pregnant woman is shot on her way to a grocery store the second day of the Los Angeles riots, in 1992. A bullet penetrates her stomach and becomes lodged near the upper limbs of the yet-to-be-born baby. Doctors perform an emergency delivery and then remove the bullet near the right elbow of the baby's arm. The mother survives and a baby girl is born virtually unscathed, except for a scar on her elbow, which, as the speaker tells the audience, will always remind her of the circumstances surrounding her birth. Like the scar on the miracle baby, the speaker informs the gathering, the scar of racial injustice remains visible today on the lives of the black poor.

The speaker then tells the audience that what happened in Los Angeles—and fifteen years later in New Orleans in the aftermath of Hurricane Katrina—is the result of a "lingering, ongoing, persuasive legacy—a tragic legacy out of the tragic history this country has never fully came to terms with." The hopelessness and the destruction in America's inner cities over the years, the speaker asserts, has led to "quiet riots." "All the hurricane did was make bare what we ignore each and every day," he continues. "There are whole sets of communities that are impoverished, that don't have meaningful opportunities, that don't have hope and they are forgotten."

The solution is clear. "If we have more black men in prison than are in college," the speaker declares, "then it's time to take the bullet out! . . . If we have millions of people going to emergency rooms for treatable illnesses like asthma," he insists, "it's time to take the bullet out! . . . If we keep sending our kids to dilapidated school buildings, if we keep fighting this war in Iraq," he says as his voice builds momentum, "a war that never should have been authorized and waged . . . A war that's costing us $275 million a day." The speaker departs from his prepared texts and jabs his fingers in the air, emphasizing the point that the money spent on the war "could have been invested in rebuilding communities all across the country."

"It's time to take the bullet out!" he again cries.

This passionate speaker for racial justice was not the Reverend Jesse Jackson nor the Reverend Al Sharpton, or any other fire-brand civil rights activist. These sentiments came from the lips of presidential candidate Barack Obama on June 5, 2007, delivered at the Annual Minister's Conference at Hampton University. Trailing Hillary Clinton among black voters for most of the first quarter of 2007, Obama found himself having to work hard at convincing black voters to support his candidacy. He did so by discussing racial injustice when he spoke before black audiences and by promoting both universal and targeted policy initiatives to solve the problems of racial inequality.[1]

This is the Barack Obama nobody knows or has forgotten.

During the early stages of the campaign in 2007, Obama's discussion of racial inequality waxed and waned. It grew stronger when he needed black support to shore up his viability as a candidate. It grew dimmer after black voters got behind his candidacy en masse after his unexpected victory in the Iowa Caucus, on January 3, 2008. Thereafter, a clear majority of blacks favored his candidacy, and Obama, as a result, switched course. As he solidified his support among black voters going into the South Carolina primary, Obama abandoned his earlier—though tempered—discussions about race (except when he was forced to during the Reverend Jeremiah Wright controversy in March of 2008). His discussions during 2007 of racial injustice and inequality were replaced in 2008 with a call for policies that benefited all Americans and tough love speeches rooted in the politics of respectability.

From a political viewpoint, it is obvious why Obama stopped talking about racial inequality once he solidified support from black voters. After all, speaking less about race helped him to negotiate walking the "racial tightrope" of building a multiracial coalition for his candidacy that included not just blacks, but whites, Latinos, and Asians. But it is less obvious why black voters got behind a candidate who was reluctant to speak out about racial injustice or discuss policies targeting poverty and racial inequality. To unravel this mystery is to delve into an unspoken practice in black politics—what I describe as a silent agreement—a wink-and-nod—between race-neutral black candidates and black voters. This agreement entails black voters giving race-neutral black politicians a pass on discussions about racial inequality in exchange for the candidates' successful elevation to high-profile political offices. Many black voters saw Obama wink when he proclaimed that when running for president he had to be the candidate for "all of America" and not just the candidate of black America. They sympathized with Obama having "to do what he has to do" to get elected, even if it meant staying silent on issues that were important to blacks, the most loyal constituency in the Democratic Party. Thus, most black voters gave Obama the nod.

However, the wink-and-nod exchange between Obama and black voters came with a cost. The agreement made it virtually impossible for black leaders—and black voters—to place issues that were particular to black communities on the political agenda.

Raising questions about the persistence of racial inequality in American life would have forced Obama—as well as the other Democratic presidential contenders—to directly discuss policy solutions to a variety of issues facing black communities. Indeed, issues that would continue to have consequences for black communities after Obama's election: The housing foreclosure crisis that disproportionately hit communities of color, growing levels of black unemployment, the persistence of the HIV-AIDS epidemic in the black population, and the War on Drugs that sends large numbers of blacks to prison for nonviolent offenses. These issues would not be substantially engaged by Obama or any of the other Democratic candidates, except John Edwards whose campaign focused on economic inequality and racial justice.

Moreover, Obama's decree to support only universal policies— that is, policies that help everyone—would only apply to blacks, but no other key constituency. Obama, for instance, met several times during the campaign with Jewish leaders and voters to clarify his positions on Middle East policy. He talked to Latino voters about immigration policy and to gay and lesbian voters about his position on gay marriage and the military's "don't ask, don't tell" policy. The candidate also met with Cuban-American leaders about the United States opening dialogue with Cuba and with feminist groups about the importance of protecting abortion rights and of ensuring equal pay for equal work for women. But again, when Obama spoke before black audiences in 2008, he talked mostly about universal policies and the need for greater personal responsibility on behalf of blacks.

That most black voters gave Obama "slack" during the campaign is partly understandable. To be a viable presidential candidate Obama had to overcome white voters' racial stereotypes about black politicians. A substantial core of white voters have traditionally thought that black politicians are less capable as public officials and more partial to helping their own racial group when they do win office. For Obama—like presidential candidates Shirley Chisholm and Jesse Jackson—running for the highest office in the land posed challenges to building, and for Obama maintaining, support among white voters. For black candidates running in white-majority jurisdictions this is a stark reality. The more powerful and influential the office, the harder black candidates must work at overcoming negative stereotypes.

In 1990 the late political scientist Linda F. Williams authored a little-known study documenting the racial stereotypes whites held about black and white politicians. The study analyzed responses from a 1987 survey that examined attitudes on the ability of black and white candidates to achieve policy goals. It also examined whether black or white politicians had the right personal attributes to succeed in public office. In considering ten policy areas, a majority or near majority of whites reported that the race of the candidate made no difference in how they evaluated the abilities of black or white politicians. But for roughly half of white respondents, they evaluated black politicians differently.

Over 90 percent of white respondents who had an opinion on the abilities of black and white politicians reported that white politicians were better at reducing drug abuse, improving public education, lowering taxes, bringing down the federal budget deficit, and increasing economic growth than black politicians. When it came to judging candidates on how well they could handle the economy, a clear disadvantage existed for black politicians. Forty-one percent of all whites—including whites who reported that race did not make a difference in their judgment of political candidates—believed that a white politician would be better at stimulating economic growth than a black politician.

A black politician fared no better at being perceived by whites as capable of reducing the federal budget deficit. Thirty-six percent of whites believed that a white politician would do a better job at reducing the deficit while only 4 percent thought that a black politician would do a better job. The only policy area that whites believed that a black politician would be better at was helping the poor and needy. During an era when social programs for the poor were being attacked, nearly 40 percent of whites agreed that a black candidate would be better at assisting the poor than a white politician (15 percent). This clearly places a black candidate at a disadvantage among moderate and conservative white voters.

Not only were black politicians thought to be less capable of achieving certain policy goals, they were also believed to be less intelligent, experienced, compassionate, and knowledgeable, as well as to lack good judgment in a crisis. Again, a near majority of whites in the survey reported that the race of the candidate made no difference in how they judged personal attributes. But for those whites who admitted to looking through a racial lens when evaluating candidates, black politicians were considered disadvantaged in all but two attributes. (The other positive attribute is that a black politician is more likely to be religious than a white politician.) The number of prejudiced white voters represented a sizeable core of white voters. For instance, when considering whites who claimed not to evaluate candidates by race, 35 percent of all whites believed that a white politician would be more intelligent than a black politician while less than 2 percent believed that a black politician would be more intelligent.

Thirty-four percent of whites thought that a white politician would have better judgment in a time of crisis. Only 1 percent of whites believed a black politician would have better judgment. And half of whites surveyed thought that a white candidate would be more experienced, and nearly one-quarter believed that a white candidate would be more trustworthy and hardworking than a black politician.

The survey also asked whether respondents would refuse to vote for a "qualified black candidate" for a range of elected public offices, including president. While few whites reported that they would refuse to vote for a black candidate for a city, county, or statewide office—indeed, opposition was in the single digits—10 percent and nearly 20 percent admitted that they would not vote for a "qualified" black person for vice president or president, respectively.

When Williams submitted the data to rigorous analysis, she discovered attitudinal patterns that would mirror white support and opposition to Obama in 2008. Williams explained that a hypothetical black candidate for president in 1987 was "handicapped" by opposition from "southern whites, low-income whites, whites who never graduated from high-school, whites aged fifty and over, whites who are conservative on racial issues." White opposition to a black presidential candidate was lowest among "western whites, college-educated whites, whites in the middle-age cohort (thirty to forty-nine years old), and whites who are liberal on racial issues."

With the exception of middle-aged white voters, Williams's findings over twenty years ago predicted patterns in white voter preference for Obama to near perfection. (Younger white voters were far more supportive of Obama than middle-aged white voters.) She summarized white voting patterns using the popular culture references of the day: "The Archie Bunker or southern redneck stereotype is not far off the mark as a description of the average racist voter, while the Berkeley yuppie profile describes

FIGURE 5.1 Booker T. Washington, first black American to dine at White House, with President Theodore Roosevelt, 1901 (*Source*: Corbis).

the white voter most likely to give a black candidate a sympathetic hearing."[2]

As the Williams study demonstrates, deeply held stereotypes of black politicians among a core of white voters had to be overcome if black politicians were going to win statewide and national offices. Decades before Obama ran as a serious contender for president, black candidates and their campaign strategists were figuring out ways to overcome whites' stereotypical views. They would do so by making black candidates more palatable to white voters by having candidates dodge race-specific issues during campaigns.

By the early 1980s, black politicians were bumping up against a glass ceiling. After the passage of the 1965 Voting Rights Act, the number of blacks elected to public office had grown exponentially, from nearly 1,400 in 1970 to nearly 5,000 in 1980. These blacks were overwhelmingly elected to local offices—school boards, city councils, and county commissions in the South—and from predominantly black jurisdictions. While there were some successes for black politicians running in white-majority jurisdictions—most notably Carl Stokes's election as Cleveland's mayor in 1967 and Tom Bradley's election as the mayor of Los Angeles in 1973—most black politicians had to rely exclusively on black voters to get elected to public office.[3]

In 1983 the Washington-based black think tank the Joint Center for Political and Economic Studies assembled political scientists, campaign managers, political consultants, pollsters, and party activists to figure out how to neutralize white voters' bias against black candidates. Jackson State University political scientist Leslie McLemore, who, in 1980, unsuccessfully ran for Congress in Mississippi, opened the discussion by raising several questions that would reverberate a quarter century later during Obama's campaign. He asked the gathering, "How does one transcend race? How do you raise issues to a level of rare and profound sophistication? How do you downplay race?" and "How do you modify or how do you lessen the impact of race?"[4]

Conference participants offered recommendations. One strategy some found effective as a neutralizing force was for a minority candidate to announce early in the campaign that racial issues were not the focal point of their platform. "When you talk about setting the environment for the definition of the campaign, it is preferable to have it revolve around something other than race, particularly in a district that is majority white," pollster Paul Maslin advised the group. "When the press and your opposition raise it as an issue, you have to confront it directly," he surmised. "I believe that you cannot run from the issue and let your opposition or the press define it." Maslin believed that black candidates would be hurt by dodging issues of race altogether, so he advised black candidates to tell voters early and often—"Don't vote for me because I am black, don't vote against me because I'm black."

Making such a declaration is important because, as the pollster explained, "That's the kind of thing you need to say as a potential candidate long before your formal announcement for office, particularly in a speech given before a black audience." Presumably, this allows black candidates to send cues to white voters that they are "race-neutral" in their approach to politics without having to directly confront white voters with the issue of race.[5]

Another suggestion offered during the conference was the need for black candidates to declare racial neutrality on policy issues. Henry "Micky" Michaux, a black candidate who in 1982 unsuccessfully ran in a racially polarized North Carolina congressional district, advised the group that a black candidate should let white voters know right away that they will be the candidate "for all the people." Doing so would preempt their white opponents from exploiting white voters' racist stereotypes. "A lot of people assume you are going to be representing solely black interests," Michaux noted, thus declarations of racial neutrality are often necessary "to get the white vote." He also believed that black candidates could circumvent race-specific policy issues by reinterpreting black issues as universal issues. "When we talked about unemployment, you're talking about black folks," Michaux advised the gathering.

"You really are, because they have the highest portion of the unemployed. When you talk about social security, work programs based on proportions, you're talking about black folks. But you've got to say that this is the type of issue that affects all people."[6]

What is troubling about the advice given at the Joint Center summit is not the appeal to universalism but that there was no discussion of—or any concern about—whether neutralizing campaign tactics undermines the ability of blacks to place their issues—other than those universal in scope—on the electoral agenda. An underlying assumption that permeates the discussions is that once a race-neutral candidate is elected, he or she will automatically address race-specific issues. Again, this implicit arrangement is simple. Black candidates wink, and black voters nod. What is considered a good campaign strategy for race-neutral black candidates is expected to be good for the interests of black communities. "Once you have established and made it known that [black] voters are the key," Michaux suggested, *"then they allow you* to go and make these other contacts and build up that 10, 15, 20 percent from the other community to bring it in . . . Black voters, contrary to what anyone else may say, are sophisticated voters. They vote with a great deal of discernment and they understand the situation."[7]

The campaign strategies and tactics that were devised to minimize white bias against black candidates running in white-majority jurisdictions began to make inroads. On Election Day, November 7, 1989, a new era of black politics was ushered in—what became known as "Black Tuesday." For the first time, a crop of race-neutral black candidates swept into city halls in districts without black majorities. David Dinkins was elected mayor of New York City; Norm Rice in Seattle; John Daniels in New Haven, Connecticut; and Chester Jenkins in Durham, North Carolina. Michael White became the second black mayor of Cleveland—defeating another black candidate—by winning a minority of the black vote and a majority of the white vote. But the crown jewel of Black Tuesday was L. Douglas Wilder's election as governor of

Virginia—the first black to be elected governor in the nation since the Reconstruction era.

The new trend got scholars of black politics thinking. Political scientists Joseph McCormick and Charles E. Jones deconstructed how and why particular black candidates appealed to white voters. They were guided by the concept of "deracialization," a perspective first coined by Charles V. Hamilton (the co-author of the 1967 classic *Black Power: The Politics of Liberation*). After Richard Nixon's 1972 landslide reelection—a campaign that tied the Democratic Party and its nominee George McGovern to racially polarized issues, such as forced busing to integrate schools, crime, and welfare—Hamilton urged the Democratic Party to be pragmatic in its approach to racial issues in the 1976 presidential election.

In a position paper Hamilton produced for the national Democratic Party, which was later explained in an essay in the journal *First World*, he advised the party to "deracialize" policy issues by promoting universal policy issues. Hamilton, who was a proponent of the issue-driven independent school of black politics, saw the practicalities of taking racial issues out of presidential politics. Doing so, Hamilton believed, would "deny the Republican Party the opportunity to use race as a polarizing issue" and facilitate a multiracial coalition for the Democrats—"Blacks, labor, liberal, white ethnics"—that the civil rights activist Bayard Rustin, a proponent of the coalition wing of black politics, called for back in 1964.[8]

By the early 1990s, "deracialization" had become a campaign strategy for race-neutral black candidates. Joseph McCormick and Charles E. Jones defined "deracialization" as a situation in which black candidates conduct "a campaign in a stylistic fashion that defuses the polarizing effects of race by avoiding explicit reference to race-specific issues." Instead of addressing the broad policy preferences of black voters—preferences that include both universal and race-specific issues—deracialized campaign tactics emphasize "issues that are perceived as racially transcendent." For black candidates, who depend on black voters as their base but need the support of white voters to win, the emphasis on racially transcendent issues allows black candidates to cultivate, as McCormick and Jones state, "a broad segment of the electorate for purposes of capturing or maintaining public office."

As McCormick and Jones explain, part of the strategy that black candidates use to build support among white voters is the candidate's campaign style. Race-neutral black candidates try to quell the concerns of whites by displaying "disarming" and "non-threatening" behavior. They also avoid making direct racial appeals to black voters. Most problematic—and indeed most consequential for the representation of black interests on the electoral agenda—is the candidate's strategy to "avoid emphasis of a racially specific issue agenda." Deracialized campaigns "deemphasize those issues that may be viewed in explicitly racial terms, for example, racial set-asides, affirmative action, or the plight of the urban underclass, while emphasizing issues that appear to transcend the racial question."[9]

As race-neutral campaigning was being perfected, a tactical playbook emerged for black candidates seeking white support: avoid talking about race, denounce black activists who are perceived too radical by white voters, and redirect or avoid questions on issues and policies that are stigmatized as black concerns. Former U.S. Senator Edward Brooke and former Virginia Governor Douglas Wilder, the first two black candidates to win high-level statewide offices, successfully used the playbook, though Brooke started before the rise of black politicians winning offices in majority-white jurisdictions during the late 1980s and 1990s.

Elected in 1966, Brooke ran in a state where less than 10 percent of the population was black. Brooke was a black politician during the rise of urban rebellions and the Black Power movement. A Republican, Brooke felt compelled to distance his victory from the civil rights and Black Power movements: "I do not intend to be a national leader of Negro people," Brooke told a reporter from *Time* magazine, "I intend to do my job as Senator of Massachusetts." In an article titled "The Senate: An Individual Who Happens to Be a Negro," it is apparent from the *Time* reporter's description that

Brooke's cool demeanor helped him gain the confidence of white voters in Massachusetts. "Some hotheads in the rights movement virtually accuse him of being an Uncle Tom," the *Time* reporter noted. "To millions of other Negroes, his image is blurred at best. Because of his pale skin, his Episcopalian faith, his reserved New England manner, he is looked upon as what might be described as a 'NASP'—the Negro equivalent of the White Anglo-Saxon Protestant." The Massachusetts senator who "happens to be Negro" felt compelled, nonetheless, to criticize Black Power, the concept that helped spawn the independent wing of black politics. "That slogan has struck fear in the heart of black America as well in the heart of white America," Brooke said. Echoing the sentiments of the coalition wing of black politics, Brooke insisted, "The Negro has to gain allies—not adversaries."[10]

Twenty years later, Douglas Wilder would steer clear of racial issues during his campaign for governor in Virginia and shed his reputation as a crusader for racial justice in the state. When Wilder ran for governor in 1989, he refused to discuss the Supreme Court's recently decided *Croson* decision invaliding the City of Richmond's set-aside programs for minority businesses. When asked about affirmative action in general, the Democratic Party nominee proclaimed that he opposed "quotas" and preferential treatment for any group, a traditional conservative response to affirmative action. When police harassed black college students during a weekend outing at Virginia Beach, Wilder issued a press release that stressed the need for "law and order" and declared that as governor he would "take whatever measures are necessary to enforce this promise."[11]

In full race-neutral campaign mode, Wilder focused on issues that transcended race. He defended the right of a woman to have an abortion, a stance that clearly separated him from his Republican opponent, J. Marshall Coleman, who trailed Wilder among women voters in the polls. Wilder also declared that he was a fiscal conservative, pledging that he would not raise taxes as governor. Wilder, who once donned an Afro hairstyle and was considered a

FIGURE 5.2 U.S. Senator Edward Brooke from Massachusetts, 1966 (*Source*: Corbis).

"militant" when first elected to the State Senate in 1969, embraced Confederate symbols during campaign stops for governor in rural Virginia, often referring to himself with pride as a "Son of Virginia."

As Obama did in 2008, Wilder distanced himself from Jesse Jackson. He feared his association with Jackson would alienate potential white voters. Wilder's campaign clearly benefited from heightened black voter participation during Jackson's presidential campaign in 1988. Indeed, Wilder's deracialized campaign tactics were so effective that the candidate's racial identity seemed to have evaporated in the minds of many white voters in Virginia. As one white voter told a reporter, "Everybody likes him so well, you forget about the fact that he's black."[12]

Though Brooke's ascendancy to a high-level office happened during the civil rights movement and Wilder's happened long after, the modus operandi for managing racial conflict in the campaigns was roughly the same. As political scientist Judson Jefferies summarized the campaign styles of these two trailblazers, both "distanced themselves from the civil rights movement and civil rights activists." Additionally, both men cautioned black candidates against soliciting the assistance of local or national black leaders whom white voters were likely to consider controversial or militant.[13]

By the time Obama ran for president, strategists working for race-neutral black candidates were creating highly sophisticated campaign techniques. Though Obama's presidential campaign adopted some of the same tactics that the first wave of deracialized black politicians adopted, Obama's biography—and the way it was sold to voters—allowed his strategists to create more nuanced tactics than could have been possible in previous high-stakes campaigns.

David Axelrod, who served as Obama's chief strategist, was a central player in packaging Obama's image to white voters. Axelrod's firm—AKP Media—developed a niche market in helping black mayoral candidates sell their image to white voters. Starting with Harold Washington's 1987 reelection campaign as mayor of Chicago, Axelrod went on to do media work for other black mayors, including Cleveland's Michael White, Philadelphia's John Street, and Detroit's Dennis Archer, among others. Axelrod's firm also conducted media work for Massachusetts gubernatorial candidate Deval Patrick in 2006. Patrick successfully ran and was reelected as governor, becoming the second black governor in modern American history after Douglas Wilder. While deracialized black candidates in the past downplayed their racial identity, Barack Obama used his identities as an asset to build support among white liberals and white moderates. Messages and images were crafted to signal to persuadable white voters that they had an opportunity to make history by electing the nation's first black president.

One of the media strategies that Axelrod's firm is known for is playing up their client's biography and deemphasizing their policy positions. "Raised by a single mother" and "worked his way up from poverty to Harvard Law," a voiceover said of Deval Patrick's up-from-poverty success story during a campaign ad. As one observer of Axelrod's strategy has noted, black candidates are marketed as hopeful figures whose success demonstrates that racial injustices can be overcome. Comparing Obama with former Chicago mayor Harold Washington, Axelrod views both these politicians—despite their different histories and views on race and racism—as hopeful symbols of American progress. "In many cases their personal stories are symbolic of the kinds of values that we as a society hold dear even if we haven't always honored them historically," Axelrod told the *Nation* editor Christopher Hayes in 2007. These well-crafted "we are about to overcome" media messages—"Yes, We Can" as the Obama campaign slogan reminded voters—convey that supporting a race-neutral black candidate allows white liberals to feel good about racial progress.[14]

As an observer explained, Axelrod has devised a "unified theory of how to elect a black candidate." Axelrod's approach not only emphasizes a candidate's biography and involves the opportunity for voters to feel good about racial progress, but it also entails making black candidates look credible in the eyes of whites. This credibility involves highly regarded whites vouching for the reputation of black candidates—what has been described as "third party authentication." Obama was authenticated by several important figures. Endorsements from Ted Kennedy and Caroline Kennedy helped Obama build support among white liberals. And support from Kansas Governor Kathleen Sebelius and Arizona Governor Janet Napolitano gave Obama credibility among white women voters, an important constituency Obama needed to make inroads into Hillary Clinton's base.[15]

Another tactic devised by Axelrod involves black candidates avoiding negative attacks on their white opponents. Axelrod's clients are convinced to take the high ground by attacking their opponents sideways, that is, by denouncing their opponent's negative ads as dishonorable and a distraction to the campaign. It is much better to give a disarming response to negative ads than for candidates like Obama and Deval Patrick to be caricatured by their opponents as an "angry black man." Another media tactic Axelrod used was for Obama to directly talk to voters with his eyes squarely fixed on the camera. As journalist Jason Zengerle interpreted the personal-touch ads, it made Obama "relatable and reasonable—not the radical figure white voters may have read about on the Internet and nothing like their worst images of a black politician." By appealing to the historic nature of his candidacy, highlighting his biography, obtaining authentication from respected white figures, and by refusing to engage in negative attack ads, Obama was able to help melt away race-infused apprehensions receptive white voters may have had about his candidacy.[16]

Cornell Belcher, who served as a pollster for Obama in 2008, noted that the candidate was able to overcome racial stereotypes as a black candidate "through a lot of hard work and a lot of strategy." As Belcher explained, the candidate had to be essentially deracialized in order for him to be elected president:

> Obama became one of the most individualized blacks in this country. He was the Michael Jordan of politics. All of the sudden he wasn't the black guy anymore because he was bigger, something larger . . . Telling his life story, making him an individual, as opposed to part of the black masses, was an important part of making him president of the United States.[17]

But Obama had another, more subtle advantage as a race-neutral black candidate: his biracial heritage and his light skin color. Though a taboo subject, particularly among African Americans, unconscious bias against darker-skinned blacks and unconscious advantages accorded to lighter-skinned blacks spills over into electoral politics. While Senator Harry Reid got in trouble for privately telling reporters that the country was ready to elect a black president—a candidate, who like Obama, is "light-skinned" and does not speak in a "Negro dialect"—the senator's assessment was not far off the mark. As research by political psychologists has confirmed, the black image in the minds of white voters has implications for which type of black candidate will be acceptable to white voters.

In a 1993 study published in the *American Journal of Political Science*, Nayda Terkildsen showed through psychological experiments that when given a choice between equally qualified candidates for governor, a white, a light-skinned black, or a dark-skinned black, white voters almost always preferred the white candidate. However, when whites in her study chose between the light-skinned and dark-skinned black candidates, whites usually preferred the light-skinned black candidate. Racial prejudice had a great deal to do with the candidate evaluations. As Terkildsen concluded, "Racially intolerant whites were particularly brutal in their evaluations of the dark-skinned black politician." And in a 2007 study by political scientists Jennifer Hochschild and Vesla Weaver, a fictitious light-skinned black Senate candidate fared better in field experiments than a dark-skinned candidate with the same credentials. As the authors found, the light-skinned candidate was perceived by whites to be "more intelligent, more experienced, more trustworthy than his dark-skinned opponent."[18]

Though it is not clear whether it was the Obama campaign's intention, campaign ads highlighting Obama's white heritage—even though Obama identifies as black rather than biracial or multiracial—constantly reminded voters of the candidate's not-completely-black identity. Campaign television ads showed photographs of Obama with his white mother and grandparents. The campaign never showed ads highlighting Obama's Kenyan roots, particularly his father, even though Obama was often described falsely as a "son of immigrants." (Obama's father, whom Obama lived with no more than a month in his entire life, was an exchange student from Kenya and never immigrated to the United States.) And the campaign rarely displayed ads that highlighted Obama's more visibly black wife and children. Indeed, Obama's biracial heritage helped the candidate to broaden his appeal in ways that were absurd. When, for instance, a white campaign worker in Nevada tried to convince a racially prejudiced white voter to support

Obama, the worker reminded the voter that Obama was not all that black. "One thing you have to remember is that Obama, he's half white and he was raised by his white mother," the campaigner told the wavering voter. "So his views are more white than black really."[19]

Indeed, Obama's biracial heritage appeared to have helped the candidate among white voters while his self-identity as a black man helped him with black voters. In a Pew Research Center poll, a majority of blacks—55 percent—reported that they thought of Obama as only black while about one-third—34 percent—viewed him as "mixed race." For whites and Latinos the perception of Obama's racial background is quite different. A slight majority of whites—53 percent—perceived Obama as mixed race while about one-quarter of whites—24 percent—thought of Obama as only black. Latinos, on the other hand, were far more likely to consider Obama mixed race than either blacks or whites. Sixty-one percent viewed Obama as mixed race while only 23 percent considered him black.[20] When you combine Obama's race-neutral campaign strategy with his light-skin privilege and biracial heritage, Obama was essentially a perfect model for a "deracialized" presidential candidate.

Given many blacks' sympathy for Obama's need to run a race-neutral campaign—and their strong desire for someone who shared their racial identity to be in the White House—it makes perfect sense why blacks would return a nod to Obama by giving him a "pass" on his silence on race-specific issues. Even in their own lives, most blacks engage in what legal scholar Kenji Yoshino describes as "covering." This happens when stigmatized minorities engage in conscious acts that "tone down a disfavored identity to fit the mainstream."[21]

Findings from an ABC News–Columbia University survey confirm that a large core of blacks supports the practice of covering. When asked, "Do you think that blacks have to play down their identity in order to get ahead or do you think they can be themselves?" nearly half of the black respondents said that blacks in general have to "play down" their race to succeed in American society. The other half said that black people could be themselves—that is freely express their "blackness"—and still get ahead in life. In further analysis, blacks who reported experiencing the greatest amount of racial discrimination were most likely to believe that blacks had to play down "being black" to get ahead. Given the large portion of blacks who endorse the concept of covering, especially among those who perceive racial discrimination in their lives the most, it is not surprising that many black voters would go along with a wink-and-nod pact between themselves and an ideologically compatible black candidate who has to tone down discussions of racial issues to win the White House.

But in the world of politics, such agreements can have unintended consequences. Since deracialized black candidates believe that an emphasis on universal policies benefits their campaigns, the strategy undermines the ability of blacks to place race-specific issues on the political agenda. The proposition is risky because the candidate can decide not to follow through on race-specific issues once he or she is elected. Thus the only benefits that blacks can be assured of getting support for are universal policies and the chance to make history. Put another way, the substance of black group interests becomes entangled—if not lost—in the symbolism of a black face in a position of power.

As law professor Lani Guinier argues in her book *The Tyranny of the Majority*, the idea that the symbolic and the substantive are the same when it comes to the representation of black interests is a suspect claim. Criticizing the theory of black electoral success—the idea that the election of black public officials automatically leads to the representation of black group interests—Guinier pinpoints how black representatives are mistakenly perceived as authentic leaders in black communities. Black politicians "who are physically and culturally similar to their constituencies, fulfill the black community's need for self-affirmation through 'role-models,'" Guinier explains. This belief is, on some level, important because racial authenticity "reflects group consciousness, group history, and group perspective of a disadvantaged and stigmatized minority." However, an overreliance on the symbolic benefits that black politicians bring to politics can have the effect of organizing race-specific issues out of the political process. As Guinier warns, "authenticity uses the normally cultural to obscure its substantively political meaning." And as a consequence, "electoral success by culturally and ethnically black candidates in majority-white electorates may not necessarily mean that black concerns will be addressed."

Indeed, black voters are at risk of having their interests ignored if they gamble on the wink-and-nod strategy. "Even where black support provides a critical margin," Guinier further explains, "successful black candidates in majority-white electorates may not necessarily feel obligated to black voters." Though race-neutral black candidates serve the psychic and cultural needs of black voters—that is, black voters develop greater confidence in the political system as a result of black politicians symbolically representing them—such politicians can easily abdicate the role of advocating on behalf of substantive race-specific issues.[22]

There is no better example of how an implicit wink-and-nod agreement can go wrong than the case of Clarence Thomas's confirmation to the Supreme Court in 1991. In the annals of black politics it was a blunder of major proportions. Despite Thomas's conservative record as a Reagan administration chair of the Equal Employment Opportunity Commission and as a Republican Party activist, many blacks believed that once Thomas made it to the Court he would be sensitive to black issues. That Thomas was descriptively black and grew up poor in racially segregated Pin Point, Georgia, was enough for many blacks to conclude he was not really that conservative. After all, Thomas was "doing what he has to do" as a black man to be appointed to the Supreme Court by a Republican president. Thomas was nominated to replace the legendary civil rights advocate on the court, Justice Thurgood Marshall, and many blacks were relieved that the opening on the Court would remain a "black seat."

Niara Sudarkasa, who in 1991 was president of the historically black Lincoln University, thought she understood Thomas's wink.

A self-described liberal and black nationalist, Sudarkasa argued in several op-ed pieces and during testimony at Thomas's hearings that blacks, in essence, should return a nod in Thomas's direction. "There is such a need on this court for someone who can reach back into his or her experience to find the compassion, courage, and conviction to stand up for justice to those who are downtrodden, excluded, or overlooked," Sudarkasa wrote in the *Philadelphia Inquirer*. "I believe Thomas will be such a person."

As a black public official culturally connected to the black community, Sudarkasa believed that Thomas had the credibility—the racial authenticity—to represent black interests on the Court. She believed that the nominee would particularly be sympathetic to the racism blacks faced in the criminal justice system. "Why would I argue for an African American to replace Thurgood Marshall?" Sudarkasa asked in the editorial. "Because if any voice is needed in those halls of justice, it is a voice for black people." Once he reached the court, Sudarkasa argued that Thomas would recognize that "black men go to prison in larger numbers, get longer sentences, and are executed more often than any other group in the nation." Despite Thomas's "presumed conservatism"—as Sudarkasa described the nominee's ideology—she believed that Thomas would be a champion for blacks once he arrived on the Court. Thomas, she thought, was a known quantity—the proverbial "bird in the hand." In Sudarkasa's wink-and-nod logic it would be too risky for blacks to press for another nominee because "we do not know who might emerge from the bush."[23]

Other supporters of Thomas thought that it would take time for the nominee to become a defender of black interests on the Court, but supported him just the same. Just give him a chance, many argued. Believing that a black conservative on the Court would be better than a white one, poet Maya Angelou, in a *New York Times* editorial titled "I Dare Hope," endorsed Thomas. Calling on the "ancestors' wisdom," Angelou asked blacks to put aside their suspicions of Thomas and "make an effort to reach, reconstruct, and save a black man from Yale." Though her argument does not have the wink-and-nod logic of other blacks who pushed for Thomas's confirmation, the hoped-for conversion of Thomas serves similar purposes. Since Thomas is culturally and nominally black and because of his credentials as a Yale-trained lawyer, he deserved black support, Angelou reasoned. Either through some ideological exorcism or through some ideological process of osmosis, the enlightened forces of blackness would, according to Angelou, bring Justice Thomas to his senses, maybe not immediately, but eventually. "Because Clarence Thomas has been poor, has been nearly suffocated by the acrid odor of racial discrimination, is intelligent, well trained, black and young enough to be won over again," Angelou wrote, "I support him."[24] (In the twenty years since Thomas has sat on the Court the ancestors' wisdom still disappoints.)

In the process of Thomas's confirmation, black supporters often dismissed his substantive shortcomings on black issues, concentrating instead on lifting Thomas up as a symbol of black progress. Believing that Americans are "not where we need to be in eliminating bigotry as a bar to opportunity in America," the president of the Liberty County, Georgia, chapter of the NAACP endorsed the nominee's confirmation. "Young people, possibly as never before, need positive role models as beacons for their lifestyles," the civil rights activist insisted. "It seems to me that Clarence Thomas, his life and accomplishment exemplify the role model that we seek for our young people."[25] A member of the black sorority Zeta Phi Beta used similar language: "We can think of no better message to send to our black youth than Judge Clarence Thomas. He should be the role model for those black youths who have lost all hope and have lost the ability to dream dreams."[26] Clearly, symbolic representation on the Court was far more important than substantive concerns. As political scientist Diane Pinderhughes observed at the time, "Blacks willing to critique Thomas were often challenged with the question, would you rather have a black conservative or a white liberal. Many found race more significant than policy."[27]

Public opinion polls during the confirmation hearings confirm blacks' stronger proclivity for symbolism over substance in their support for Thomas. During the early phase of the confirmation hearings black support for Thomas was soft, but gradually a majority of blacks came around to back the nominee. When pollsters asked blacks whether they share Thomas's views on affirmative action, only one in six reported that they did (most blacks strongly supported affirmative action policies). And while a large portion of blacks—about 40 percent—thought that Thomas did not share and understand black concerns, a clear majority—58 percent—approved of his nomination. Indeed, a greater share—61 percent—thought that Thomas should be confirmed. After Anita Hill accused Thomas of sexual harassment, Thomas's black support solidified even more, especially after the nominee testified that his treatment as a black man during the hearings amounted to a "high-tech lynching."[28]

Many years later, Thomas is no longer lifted up as a symbolic role model for black youth to emulate or trusted by the black community "to do the right thing" on the Court; his popularity in the black community has plunged. In a 2007 Pew Research Center survey that asked blacks whether fourteen black newsmakers had either a good or bad influence on the black community, Thomas was one short of last place on the list, just ahead of gansta rap artist 50 Cent.[29] Considering that Thomas is one of the most conservative justices on the Supreme Court, particularly in the areas of civil rights and criminal justice, the implicit wink-and-nod pact between Thomas and blacks was a serious miscalculation. It demonstrates what the risks and consequences can be when symbolism overrides substantive judgments about political decisions.

Obama, by any stretch of the imagination, is not Clarence Thomas. But the implicit wink-and-nod agreement between Obama and black voters operated—and still operates—in similar ways. The belief that the symbolism of having Obama president would lead the candidate to represent blacks' substantive issues—both universal *and* race-specific—once he entered the White House, was to give way into the same faulty assumption. What complicated the implicit wink-and-nod agreement between Obama and black voters were two factors: a race-neutral black candidate at the top of the Democratic Party's ticket and the Democratic Party nominee's traditional move to the center after winning the nomination. In their quest to capture as many "median voters" as possible, nominees of both parties soften their positions on issues that are favored by their left-of-center or right-of-center constituencies.

Not surprisingly, after the Democratic Party's nominee has been determined, the influence of black voters diminishes. As the late political scientist Ron Walters argued, the strongest influence black voters have in presidential elections is during the Democratic primaries. Black voters are able to use what Walters described as "dependent leverage," that is, black voters are able to leverage their collective voting power for a Democratic presidential candidate who—if he or she wins the nomination—will prioritize blacks' issues once the candidate is elected president. The dependent-leverage strategy provides black voters the greatest opportunity to exert their collective power in presidential elections because black voters constitute approximately 20 percent of Democratic primary voters. And in the South, black voters exert even greater influence. The percentage of black Democratic primary voters participating in primaries constitutes about 40 percent and should expand as black in-migration to the South grows and as southern whites continue to abandon the Democratic Party.

Since half the black population is concentrated in reliably red states in the South, and large numbers of blacks are clustered in reliably blue states in the Northeast and in California, black voters have considerably less influence in general elections. What influence black voters do have are in battleground states. High black turnout could make a difference in closely contested races in Florida, Michigan, Ohio, and Pennsylvania. But black voters are nonentities in other battleground states like Colorado and Nevada. That is why blacks' choice of candidate in the Democratic primary is crucial for black voters having their issues placed on the electoral agenda. In the presidential elections sweepstakes, black voters have only one chance to get it right. And a

wink-and-nod arrangement between a race-neutral primary candidate and black voters, who have race-specific policy goals,
maximizes the risk that their concerns will be ignored. Since
black voters have nowhere else to go—indeed, many would rather
not vote than vote for a Republican candidate—they are a constituency captured by the Democratic Party. The party's stand-
ard-bearer can ignore their demands in the general election
campaign and, if elected, continue to ignore them once he or she
reaches the White House.

But having your group's interests captured by a political party
does not necessarily mean that your group has no influence. When
we consider the agenda-setting strategies of the Religious Right—
a captured constituency that, like black voters, has no other place
to go—the importance of group issues far outweighs the symbolism of a born-again Christian in the White House. During the
2000 presidential election, Religious Right leaders and voters
expected they would have in George W. Bush both a born-again
Christian who symbolized the movement and a president who
supported the Religious Right's policy agenda.

Indeed, during the primary, Bush let Christian Right leaders
and voters know that he was one of them and on their side. When
asked during a televised debate who was his favorite political
philosopher, Bush answered as if confessing at the church altar:
"Jesus Christ because he saved my life." After receiving the Republican nomination, Bush moderated his conservative views. He
described himself during the general election campaign as a "compassionate conservative," a move that allowed him to win the
support of independent voters. However, unlike Obama and other
Democratic Party nominees who gravitate toward the center and
steer clear of race-related issues, Bush never downplayed issues
important to the Religious Right, his core base. For these captured
voters within the Republican Party any distancing from policy
issues that were near and dear to the Religious Right would have
amounted to treason. George W. Bush—and none of his campaign
surrogates—would have uttered the following during the campaign:

"I'm a presidential candidate who just happens to be a born-again Christian."

"Don't vote for me because I'm a born-again Christian, but don't vote against me because I'm a born-again Christian either."

"George Bush can't be the president of born-again Christians; he has to be president of all the people."

Nor would the Religious Right stand for a candidate who attempted to widen his or her electoral coalition by promoting only policies that helped everyone. A "born-again-neutral" campaign strategy, that asked "sophisticated" believers to remember what the candidate had done in the past rather than what he plans to do once in office, would be considered absurd. Imagine surrogates for any Republican presidential nominee asking supporters to indulge the candidate's insufficient attention to Religious Right issues by proclaiming that the candidate must "do what he has to do" to get elected president. "Just wait until John McCain gets into the White House," a wink-and-nod surrogate would plead, "then he will address issues important to the Religious Right."

To this constituency, the stakes are too high to let candidates conceal or ignore policy stances on issues deemed integral to the movement. Indeed, because the Religious Right did not trust John McCain, who had previously described its leaders as "agents of intolerance," the Republican nominee was forced to select a born-again candidate, Sarah Palin, as his running mate. However, the overture was not enough. The lack of substantive clarity on key issues mattered more than the symbolism of a born-again Christian on the ticket. Instead of jumping ship by voting for Obama, many Religious Right voters decided to stay home on Election Day. They held their party's presidential candidate accountable for being too moderate on issues they cared about the most.

Although kept quiet, the Religious Right has authenticity litmus tests for presidential candidates. In the 2008 election, the movement's quest for authenticity not only impacted John McCain's candidacy, it also affected Mitt Romney's. While questions were raised about whether Obama was "black enough" to gain the support of black voters, similar questions were asked, and continue to be asked, about whether Romney, a Mormon, is "Christian enough" to be the candidate of the Religious Right.

The Democratic Party does not pay nearly as much attention to the concerns of its black members (despite their fierce loyalty to the party) compared with the Republican Party's response to the Religious Right. Like blacks, the Religious Right has no other party to turn to when choosing which candidate to support for president. But despite being captured voters of the Republican Party, the Religious Right is far more effective in placing issues on their party's agenda than civil rights organizations and black voters. When it comes to whether candidates support stem-cell research, abortion, or gay marriage, there are no wink-and-nod arrangements between Republican presidential candidates and Religious Right voters.

Part of the difference is black voters underestimating their own power and influence in the Democratic Party's nominating process. When presidential candidates are competing for the black vote—rather than taking black voters for granted—policy discussions about racial inequality come into view. Before Obama was transformed into a symbol of black progress, the candidate spoke with greater clarity about race-specific issues when he met with black audiences. Having to compete for black voters necessitated Obama's forcefulness when speaking out on some race-specific issues. What pushed Obama was that he was losing ground among blacks. By the summer of 2007, Clinton was gaining momentum over Obama among black voters. A June Gallup poll showed blacks evenly split between the two candidates—43 percent for Clinton and 42 percent for Obama. But a July Pew Research Center poll showed Clinton polling 47 percent among blacks compared to Obama's 34 percent.[30]

On September 28, 2007, Obama gave a speech at Howard University's annual convocation. It was delivered eight days after 15,000 to 20,000 blacks marched in support of the "Jena Six," a group of black male teenagers who were arrested and charged for attempted murder after a schoolyard brawl with a white male classmate in Jena, Louisiana. Some black leaders criticized Obama for declining to attend the march. For one brief moment in the campaign, race and the criminal justice system had been placed on the forefront of the political agenda, and Obama, who rarely discussed racial issues, spoke to the incident.

"Thurgood Marshall did not argue *Brown* so that we would accept a country where too many African-American men end up in prison because we'd rather spend more to jail a twenty-five-year-old than to educate a five-year-old," the candidate told the audience. Turning to the effects of Hurricane Katrina, Obama continued to raise issues of racial inequality. "Dr. King did not take us to the mountain top so that we would allow a terrible storm to ravage those who were stranded in the valley; he would not have expected that it would take a breach in our levees to reveal a breach in our compassion." He went on, "And I am certain that nine children did not walk through the doors of the school in Little Rock so that our children would have to see nooses hanging at a school in Louisiana."

Praising President Dwight Eisenhower's decision in 1957 to send federal troops to desegregate Central High School in Little Rock, Arkansas, Obama told the Howard University audience that "there are moments when what's truly risky is not to act." He then expounded at length on race-specific issues—the tragedy of the Jena Six, the unfairness of the criminal justice system, opposition against affirmative action, and the racial bias of the Bush administration's Justice Department:

Like Katrina did with poverty, Jena exposed glaring inequities in our justice system that were around long before that schoolyard fight broke out. It reminds us of the fact that we have a system that locks away too many young, first-time, nonviolent offenders for the better part of their lives—a decision that's made not by a judge in a courtroom, but by a politician in Washington. It reminds us that we have certain sentences that are based less on the kind of crime you commit than on what you look like and where you come from. It reminds us that we have a Justice Department whose idea of prosecuting civil rights violations is trying to roll back affirmative action programs from our college and universities; a Justice Department whose idea of prosecuting voting rights violations is to look for voting fraud in black and Latino communities where it doesn't exist.

Obama's address not only reminded the audience of the racial disparities in the criminal justice system, it also proposed new policies to address those disparities. Obama, later known as the presidential candidate who happens to be black, found his voice on racism in the criminal justice system when he needed the support of black voters. He proposed recruiting more public defenders so that every citizen—regardless of race, age, or social status—would have a qualified attorney available to them. He also proposed forgiving college and law school loans for law graduates who decide to become public attorneys. This would, Obama believed, provide incentives for the best and the brightest law students to become public attorneys. The candidate promised as well to push for a federal racial profiling law that would bar police from singling out blacks and other minorities based on their race during criminal investigations. And if elected, he also promised to encourage states to reform the death penalty to ensure that innocent people would not be executed.

The candidate did not stop there. He proposed additional reforms, including *closing the disparities* in punishment for possessing powder cocaine versus crack cocaine. Blacks use crack cocaine more than whites. However, the punishment for possession of crack cocaine is more severe than powder cocaine, although there is no difference in the psychological and physical effects on individuals.[31] "The real difference between the two is the skin color of the people using them," Obama told the audience. The candidate also supported drug rehabilitation programs for first-time, nonviolent drug users instead of serving time in prison. "When I'm president," he promised the students and faculty at Howard, "we will review these sentences to see where we can be smarter on crime and reduce the blind and counterproductive warehousing of nonviolent offenders." He went further, "And we will give first-time, nonviolent drug offenders a chance to serve their sentence, when appropriate, in the type of drug rehabilitation programs that have been proven to work better than a prison term in changing bad behavior." (In 2010 Obama signed into law legislation that narrows but does not close the sentencing disparity between crack and powder cocaine.)

Unlike the speeches on respectability that would dominate his repertoire when addressing black audiences after he clinched the nomination in the spring of 2008, the struggling candidate only devoted a few lines to the idea of personal responsibility in the fall of 2007. "We need parents to start acting like parents and spend more time with their children and read to them once in a while," the candidate advised the audience of potential voters. These views on the need for fairness in the criminal justice system were short-lived. Once Obama no longer needed to work hard at getting the black vote, the candidate lost his voice on racial justice. Discussions of substantive policy issues on race would be replaced by the symbolism of a black candidate making history as a serious contender for the presidency.

When we take stock of the policy priorities of black voters, it is not a one-dimensional, narrow focus on issues that directly help everyone. Given the complexity of issues black voters face, both universal and targeted policies are necessary to tackle racial inequality and poverty. As the ABC News–Columbia University survey showed, blacks, whites, and Latinos reported—just two months prior to the November 2008 general election—that the next administration should give its highest priorities to addressing the economy, health care, and education. Clearly these are issues that may be looked at as universally affecting all Americans.

But in contrast to whites, a majority of blacks—and a majority or near majority of Latinos—also believed that the "highest priority" should be given to raising the minimum wage, fairness in the criminal justice system, and addressing poverty. Blacks and Latinos expressed greater interest in the next administration addressing the minimum wage (52 percent of blacks and 57 percent of Latinos) than whites (26 percent). Similarly, blacks and Latinos placed a higher priority on poverty (65 percent of blacks and 63 percent of Latinos) and fairness in the criminal justice system (51 percent of blacks and 46 percent of Latinos) than whites (38 percent and 34 percent, respectively). Not surprisingly none of the racial/ethnic groups—including blacks—thought that the hot-button issue of reparations for slavery should be a priority of the next administration (24 percent for blacks, 8 percent of whites, and 19 percent of Latinos). With the exception of the minimum wage, poverty and fairness in the criminal justice system are problems so entrenched in black and Latino communities that they require targeted policies to solve.[32]

The eminent sociologist William Julius Wilson likes to tell the story of a black taxicab driver in South Bend, Indiana, he met during the 2008 campaign. Like the wise and down-home fictional character Jesse B. Semple, whom Langston Hughes wrote about during the 1950s, Wilson uses the perspective of the South Bend black taxi driver to illustrate the "sophisticated" support black voters gave Obama.

Responding to a story about Jesse Jackson's public criticism of Obama, the cab driver asked the sociologist, "What is wrong with Jesse Jackson? Let the man get elected, then we can raise questions about how he plans to deal with the problems of Blacks!" The sociologist interpreted the cab driver's lament: "That's a very sophisticated remark, much more sophisticated than a lot of these Black Intellectuals who have been trashing Obama because his messages were not tailored to Black people." Wilson went on to argue that black voters gave Obama the "slack" he needed to navigate the "racial terrain" during the election.[33]

But the "slack" that black voters gave Obama—or what could be viewed as a greater preference for symbolism than for having the totality of their policy priorities addressed—meant that black voters put aside policy demands for the prize of electing one of their own to the White House. The same logic pervaded Obama's governing style once he reached the White House. When it comes to directly addressing issues of racial inequality, the wink-and-nod agreement continues to dictate Obama's relationship with the most loyal constituency of the Democratic Party, which just happens to be black, disproportionately poor, and severely unemployed.

The Price of the Ticket

ON WEDNESDAY EVENING, April 30, 2009, President Obama marked the one-hundredth day of his administration by holding a live press conference. Midway through the exchange with reporters, Obama took a question from Andre Showell, a news correspondent from Black Entertainment Television (BET). The reporter asked the president if he had a plan to address the rapidly growing unemployment rate in black and Latino communities. Noting a double-digit national black unemployment rate and the nearly 50 percent black male unemployment in New York City, the journalist's question was direct and to the point: "Given this unique and desperate circumstance, what specific policies can you point to that will target these communities, and what's the timetable for us to see tangible results?"

The president responded in the same way he did when issues of race came up during the presidential campaign: "Well, keep in mind that every step we are taking is designed to help all people." Because blacks and Latinos are disproportionately affected by the economy, Obama asserted that aspects of the Recovery Act were going to fix the growing problem of black and Latino unemployment. The president mentioned the act's unemployment insurance and the opportunity for the unemployed to keep their health benefits from their former employer. The president then commented on additional initiatives that were passed on his watch that would benefit struggling communities, particularly funding for community health centers and expanded health care coverage for children. These programs, Obama believed, would trickle down to black and Latino communities to help them weather the great recession.

But the main goal, the president insisted, was getting the economy out of recession. To the disappointment of many, including to members of the Congressional Black Caucus, Obama pursued a recovery strategy in the first two years of his administration without offering a jobs bill. "So my general approach is that if the economy is strong that will lift all boats," Obama continued. Lifting the economy, the president believed, could be accomplished by giving tax cuts to the middle class, making college affordable for everyone, and initiating job-training programs.[1] But the Recovery Act, as it became clear three years into his administration, would hardly assist those who had no boats to begin with. There would be no massive back-to-work initiatives targeting resources to the communities hardest hit by the recession. As months passed, rising unemployment, and particularly rising black unemployment, was turning into a national crisis. Though black unemployment stood at 8.4 percent prior to the recession, it was growing at a faster rate than the national unemployment rate and at a faster rate than in any other racial group. By the summer of 2009, black unemployment had climbed to an astonishing 15 percent.[2]

Obama's disregard of targeted remedies to address minority unemployment continued throughout his first year in office. On June 23, 2009, the president was asked again at a press conference about the mounting problem of black unemployment. April Ryan, a journalist with American Urban Radio, noted in her question predictions by some economists that black employment could soar as high as 20 percent by the end of that year. "Why not target intervention now to stop the bloodletting in the black unemployment rate?" Obama provided the same pat answer. The president acknowledged that black and Latino workers were disproportionately affected by the great recession, but he still insisted that policies that helped everyone would cure the catastrophic unemployment rate in minority communities. "Well, look . . . first of all," he persisted, "if the economy as a whole is doing poorly, then you know the African American community is going to be doing poorly, and that they are going to be hit even harder." The solution was "to lift the economy overall, and that's what my strategy is focused on." When the reporter attempted to follow up, asking if his strategy was "targeted enough" to make a dent in minority communities, Obama moved on to take a question on violence in Iran.[3]

April Ryan got another opportunity to ask the president about black unemployment and received a similar response, even though black unemployment was climbing even higher. In a one-on-one interview in the Oval Office on December 21, 2009, Ryan asked the president about the growing and disproportionately high black unemployment rate, which was at nearly 16 percent. "The only thing I can do is, you know, by law I can't pass laws saying I'm just helping black folks. I am the president of the entire United States," he quipped. "What I can do is make sure that I am passing laws that help all people, particularly those that are most vulnerable and most in need. That in turn is going to help lift up the African American community."[4]

The president's comment on his inability to pass a bill "just helping black folks" was a red herring. What some members of the Congressional Black Caucus actually proposed was a jobs bill that incorporated the principle of "targeted universalism"; an approach that would geographically target government-sponsored job projects in communities most affected by the recession and with the greatest concentrations of poverty. By default, such legislation would not help everyone equally but benefit those most affected by the recession. Nevertheless, the president continued to govern on matters of race the same way he campaigned—"neutral" on issues specific to race.[5]

Malcolm X's vision of black politics, centered on putting community issues first, has collapsed under the weight of the Democratic

Party's general uneasiness about tackling racial inequality and under the guidance of a race-neutral black president who distances himself from issues and policies targeted at eradicating racial inequality. What has been accomplished during the presidency of Barack Obama is history being made "in our lifetime," but on the condition that issues specific to racial inequality will not be prioritized in his administration.

Indeed, Obama's race-neutral campaign strategy has spilled over to his approach to governing. The strategy has exacted a heavy cost to politics once dominated by strategies that overtly challenged racist practices and institutions. Though Obama's success as a presidential candidate is a testament to the success of coalition politics, as well as to the effectiveness of race-neutral campaign strategies, these approaches to black politics have actually marginalized rather than elevated race-specific issues onto the national political agenda. Symbolically, the election of Obama as the first black president represents the apex of black politics. Substantively, however, Obama's ascendancy illustrates the continuing decline of black politics' inability to set a political agenda in national politics. As a consequence, the rise of black politics during the Obama presidency has more to do with the symbolism of being the first black president and less to do with addressing substantive issues that face black America.

Universalism, once a policy doctrine, has now morphed into a color-blind approach to politics and public policy. Because many black voters feel that Obama should be protected from his political enemies on the Right, they are reluctant to press him into action on race-specific issues or any issue facing their communities. Thus, blacks are confined to the sidelines while the political game in Washington is played. Instead of putting pressure on Obama to address particular policies, black leaders and black voters function more like cheerleaders than players suited up to play. They stand on the sidelines cheering on the team's first black quarterback. In the meantime, points are scored by the opposing teams, but not in the interest of black communities.

On matters of race and criminal justice—a focus on policy less amenable to the dictates of universalism—the president's response has been muted. Though blacks assign high priority to policies that assure fairness in the criminal justice system, the Obama administration has done little on that front. The high-profile police shootings of unarmed black men on the eve of Obama's inauguration—most notably the murder of Oscar Grant in Oakland and the shooting of Robbie Tolan in a suburb outside of Houston—went without comment by the president-elect. But the July 16, 2009, arrest of Harvard University Professor Henry Louis Gates—who is a friend of the president—provided an opportunity for Obama to articulate his policy views on the need for criminal justice reform.

When first asked about the incident during a press conference, the president gave a gut response that briefly unmasked his personal feelings about bias in the system: "The Cambridge police acted stupidly in arresting somebody when there was already proof that they were in their own home." His honest response led to a firestorm of criticism by the Right. To quell the perception that his comments were unsympathetic to the work of police officers, Obama invited Sergeant James Crowley, the arresting officer, and Professor Gates to the White House for beer and conversation. That was the end of that.

Obama did not allow the Gates incident—which is a reminder of the type of negative encounters black men regularly have with police officers—to become a teachable moment. Though Obama probably dropped the subject out of fear that a white backlash would consume his efforts to shore up public support for his health care campaign, his silence demonstrates, once again, how race-specific issues are placed on the back burner in the Obama administration. There would be no follow-up discussions about Obama's campaign promise to pursue a federal racial-profiling law. Obama's missed opportunity in the Gates affair and his unwillingness to adopt targeted policies to address the rapid rise of minority unemployment also illustrate that black issues get low priority in the Obama administration.

The vision of independent black politics—which places community issues above all else—would have predicted that the rise in black political empowerment, symbolized by the election of Obama as president, would produce more substantive policy outcomes for black America. That having a black president, a black attorney general (Eric Holder), and a black chairman of the House Judiciary Committee (John Conyers, when the Democrats were in the majority during the first two years of Obama's presidency) has not resulted in any major reform in the criminal justice system shows the substantive limits of black politics at its peak of "empowerment."

There have been, however, two constituencies more effective than blacks at setting the agenda during Obama's presidency— the Tea Party on the Right and the gay and lesbian movement on the Left. The Tea Party, in collaboration with House Republicans, has set the agenda on economic policy following the recapture of the House after the 2010 midterm elections. During the summer of 2011, the House Republicans turned a standard voting procedure on the extension of the nation's debt ceiling into a full-blown crisis and altered the debate about how to stimulate the economy.

Congressional Republicans linked their support of the debt-ceiling extension to reductions in government spending. Reductions included cuts in long-standing safety net programs targeted to the poor and/or elderly, such as Medicare. Though a majority of Americans believed that stimulating the economy was the number one issue facing the nation and most agreed that tax increases for the rich should be enacted, the Tea Party and the House Republicans shifted the debate in Washington. Indeed, as of this writing, the Tea Party and the House Republicans continue to get their way on economic policies despite their widespread unpopularity among the American public.

On the Left, the gay and lesbian movement has been effective at pushing its policy goals. Though the nation is divided over gay rights—especially gay marriage—Obama has risked political capital and managed to use the bully pulpit and executive orders to support gay and lesbian rights.

The attention that the Obama administration has given to gay and lesbian issues compared with the lack of attention given to race-specific issues is a study in contrasts. On June 29, 2011, the president made a short speech in celebration of Lesbian, Gay, Bisexual, Transgender (LGBT) Pride Month at the White House. In an event that resembled a pep rally, Obama told the gathering what policy goals he had accomplished for them during his tenure as president. While Obama has repeatedly told black leaders and black voters to be patient with the slow pace of change regarding his economic policies, Obama vowed to "never counsel patience" regarding the LGBT community.

The accomplishments on behalf of the LGBT community are impressive, and the president named them one by one during his talk. He told the crowd that he had signed into law hate crime legislation that included protections for gays and lesbians and that the legislation had been named in memory of Matthew Sheppard, who, in 1998, was murdered and tortured in Wyoming because he was gay. Obama then informed the gathering that he had lifted the HIV travel ban and that his administration had developed a national strategy to fight HIV/AIDS.

The president related how he had pushed for the repeal of the "don't ask, don't tell" policy that was, at the time, on the cusp of implementation. He followed by declaring that his administration refused to defend in court the Defense of Marriage Act, which hampers efforts to expand recognition of gay marriage in federal law, because the act defines marriage to be between a man and a woman. "I met my commitments to the LGBT," Obama proclaimed. "I have delivered on what I promised."

The president promised to do more in the future and acknowledged the pressure that the LGBT community placed on him to act. "That does not mean our work is done. There will be times when you are still frustrated with me." He continued, "I know there will be times when you are still frustrated with the pace of change. I can count on you to let me know. This is not a shy group." Along with the policy successes that Obama enumerated in his talk, the president has also used the bully pulpit to prioritize the goals of the LGBT community. He invited, for instance, children of gay and lesbian families to the annual White House Easter egg hunt. He also recorded a promo for the "It Gets Better" anti-bullying campaign for gay and lesbian youth.[6]

The Obama administration has responded to LGBT issues even when doing so carried political risks. Support for LGBT goals offers minimal benefit to Obama in his quest to expand voters for his reelection campaign. He could have simply decided to ignore LGBT concerns. Like black voters, many gay and lesbian voters are a captured constituency of the Democratic Party. They have no other place to go. The LGBT community can either vote for the Democratic presidential nominee or not vote at all because the Republican Party is opposed to their policy demands. Furthermore, LGBT political influence in presidential elections is confined to reliably blue states like New York and California. Indeed, Obama's LGBT policy successes may not help him with some independent voters and will certainly not help him win over conservative voters. Despite potential risks, Obama has been willing to go to bat for LGBT issues but unwilling to go to bat for issues that are top priorities for black communities. Far from telling black leaders that they should not be patient with the slow pace of change in black communities—as he told LGBT activists about their concerns—Obama berated members of the Congressional Black Caucus and other black critics during the CBC's 2011 awards dinner to "stop complaining, stop grumbling, stop crying" and get behind his reelection campaign.[7]

A look at the White House's webpage featuring Black History Month illustrates, once again, how low a priority race-specific policy issues are to the Obama administration. With the exception of modest initiatives to strengthen historically black colleges, which Obama noted with an air of defensiveness during a speech—"every president since Ronald Reagan has supported black colleges"—the website focuses almost exclusively on cultural events and personal testimonies of black success. Included were excerpts of "Motown

Night" at the White House and the screening of the HBO film on Thurgood Marshall, among other cultural events. The site also includes what can be described as a virtual black history poster highlighting black staff working in the Obama administration.

As if extolling the politics of respectability, this feature of the White House Black History Month website allows black staffers to tell uplifting stories. They recount fond memories of reciting Bible verses as kids, being raised in families with strong work ethics, the value placed on education in their families, and stories about overcoming racial discrimination. There is a lot of pride expressed on the website, but very little policy content.[8] While the LGBT community demands, lobbies, and demonstrates, blacks celebrate, protect, and wait. When it comes to blacks scoring points on the field by getting policy goals enacted, the expectations have been lowered and the goalpost keeps moving farther away. "Just wait until Obama gets elected, then he can focus on black issues," many said during the 2008 campaign. "Just wait until after the midterm," many said after he was elected. "Just wait until after he wins a second term," many now say. Just wait.

In order for a group to have its voice heard in the political process—as the political scientist E. E. Schattschneider observed nearly fifty years ago in his classic book the *Semisovereign People*—conflict and the number of players in the political game are essential to setting a group's political agenda. The greater the number of participants in the process the more likely issues will be placed on the agenda. "The number of people involved in any conflict determines what happens," Schattschneider wrote. "Every change in the number of participants, every increase or reduction in the number of participants, affects the results."[9] In essence, if organized groups don't allow their voices to be heard on issues important to them, then the political system will not respond. Or, as nineteenth-century abolitionist Frederick Douglass said succinctly, "Power concedes nothing without demand. It never did and it never will."

The irony here is that both the Tea Party and the LGBT community—despite being on opposite ends of the political spectrum—have scored points by becoming actively engaged in the political process. In both cases, the injection of their issues on the agenda led to conflict. What were once "nonissues" became issues that Obama prioritized. Adopting a mix of protest tactics and electoral politics, combining insider and outsider roles to press for change, the Tea Party and the LGBT community adopted a strategy of politics, which pressed Obama into action, that was once an integral part of black politics. But instead of pushing the Obama administration to prioritize community issues, most black leaders and many black voters have become his protectors by shielding the president from criticism.

Advocates of black causes are fearful that the Right will discredit Obama by exploiting black demands. This fear allows community issues to remain dormant in the political process. The idea that demands cannot be made on the standard bearer of the Democratic Party because it hurts the president's standing bestows too much power and influence on the Right. It virtually amounts to the Right dictating when and if blacks can set their own agenda. Imagine, if you will, Martin Luther King and other civil rights leaders deciding not to engage in protest demonstrations because doing so would be used by white supremacists to undermine Lyndon Johnson's ability to win support for civil rights legislation. There has been—and will likely be for quite some time—strong opposition by the Right to policies aimed at addressing racial inequality. Remaining silent on racial inequality will do little to eliminate it.

When the political scientist Charles V. Hamilton proposed a deracialized strategy for the Democratic Party in 1976, he believed the strategy could circumvent the Republican Party's exploitation of the Democratic Party's support of race-specific policies. By emphasizing universal policies, the Democratic Party could recapture southern whites and white working-class voters who were driven away by liberal racial policies of the Democratic Party. In 1976, Carter won as a moderate Democrat and did not place black demands at the top of his domestic policy objectives. Although the implicit agreement comes with obligations on the part of black voters, the strategy does not mean, as Hamilton argued, granting blind loyalty to the Democratic Party or its standard bearer. If the strategy is to function, black voters have to be prepared to reward or punish the Democratic Party. "Precisely because Black voters were so instrumental in electing Carter the next task is to operate in a manner to hold the new administration accountable," Hamilton wrote in a *New York Times* op-ed piece. Accountability required "diligent" political mobilization on the part of black voters. "One should not assume that the Carter administration will recognize its political debt to the Black masses and act responsibly," Hamilton asserted. "That would be expecting more from the political process than history would justify."[10]

As Hamilton observed, a problem with a deracialized, wink-and-nod strategy "lies essentially in having to articulate a position openly." Thus, in order for the strategy to benefit community interests, neither the winkers nor the nodders can publicly reveal the agreement. This situation, Hamilton noted, creates a "special dilemma" for black voters. "It is precisely because racism is still (and will probably remain so for some time) a most prevalent, oppressive force in this society that Blacks—as Blacks—must be ever mindful of collective interests, our collective resources, and our collective capabilities." The burden for black voters and black leaders, then, is to be "collectively calculating" in their decision to support candidates.[11]

But as Hamilton pointed out, the wink-and-nod and wholesale focus on coalition politics to win elections have placed limits on the types of policies that can be pursued. It is not as if blacks haven't tried to build multiracial coalitions with whites, especially alongside the white poor and working classes, in the past. As Hamilton rightly noted, the problem has not been "black unwillingness but white unavailability." Rather than support Democratic presidential candidates who move toward the center, in search of support from the elusive "median voter," whose policy preferences are to the right of the average black voter, a true test for the viability of coalition politics is to see if "the country is prepared to join with blacks in moving toward truly progressive policies." Deracialization, to quote Hamilton, should not be thought of as a "means of co-opting black demands."[12]

Today, community interests are not being co-opted by the Democratic Party; they are being organized out of national politics altogether. When it comes to the two political parties addressing issues related to racial inequality, the ascendancy of Barack Obama as the standard bearer of the Democratic Party and the short-lived rise of Republican presidential candidate Herman Cain represent two sides of the same coin.

Cain reinforced the racial prejudices of right-wing Republicans by saying things about blacks and poor people that white Republicans would get called on as racist and insensitive. A favorite of the Tea Party, Cain continued the Republican Party's "Southern Strategy" tradition by serving as a mouthpiece for mean-spirited denouncements against blacks and the poor. Cain's opinions provided cover for the Tea Party, which has been accused of harboring racist views. Speaking in their defense, Cain told Tea Party activists that he too had been called racist because "I disagree with the president who happens to be black . . . I got breaking news for you, you are not racists you are patriots," Cain declared. When talking about the effects of the recession on rising levels of black unemployment, Cain argued that unemployed blacks "aren't held back because of racism." They just need the right attitude, Cain offered. "People sometimes hold themselves back because they want to use racism as an excuse for them not being able to achieve what they want to be achieved," the Republican candidate proclaimed.[13]

When you place Cain next to Obama, who appears to be too timidly strategic to raise questions about—and work overtly against—racial inequality, the actions (or in the case of Obama inactions) of both diminish black interests on the national political scene. One black candidate for president spouts bigoted views about blacks and the poor. The other is silent on issues of racial inequality and poverty. In the end, neither political party is a vehicle for blacks to directly confront inequality, because both parties push black-specific issues to the margins of national policymaking. This development tells us something about the durability of racism as an ideology in American politics. Instead of fading away in an era celebrated as "postracial," race as ideology demonstrates convincing staying power, endowed with the ability to readapt and readjust as new political situations arise.

To understand the significance of Obama to black communities is to understand how the symbolic aspects of representation operate in black politics. As a black person elected to the most powerful position in the nation—if not the world—it is no wonder that Obama stands as a powerful symbol of black aspirations and why black voters are willing to give him slack. The symbolic side of black politics also highlights how the role-modeling assumptions of black leadership—both elected and nonelected leaders—permeates black politics. This aspect of political representation in black politics fuels the wink-and-nod strategies of race-neutral black candidates who usually need the support of black voters to win office. The level of trust—and deference—to black politicians is greater when those politicians become black "firsts." They then easily become symbols of black progress, conveying the message that the system works for those willing to take advantage of opportunities, irrespective of the societal barriers in their way.

As law professor Lani Guinier explains:

As role models these black achievers presumptively represent equal opportunity. With few exceptions, their election signals that society's institutions are "color-blind" pure meritocracies. Role models, who convey the message "We Have Overcome," also inspire those not yet overcoming. Thus in general, black role models are powerful symbolic reference points for those worried about the continued legacy of past discrimination.[14]

Thus, the trust that accompanies symbolic firsts—and oftentimes symbolic seconds, thirds, and fourths—has the effect of insulating these politicians against accountability by black voters. As long as trusted black politicians are viewed as symbols of black progress, it is assumed that they are automatically providing substantive representation for blacks. The black politician as "role model" can exert a powerful influence in black communities and that partly explains why the overwhelming majority of blacks has provided unwavering support to Obama—never lower than 80 percent in favorability polls—since the day he stepped into the White House.

In Richard Fenno's book *Going Home: Black Representatives and Their Constituents*, published in 2003, the legendary congressional scholar documents how black members of Congress interact with black constituents in their districts. Fenno, who has written numerous books on the ways members of Congress connect to their constituents, returned to his field notes from the 1970s and rethought his earlier observations of two black members of Congress— Cleveland's Louis Stokes and Houston's Barbara Jordan. Three decades later Fenno revisited Stokes's congressional district, which was then represented by the late Stephanie Tubbs-Jones. He also followed Congressman Chaka Fattah around black neighborhoods in his Philadelphia district. (Barbara Jordan did not seek reelection in 1978. She died in 1992.)

In addition to studying their career ambitions, links to political organizations, and policy goals, Fenno discovered an aspect of political representation that had escaped him decades before. Observing these members in their districts while attending campaign rallies, ribbon-cutting ceremonies, school events, and church services, Fenno discovered the enormous pull of symbolic representation. It was a style of representation that he had not encountered in his studies on white members of Congress.

When Fenno, for instance, shadowed Carl Stokes in the mid-1970s and again in the 1990s, he gained insight into how the symbolism of being a "black first" influenced the way constituents perceived Stokes as an "exalted" member of Cleveland's black community. (Fenno also shadowed Tubbs-Jones in the district after Stokes retired in 1998.) For black public officials, especially those who were first to break the color barrier, the symbolism of being a pioneer meant that black voters had an inordinate degree of confidence and trust in them. When Fenno asked Stokes how he perceived his relationship with voters back home, Stokes answered that he—as a black man—embodied the wishes of his constituency simply because he was black. "When I vote as a black man, I necessarily represent the black community. I don't have any trouble knowing what the black community thinks or wants," Stokes told Fenno. "I don't know whether my district is peculiar or strange or what, but I don't get letters asking me to vote such and such a way on such and such bill." Stokes understood his constituents provided him a great deal of leeway in making decisions for them. "They say to themselves that everything they know about Lou Stokes tells them 'he's up there doing a good job for us.' It's a blind faith type of thing."[15]

Fenno, whose method of observation makes him akin to a political anthropologist, reveals how Stokes was treated like royalty in black Cleveland. "As we drove around the city in a staff-driven Cadillac or Lincoln, people often waved," Fenno noted. "At stoplights, they would roll down the window and call on him." At an event sponsored by a black sorority, Fenno observed how the Cleveland congressman received red-carpet treatment, a rare occurrence for a member of Congress greeting his constituents. As Fenno described the scene, "He was introduced as 'our leader,' as a man who has known poverty and overcome it, a man who knows what it means to be part of an oppressed people—'our people,' and a man with 'many, many awards and accomplishments and many, many qualifications.'" Stokes then received a standing ovation before and after his speech. "No other congressman I've seen gets that," Fenno noted with bewilderment. Even more surprising from Fenno's observations was the adoration members of the audience expressed for their representative in Washington. Fenno further wrote, "After the talk [Stokes] was mobbed by these mature, college-educated, professional women—for his autograph. I never saw that before."[16]

When Fenno followed Chaka Fattah in the black neighborhoods of his district, the political scientist saw the same symbolic dynamics at play. Even though Fattah is the *fourth* black congressman elected from Philadelphia over the span of forty years, the congressman is still seen as a symbol, a role model for black aspirations. Fattah explained to Fenno why this is the case. Since there have been so few blacks elected to Congress, being a black congressman in Philadelphia—and presumably elsewhere—is "considered the pinnacle of political success." Fattah described his situation at the time: "I am the highest ranking African-American elected official in the city and the highest ranking elected official in the state, and that gives me a higher standing in my district." He continued, "Because of that, my constituents hold me in esteem—almost reverence. When I come into the church, for example, people stand up." Because of the high regard many of his black constituents hold of him, Fattah reported to Fenno that "people give me added leeway in what I do here and what I do in Congress."[17]

For many black voters the symbolism of a black president and a black family in the White House is well worth the price of the ticket. And many blacks believe it is their duty to protect the symbol. With some exceptions, black America has embraced a "close ranks" policy when it comes to standing behind the president. Black America has built a shield of protection around Obama composed of all strata of black life—from ordinary working people to Ivy League professors and Wall Street executives. Public criticism of the president by other blacks is considered by many blacks to be a violation of community solidarity, if not outright treason. Tom Joyner, the popular black syndicated radio host and a surrogate for the Obama administration, has admonished his listeners to "stick together, black people." "Let's not even deal with facts right now," Joyner wrote on his blog. "Let's deal with our blackness and pride—and loyalty." He continued, "We have the chance to re-elect the first African-American president, and that's what we ought to be doing. And I'm not afraid or ashamed to say that as black people, we should do it because he's a black man."

And the Reverend Al Sharpton—who has been transformed from a protest activist to an advisor for the Obama administration—has even threatened the president's black critics with public denunciations. "I'm not telling you to shut up," Sharpton told listeners during one of his radio talk shows when speaking about the president's black critics. "I'm telling you don't make some of us have to speak up." For the president who "just happens to be black," it is curious—if not hypocritical—that many of his black surrogates wave the banner of racial solidarity to silence black critics and to keep black voters solidly in his corner for the 2012 election. It seems the only time the president sanctions racial solidarity is when he needs the support of black voters. It is no wonder, then, why "I got his back" is an Obama campaign slogan for 2012.[18]

As a historically marginalized group it is not surprising that many blacks see Obama as a person who stands in for them, who makes them proud, who provides them with overdue recognition for their long struggle for acceptance and dignity. Indeed, Obama has entered the pantheon of great black leaders—alongside Martin Luther King, Frederick Douglass, Booker T. Washington, W. E. B. DuBois, and Malcolm X—not because of what he's done to break down the barriers of racial inequality but merely for being the first black president.

But too strong of a desire for recognition can have unintended consequences for marginalized groups. Recognition and social change are similar but different factors in the life of those near the bottom of society. If recognition is achieved for black Americans but structural barriers remain intact and unchallenged, then recognition without a commitment to eradicating racial inequality may actually end up further perpetuating inequality, despite the visible gains made by some.

Indeed, the very idea of an elected official as role model for any constituency is incompatible with accountability, a central tenet of representative democracy. Role models are to be lifted up, placed on pedestals, and emulated. They stand as symbols of community progress and are to be protected. Therefore, role models are not to be criticized, questioned, or asked to account for failures. Acknowledging the shortcomings of role models by those who wish to emulate them would be a difficult exercise. And feelings of disappointment toward role models may actually further internalize negative stereotypes about the inability of blacks as a group, which is why rooting for role models is so embedded in black culture. To place community interests above symbolism is not to ask what the first black president is doing for blacks. Rather it is to ask what is a Democratic president doing for the most loyal constituency of the Democratic Party, which just happens to be black, and which happens to have issues that need to be prioritized. Unfortunately, when it comes to the Obama presidency and black America, the symbolic and the substantive are assumed to be one.

This is the price of the ticket.

But it is not the only price. The nation's fiscal crisis has affected the president's ability to deliver on universal policies and on the modest policies he proposed as a candidate to tackle racial inequality. The crisis has made Obama—the nation's first black president—a "hollow prize" for black America. Like the first black mayors who came of age during the 1960s and 1970s in cities that were in decline—cities like Gary, Indiana; Newark, New Jersey; and East St. Louis, Illinois—Obama inherited an economy that was on the verge of ruin. Those early black political firsts had to contend with white flight from cities, a declining revenue base, and the rising social costs of a growing black and increasingly poor population. As Coleman Young, the first black mayor of Detroit, once said, black mayors are either "undertakers or saviors of cities." It is difficult to be the captain of a sinking ship. And it is troubling when the captain of the *Titanic* tells those barely holding on for survival that a "rising tide lifts all boats," as Obama did when asked about the mounting rate of black unemployment.[19]

There have been some policy accomplishments under Obama that will benefit black communities in the long run. Obama signed into law a form of expanded health care that will provide additional

blacks—an estimated one-fifth that are currently uninsured—
health care coverage. If the law survives legal scrutiny it will help in
the fight to close the racial gap in various health disparities. Obama
also signed into law reforms that lessen—but do not eliminate—
the disparity in sentencing between those possessing crack cocaine
and those possessing powder cocaine. As mentioned, even though
researchers have shown there are no scientific differences in the
effects each drug has on individuals, the new sentencing guidelines
will still place black violators at a disadvantage since blacks are
more likely to be caught with crack cocaine than whites. Additionally, the new sentencing guidelines are not retroactive, which means
that thousands of nonviolent offenders charged with the possession
of crack cocaine remain in jails. However, even with those reforms,
the debt crisis and austerity proposals aimed at cutting long-standing programs that benefit the black poor and elderly—such as Social
Security, Medicare, and Medicaid—are rendering Obama's universal
approach to addressing racial inequality insufficient.

Now that it has happened in our lifetime, black Americans can
move on and begin anew, placing interest above pride. We protect
more than we demand, because we fear that the forces of the
Right will destroy the thing—the very person—that has made us
prideful. But pride, with its ability to soothe doubts, to lift us as
individuals and as a people, has its limits. Symbols can act as
double-edged swords. They can serve as a source of inspiration,
but they can also have the effect of legitimizing conditions as
they are. Pride cannot stand in as a cure for depression-level
unemployment, for a community on the front line of the mortgage
foreclosure crisis, for the ravages of AIDS, or for the hope that a
rising tide will lift all boats.

This surge of pride has occurred during an era of an imagined—if
not willed—view of a color-blind society. What is at stake in this
new era is the erasure of memories of past group struggles. Black
America's collective memory—a memory handed down by those who
bore witness to things as they really were—is being recast as a
lopsided, triumphant story of progress over America's racist past.

Obama's rise as the nation's first black president has created a new story of American progress; one that may have the effect of obliterating the collective memories of past black struggles and triumphs. The emerging official story of American progress goes something like this: Obama's ascendancy proves, once and for all, that America has overcome its racism. Though it may have taken a long time for American society to change—over 250 years from slavery to citizenship with fully designated legal rights—the American economic and political order was flexible enough to accommodate the descendants of slaves and the survivors of state-sanctioned segregation.

This new era of an imagined color-blind society will alter America's sense of time. In the past, time was marked by the oppression blacks endured and the freedom they fought for and won. From "slavery to freedom," from "civil rights to post–civil rights"—these experiences marked black people's journey in America. The election of Barack Obama as president of the United States—a triumph for many that is akin to a Second Emancipation Proclamation—seems to mark a new (postracial) time in America. It might be that future generations of black America will mark time of the black experience in America by the initials B.B.O and A.B.O.—"Before Barack Obama" and "After Barack Obama."

It was James Baldwin—who always encouraged survivors to bear witness—who wrote, "The Negro has been formed in this Nation, for better or for worse, and does not belong to any other . . . The paradox is that the American Negro can have no future anywhere, on any continent as long as he is unwilling to accept his past." What does it mean for the story of your people's triumphs and tragedies to be told by those who are unwilling to disturb the nation's image as the beacon of equality?

It is possible that the newest descendants of the survivors will hear the official story of overcoming tragedy not by those who bore witness or by those who witnessed the bearing of witnesses, but by those who desire to maintain the nation's reigning myths and ideas about equality and opportunity. The diminishing of black America's memory will have consequences for future generations of blacks. Will the "official" national history really tell them about how battles were won and of casualties lost along the way, so that tragedies will not be repeated?

Perhaps this is why the monument to Martin Luther King, Jr., on the National Mall—and the many comparisons of President Obama to the civil rights leader—disturbs memory but makes great history. Obama has been lifted up as the fulfillment of Martin Luther King's dream. That dream was realized when the nation elected Obama—a black man—president of the United States. His election is a testament that he has been judged—and presumably all blacks are now judged—by the content of his character and not by the color of his skin, as King proclaimed in his 1963 speech on the steps of the Lincoln Memorial. How future generations of Americans—both blacks and nonblacks—will interpret black America's struggle from slavery to freedom, from civil rights to

FIGURE 6.1 James Baldwin (center) at the 1963 March on Washington (*Source:* Getty Images).

post–civil rights to the present day's persistence of racial inequality, will be dominated by triumphant narratives extolling Barack Obama as the forty-fourth president of the United States.

Like King's granite image on the National Mall, the civil rights leader's *national* memory is frozen in 1963, when King gave his "I Have a Dream" speech. The selective passages from King's famous speech convey the spirit of the American promise and hope that the nation will one day live up to its true values of freedom and opportunity. But the King on the National Mall and the president in the White House are where memory fades and national mythology begins.

Now that King is a national hero—whose ideas and actions are no longer a threat to the American way of life—it is easy to erase from memory the last two years of his life, in 1967 and 1968. It was then when King became increasingly critical of America's failure to deal with poverty and the war in Vietnam. King believed that the bombs that were being dropped in Vietnam were taking away resources that could attend to the poor in the United States. He believed that the "triple evils" of racism, poverty, and militarism worked together to perpetuate inequality in the nation.

In one of King's most moving but lesser-known speeches— "Remaining Awake during a Great Revolution," delivered on March 31, 1968, the last Sunday before his death—the civil rights leader leaves us a vision of what it will take for real change to come to America. "We are coming to demand that the government address itself to the problem of poverty," King told those gathered at the National Cathedral that morning. Citing lines from the Declaration of Independence, as he did in his 1963 March on Washington speech, King reminded the audience of the unfulfilled promise of the American creed. "We hold these truths to be self-evident that all men are created equal" and that "all men are endowed with inalienable rights of life, liberty, and the pursuit of happiness," King restated. He continued, "But if a man does not have a job or income, he has neither life or liberty nor the possibility of the pursuit of happiness. He merely exists."

For King the pursuit of happiness would be a continuous struggle to pursue equality through political agitation designed to push
government to act. "It is our experience that the nation doesn't
move around questions of genuine equality for the poor and for
black people until it is confronted massively, dramatically in terms
of direct action," King stated.[20]

King never made it to Washington to lead a poor people's campaign; he took a detour to Memphis to help poor striking garbage
workers gain dignity and a fair wage. There he was murdered on
April 4, 1968, and became, forty-three years later, with Jefferson
and Lincoln, sketched in stone as a hero on the National Mall. King
told black America in his final public address, the night before his
assassination, that he would not make it to the Promised Land with
them but that "we, as a people, would get to the Promised Land."

As the Moses of a historically despised people, "great history"—
not memory—will record King passing on the torch of the freedom
movement to Obama, who is standing in as the biblical Joshua on
the cusp of entering the Promised Land. But it remains to be seen
if this Joshua—and his generation—will ever lead his people
there. As the biblical story of the Exodus instructs, the Battle of
Jericho has to be won—walls will have to tumble down—before
entering the land of milk and honey. Black America is still battling structural inequalities, manifested in racial disparities in
education, health, wealth, and justice. Obama is expected to lead
black America to the Promised Land not as a voice of opposition to
the government, demanding it act on behalf of the poor and the
outcast, but as the commander in chief of the American empire.

One day the question will be asked—years if not decades from
now—whether the sacrifices of previous generations were worth
the rise of a "race-neutral" black president, whose ascendancy was
made possible by their efforts. As it stands now, the price has not
yet proven its worth in sacrifice, to the memory of those lost in
battle, nor for those who still sit at the very bottom of society, still
believing and hoping in the possibilities of change.

Notes

CHAPTER 1

1. Frank Lynn, "New Hat in Ring: Mrs. Chisholm's," *New York Times* [hereafter *NYT*], January 26, 1972; Stephen Isaacs, "Shirley Chisholm Makes It Formal: She's a Candidate," *Washington Post* [hereafter *WP*], January 26, 1972.
2. Malcolm X, "The Ballot or the Bullet," and "Statement of the Organization of Afro-American Unity," in *Let No Body Turn Us Around*, edited by Manning Marable and Lee Mullings (Lanham, MD: Rowman and Littlefield, 2000).
3. Bayard Rustin, "From Protest to Politics: The Future of the Civil Rights Movement," *Commentary*, February 1965.
4. William L. Clay, "Emerging New Black Politics," *Black World*, October 1972, 37–38.
5. Carl Stokes and Percy Sutton quoted in "Blacks Eye U.S. Presidency, Audacious," *Jet*, May 27, 1971.
6. Carl Stokes quoted in Stephan Lesher, "The Short, Unhappy Life of Black Presidential Politics," *NYT*, June 25, 1972; Jesse Jackson quoted in Ronald E. Kisher, "Blacks Pick Man They Prefer as a Candidate for U.S. President," *Jet*, August, 26, 1971.
7. Frank Lynn, "What Makes Shirley Run?" *NYT*, January 30, 1972; Lynn, "New Hat in Ring."
8. Thomas A. Johnson, "Blacks, in Shift, Forming Unit for Mrs. Chisholm," *NYT*, February 4, 1972.
9. Austin Scott, "Black Voter Strategy Is Split Four Ways," *WP*, May 8, 1972.

10. Austin Scott, "In Waning Hours, Mrs. Chisholm Courted 1st-Ballot Support," *WP*, July 13, 1972.
11. James Richardson, *Willie Brown: A Biography* (Berkeley: University of California Press, 1996).
12. Scott, "In Waning Hours, Mrs. Chisholm Courted 1st-Ballot Support."
13. Shirley Chisholm, *The Good Fight* (New York: Harper and Row, 1973), 116–117.
14. Lesher, "The Short, Unhappy Life of Black Presidential Politics."
15. Quoted in Chisholm, *The Good Fight*, 31.
16. Lesher, "The Short, Unhappy Life of Black Presidential Politics."
17. Johnson, "Blacks, in Shift, Forming Unit for Mrs. Chisholm."
18. "Rep. Chisholm Asks Black Men to Get Off Her Back," *Jet*, October 28, 1971; Chisholm, *The Good Fight*, 32.
19. Chisholm, *The Good Fight*, 161–163.
20. Lucius Barker, *Our Time Has Come: A Diary of Jesse Jackson's 1984 Presidential Campaign* (Urbana: University of Illinois Press, 1988).
21. Thomas E. Cavanagh and Lorn F. Foster, *Jesse Jackson's Campaign: The Primaries and the Caucuses* (Washington, DC: Joint Center for Political Studies, 1984).
22. Barker, *Our Time Has Come*, 22–23.
23. Linda Williams, *The Constraint of Race: The Legacies of White Skin Privilege in America* (University Park: Pennsylvania State University Press, 2003), 187–188.
24. Cavanagh and Foster, *Jesse Jackson's Campaign*.
25. Ethel Payne, "Few Gains for Minorities at the Democratic Convention," *Baltimore Afro-American*, August 4, 1984; George Curry, "Blacks Boo Coretta Scott King," *Chicago Tribune*, July 19, 1984; Milton Coleman, "Jackson Rebukes Hecklers," *WP*, July 19, 1984.
26. Thomas E. Cavanagh, *Inside Black America: The Message of the Black Vote in the 1984 Elections* (Washington, DC: Joint Center for Political Studies, 1985).
27. Sam Allis, Jack E. White, and William R. Doerner, "A Long-Awaited Embrace," *Time*, September 10, 1984.
28. D. Michael Cheers, "Jesse Jackson Takes First Step Toward Another Run for President of the United States," *Jet*, April 13, 1987.
29. Donald L. Rheem, "Jackson Win in Michigan Said to Create 'A New Political World,'" *Christian Science Monitor*, March 28, 1988; Ellen Hume, "Jackson's Big Michigan Victory Leaves Democrats in a Quandary over Nominee," *Wall Street Journal*, March 28, 1988.
30. R. W. Apple, Jr., "Jackson Triumph Changes Outlook for Top Democrats," *NYT*, March 28, 1988; Dennis Schatzman, "Stop Jackson Move Underway," *New Pittsburgh Courier*, April 16, 1988.
31. Bernard Weinraub, "Gore Assails Dukakis over Jackson," *NYT*, April 4, 1988.
32. Manning Marable, "The 'Stop Jesse Jackson' Movement," *New Pittsburgh Courier*, May 14, 1988.

33. Harold Stanley, "Assessing the Presidential Candidacies of Jesse Jackson," in *Prejudice, Politics, and the American Dilemma,* edited by Paul M. Sniderman, Philip E. Tetlock, and Edward G. Carmines (Stanford, CA: Stanford University Press, 1993).

34. Jesse Jackson, "What We Must Do," *Ebony,* October 1988.

35. Brazile quoted in Kevin Merida, "A Leader Left Behind?" *WP,* July 14, 2008; Roger Burns, *Jesse Jackson: A Biography* (Westport, CT: Greenwood, 2005).

36. Coleman, "Jackson Rebukes Hecklers."

CHAPTER 2

1. Shirley Chisholm, *The Good Fight* (New York: Harper and Row, 1973), 28–30.

2. Lynn Sweet, "Jones' Obama Pitch to Black Democrats Stirs Controversy," *Chicago Sun-Times* [hereafter *CST*], February 6, 2007.

3. Quoted from *Washington Tribune* in Harold Gosnell, *Negro Politicians: The Rise of Negro Politics in Chicago* (1935; repr., Chicago: University of Chicago Press, 1967), 184–185.

4. Ibid., 195.

5. Ted Kleine, "Is Bobby Rush in Trouble?" *Chicago Reader,* March 17, 2000.

6. William Grimshaw, "Harold Washington: The Enigma of the Black Political Tradition," in *The Mayors: The Chicago Political Tradition,* 3rd ed., edited by Paul M. Green and Melvin G. Holli (Carbondale: Southern Illinois University Press, 2005), 183.

7. Gary Rivlin, *Fire on the Prairie: Chicago's Harold Washington and the Politics of Race* (New York: Henry Holt, 1992), 26–38.

8. Charles Payne, *I've Got the Light of Freedom: The Organizing Tradition and the Mississippi Freedom Struggle* (Berkeley: University of California Press, 1995).

9. Vernon Jarrett, "For Washington, the Party's Over," *Chicago Tribune,* May 11, 1977, A4.

10. Abdul Akalimat and Doug Gills, *Harold Washington and the Crisis of Black Power in Chicago* (Chicago, IL: Twenty-First Century Books and Publications, 1989), 73.

11. Paul Kleppner, *Chicago Divided: The Making of a Black Mayor* (DeKalb: Northern Illinois University Press, 1985), 154–155.

12. Quoted from "Harold," *This American Life,* episode 84, November 21, 1997, National Public Radio, http://www.thisamericanlife.org/radio-archives/episode/84/Harold.

13. Ibid.

14. Kleppner, *Chicago Divided,* 173.

15. Paul Kleppner, "Mayoral Politics Chicago Style: The Rise and Fall of a Multiethnic Coalition, 1983–1989," *National Political Science Review,* 5 (1994): 152–180.

16. Ibid.

17. Christopher Hayes, "Obama's Media Maven," *The Nation*, February 6, 2007.
18. Paul M. Green, "Braun's Dazzling Win as Downstate Fails Dixon; Bush and Clinton Pile Up Delegates," *Illinois Issues*, June 1992.
19. Basil Talbott, "Braun Surges in Victory—and a Place in History," *CST*, November 4, 1992; George F. Will, "Primary Has Had Secondary Effect," *CST*, September 20, 1992.
20. Florence Hamlish Levinsohn, "The Street Scrapper and the Rhodes Scholar," *Chicago Reader*, March 9, 1990.
21. Ibid.
22. Ibid.
23. Paul Merrion, "Reynolds Groundswell Poses Savage Threat; Cash, Backing Help Challenge to Troubled Rep," *Crain's Chicago Business*, January 29, 1990.
24. Levinsohn, "The Street Scrapper and the Rhodes Scholar."
25. Ibid.
26. George F. Will, "Worst Member of Congress Faces Tough Fight for Re-Nomination," *Baltimore Sun*, March 5, 1992.
27. George Will, "The Worst Congressman," *Orlando Sentinel*, March 5, 1992.
28. George Will, "Savage Is Seen as Worst in Congress," *CST*, March 5, 1992.
29. Ibid.
30. Steve Neal, "Top Democrat Guns Take Aim at Savage," *CST*, August 30, 1991; Steve Neal, "Reynolds Is Upbeat about His Third Race," *CST*, January 3, 1992.
31. Kleine, "Is Bobby Rush in Trouble?"
32. Steve Neal, "New African-American Leaders Are Emerging," *CST*, September 1, 1999.
33. Kleine, "Is Bobby Rush in Trouble?"
34. Ibid.
35. Carter G. Woodson, *Mis-Education of the Negro* (Trenton, NJ: African World Press, 1998), 6.
36. Peter Slevin, "Obama Forged Political Mettle in Illinois Capitol," *Washington Post*, February 9, 2007; Todd Purdum, "Raising Obama," *Vanity Fair*, March 2008.
37. John O'Connor, "Illinois State President Emil Jones Retiring after Term Ends in January," Galesburg.com, August 19, 2008.
38. Robert McClory, "The Invisible Man: Richard Newhouse Has Done So Much. Why Is He Seen So Little?" *Chicago Reader*, September 13, 1990.
39. David K. Fremon, *Chicago Politics, Ward by Ward* (Bloomington: Indiana University Press, 1988), 138.
40. McClory, "The Invisible Man."
41. Tracey Robinson-English, "State House Clout: Emil Jones, Jr., President of the Illinois Senate, Is One of the Nation's Most Powerful Politicians," *Ebony*, April 2005.
42. Scott Fornek, "Obama for President?" *CST*, November 4, 2004. [Emphasis mine.]

CHAPTER 3

1. Reverend Jeremiah Wright, "Confusing God and Government" (transcript, April 13, 2003), BlackPast.org, http://www.blackpast.org/?q=2008-rev-jeremiah-wright-confusing-god-and-government.
2. Reverend Wright's most irresponsible comments were not "God Damn America" but his remarks that the government injected syphilis in the infamous government-funded Tuskegee experiment and that the government invented "the HIV-virus as a means of genocide against people of color." The syphilis experiment refused to treat men who already had contracted syphilis even though there was a cure, and there has been no evidence that the government created the HIV virus. Unfortunately, it is the perpetuation of these myths that create distrust of black Americans against medical institutions. This distrust discourages many black Americans from seeking early treatment for curable but deadly diseases.
3. David Walker, *David Walker's Appeal*, with an introduction by Sean Wilentz (New York: Hill and Wang, 1995), 3.
4. Frederick Douglass, "What Is the Slave to the Fourth of July?"in *Let Nobody Turn Us Around: An African-American Anthology*, 2nd ed., edited by Manning Marable and Leith Mullings (Lanham, MD: Rowman and Littlefield, 1993), 87.
5. Malcolm X, "God's Judgment of White America" (transcript, December 4, 1963), http://www.malcolmxonline.com/speeches-gods-judgement.html.
6. Fredrick C. Harris, "Black Churches and Civic Traditions: Outreach, Activism, and the Politics of Public Funding of Faith-Based Ministries," in *Can Charitable Choice Work? Covering Religion's Impact on Urban Affairs and Social Services*, edited by Andrew Walsh (Hartford, CT: Pew Program on Religion and the News Media and Greenberg Center for the Study of Religion in Public Life, Trinity College, 2001), 140–156.
7. Robert M. Franklin, *Crisis in the Village: Restoring Hope in African-American Communities* (Minneapolis, MN: Fortress Press, 2007), 112–113.
8. Milmon F. Harrison, *Righteous Riches: The Word of Faith Movement in Contemporary African-American Religion* (New York: Oxford University Press, 2005).
9. Michael Dawson, *Behind the Mule: Race and Class in African-American Politics* (Princeton, NJ: Princeton University Press, 1994), 11.
10. See Eugene Genovese, *Roll, Jordan, Roll: The World the Slaveholders Made* (New York: Vintage Books, 1974); and Albert J. Raboteau, *Slave Religion: The "Invisible Institution" in the Antebellum South* (New York: Oxford University Press, 1978).
11. C. Eric Lincoln and Lawrence H. Mamiya, *The Black Church in the African-American Experience* (Durham, NC: Duke University Press, 1990), 3–5.
12. Michael C. Dawson, *Black Visions: The Roots of Contemporary African-American Political Ideologies* (Chicago: University of Chicago Press, 2001), 11.

13. "Black Leaders Blast Mega Churches, Say They Ignore Social Justice," Associated Press, June 29, 2006.
14. "Black Baptists Eschew 'Prosperity Preaching,'" transcript, WFAA TV, Dallas, September 7, 2006.
15. Frederick K. C. Price, *Prosperity on God's Terms* (Tulsa, OK: Harrison Press, 1990), 8–9.
16. Ralph E. Luker, *The Social Gospel in Black and White* (Chapel Hill: University of North Carolina Press, 1991).
17. Albert J. Raboteau, "African-Americans, Exodus, and the American Israel," in *African-American Christianity: Essays in History*, edited by Paul E. Johnson (Berkeley: University of California Press, 1994), 9.
18. Eddie S. Glaude, Jr., *Exodus! Religion, Race, and Nation in Early Nineteenth Century Black America* (Chicago: University of Chicago Press, 2000).
19. Harris, "Black Churches and Civic Traditions," in *Can Charitable Choice Work?*
20. Howard Thurman, *Jesus and the Disinherited* (1949, repr., Boston: Beacon Press, 1996), 17–18.
21. Albert B. Cleage, Jr.,"The Black Messiah," in *Black Theology: A Documentary History Volume One: 1966–1979*, edited by James H. Cone and Gayraud S. Wilmore (Maryknoll, NY: Orbis Press, 1993).
22. James H. Cone, *A Black Theology of Liberation* (Philadelphia: J. B. Lippincott, 1970).
23. John Blake, "Bishop's Charity Generous to Bishop," *Atlanta-Journal Constitution*, August 28, 2005.
24. In 2007, the Senate Finance Committee launched an investigation of Bishop Long and other prosperity gospel ministers. The committee was looking into whether particular ministries operate more like for-profit institutions than non-profit institutions that are tax-exempt. Senator Chuck Grassley (R-IA), the ranking minority leader of the Senate Finance Committee, has requested financial documents from various ministers and churches. Other ministers under investigation include Kenneth and Gloria Copeland, Creflo Dollar, Benny Hinn, Joyce Meyer, and Paula White. The investigation was hampered because of the difficulties in getting ministers to surrender financial documents to the committee. A report was completed in 2011 that documented the need for significant reforms in how megachurches conduct their finances.
25. John Blake, "Long Not Welcomed by All at Seminary, Graduation Provokes Protest," *Atlanta-Journal Constitution*, May 11, 2006.
26. Edith L. Blumhofer, *Restoring the Faith: The Assemblies of God, Pentecostalism, and American Culture* (Urbana: University of Illinois Press, 1993), 16.
27. W. J. Hollenweger, *The Pentecostals: The Charismatic Movement in the Churches* (Minneapolis, MN: Augsburg Publishing House, 1972), 20.
28. Quoted in ibid., 23.

29. Hollenweger, *The Pentecostals*; and Harrison, *Righteous Riches*.

30. John Avanzini, *Rich God, Poor God: Your Perception Changes Everything* (Tulsa, OK: Abel Press, 2001), viii.

31. John Blake, "Was Jesus Rich? Swanky Messiah Not Far-fetched in Prosperity Gospel," *Atlanta-Journal Constitution*, October 22, 2006.

32. Creflo A. Dollar, *Total Life Prosperity: 14 Practical Steps to Receiving God's Full Blessing* (Nashville, TN: Thomas Nelson, 1999), 4.

33. Kirbyjon Caldwell with Mark Seal, *The Gospel of Good Success* (New York: Simon and Schuster, 1999), 17.

34. Quoted from transcript, "Prosperity Gospel," *Religion and Ethics*, August 17, 2007.

35. Laurie Goodstein, "Without a Pastor of His Own, Obama Turns to Five," *NYT*, March 14, 2009.

36. See Robert Weisbrot, *Father Divine and the Struggle for Racial Equality* (Urbana: University of Illinois Press, 1983); and Marie Dallam, *Daddy Grace: A Celebrity Preacher and His House of Prayer* (New York: New York University Press, 2007).

37. Hans A. Baer and Merrill Singer, *African-American Religion in the Twentieth Century* (Knoxville: University of Tennessee Press, 1992), 62–63.

38. Lee Shayne, *America's New Preacher: T. D. Jakes* (New York: New York University Press, 2005), 103.

39. Stepanie Mitchem, *Name It and Claim It? Prosperity Preaching in the Black Church* (Cleveland, OH: Pilgrim Press, 2007).

40. See Fredrick C. Harris, *Survey on Race, Politics, and Society* (Center on African-American Politics and Society, Columbia University, September 2008).

41. Ibid.

CHAPTER 4

1. Lynn Sweet, "Obama Tells Blacks: Shape Up," *CST*, February 29, 2008.

2. For an excellent analysis of the oversaturation of fast-food chains in poor and minority communities, see Naa Oyo A. Kwate, "Racial Segregation and the Marketing of Health Inequality," in *Beyond Discrimination: Racial Inequality in a Post-Racial Era?* edited by Fredrick C. Harris and Robert C. Lieberman (New York: Russell Sage Foundation Press, forthcoming, 2013).

3. Evelyn Brooks Higginbotham, *Righteous Discontent: The Women's Movement in the Black Baptist Church, 1880–1920* (Cambridge, MA: Harvard University Press, 1994).

4. Kevin K. Gaines, *Uplifting the Race: Black Leadership, Politics, and Culture Since the Turn of the Century* (Chapel Hill: University of North Carolina Press, 1996), 6.

5. For further discussion of racial inequality and neoliberalism, see Cathy J. Cohen, *Democracy Remixed: Black Youth and the Future of American*

Politics (New York: Oxford University Press, 2010); and Cedric Johnson, ed., *The Neoliberal Deluge: Hurricane Katrina, Late Capitalism, and the Remaking of New Orleans* (Minneapolis: University of Minnesota Press, 2011).

6. All quotes are from Margaret Murray Washington, "We Must Have a Cleaner Social Morality" (September 13, 1898, Charleston, South Carolina), http://www.blackpast.org/, accessed February 18, 2011.

7. James R. Grossman, *Land of Hope: Chicago, Black Southerners, and the Great Migration* (Chicago: University of Chicago Press, 1989), 140.

8. Ibid., 150.

9. Ibid., 154.

10. Julius Lester, ed., *The Seventh Son: The Thought and the Writings of W.E.B. Dubois*, vol. 2 (New York: Random House, 1971), 61.

11. W. E. B. DuBois, "The Talented Tenth: Memorial Address," in *W.E.B. DuBois: A Reader*, edited by David Levering Lewis (New York: Henry Holt, 1995).

12. Brook Barnes, "From Footnote to Fame in Civil Rights History," *NYT*, November 25, 2009.

13. Phillip Hose, *Claudette Colvin* (New York: Farrar Straus Giroux, 2009).

14. Hobart Sidney Jarrett, *The History of Sigma Pi Phi: First of the African-American Greek-Letter Fraternities*, vol. 2 (Philadelphia: Quantum Leap, 1995), 50–52.

15. Pew Research Center, *Blacks See Growing Values Gap between Poor and Middle-Class*, November 13, 2007, http://pewsocialtrends.org/assets/pdf/Race.pdf.

16. Quoted in Adolph Reed, Jr., *Class Notes: Posing as Politics and Other Thoughts on the American Scene* (New York: New Press, 2000), 56, 58.

17. Glenn Loury, "The Moral Quandary of the Black Community," in *Gaining Ground: New Approaches to Poverty and Dependency*, edited by Michael Cromartie (Washington, DC: Ethics and Public Policy Center, 1985).

18. Bill Cosby, "Address at the NAACP on the 50th Anniversary of *Brown v. Board of Education*" (transcript, Washington, DC, May 17, 2004), http://www.americanrhetoric.com/speeches/billcosbypoundcakespeech.htm. Anna Marie Smith, *Welfare Reform and Sexual Regulation* (New York: Cambridge University Press, 2007), 148.

19. Cosby, "Address at the NAACP on the 50th Anniversary of *Brown v. Board of Education*."

20. Leesha McKinzie, "Hampton Business School Sticks by Requirement for 'Conservative Hairstyles,'" *Black College Wire*, March 26, 2006, http://www.blackcollegewire.org/.

21. Hampton University, "Dress Code," http://www.hamptonu.edu/student_life/dresscode.cfm, accessed February 20, 2011.

22. Bennett College, Bennett Belle Book, *Student Handbook*, 2008–2009, http://www.bennett.edu/pdf/Student%20Handbook%202008-2009.pdf.

23. David Zucchins, "Obama Dress Code: 'Pull Up Your Pants,'" *The Swamp*, January 30, 2009, http://www.swamppolitics.com/news/

politics/blog/2009/01/obamas_dress_code_pull_up_your.html; Mashaun D. Simon, "Morehouse Dress Code Seeks to 'Get Back to Legacy,'" *Atlanta Journal Constitution*, October 16, 2009; "Morehouse College Appropriate Attire Policy," *Maroon Tiger*, October 6, 2009.

24. "Morehouse Dress Code Debate," CNN, October 17, 2009, http://newsroom.blogs.cnn.com/2009/10/17/morehouse-dress-code-debate/.

25. Cohen, *Democracy Remixed*.

26. Chris Rock, *Bring the Pain*, DVD, 1996.

27. Tyler Perry, *Madea's Family Reunion*, DVD, 2006.

28. Bill Clinton, "Speech in Memphis" (transcript, November 13, 1993), http://www.presidentialrhetoric.com/historicspeeches/clinton/memphis.html.

29. Hank De Zutter, "What Makes Obama Run?" *Chicago Reader*, December 7, 1995.

30. Quote is from Devah Pager, *MARKED: Race, Crime, and Finding Work in an Era of Mass Incarceration* (Chicago: University of Chicago Press, 2007).

31. Barack Obama, "Father's Day Speech" (Apostolic Church of God, Chicago, Illinois June, 15, 2008), http://www.youtube.com/watch?v=Hj1hCDjwG6M.

32. Barack Obama, "2008 NAACP Barack Obama Speech" (99th Annual NAACP Convention, July 15, 2008), http://www.youtube.com/watch?v=L0JAIG-qLKo, accessed February 25, 2011.

33. Chris Harris, "Barack Obama Weighs In on Sagging Pants, 'Brothers Should Pull Up Their Pants,'" *MTV News*, November 3, 2008.

34. See Fredrick C. Harris, *Survey on Race, Politics, and Society* (Center on African-American Politics and Society, Columbia University, September 2008).

35. Cynthia M. A. McIntyre, "Respect for the President-Elect," national president, Delta Sigma Theta, e-mail received on December 18, 2008.

CHAPTER 5

1. Lynn Sweet, "Sweet Blog: Obama Warns of Despair Leading to 'Quiet Riots' in Address at a Va. Black U.," Remarks of Senator Barack Obama, Hampton Ministers Conference, June 5, 2007, as prepared for delivery, *CST*, June 5, 2007.

2. Linda F. Williams, "White/Black Perceptions of the Electability of Black Political Candidates," *National Political Science Review*, 1990, 58.

3. Davis Bositis, *Black Elected Officials: A Statistical Summary* (Washington, DC: Joint Center for Political and Economic Studies, 2001), http://www.jointcenter.org/research/black-elected-officials-a-statistical-summary-2000.

4. Thomas E. Cavanaugh, *Race and Political Strategy: A JCPS Roundtable* (Washington, DC: Joint Center for Political Studies, 1983), 3.

5. Ibid., 7.

6. Ibid., 15.

7. Ibid., 47.

8. Charles V. Hamilton, "De-racialization: Examination of a Political Strategy," *First World: International Journal of Black Thought* (March–April 1977): 3–5.

9. Joseph E. McCormick II and Charles E. Jones, "Deracialization Revisited: Thinking through a Dilemma," in *Dilemmas of Black Politics: Leadership, Strategy, and Issues*, edited by Georgia A. Persons (New York: HarperCollins, 1993), 77.

10. "The Senate: An Individual Who Happens to Be a Negro," *Time*, February 17, 1967.

11. Judson Jefferies, *Virginia's Native Son: The Election and Administration of Governor L. Douglas Wilder* (West Lafayette, IN: Purdue University Press), 24.

12. Ibid.

13. Judson Jefferies, "U.S. Senator Edward W. Brooke and Governor L. Douglas Wilder Tell Political Scientists How Blacks Can Win High-Profile Statewide Office," *PS Political Science and Politics* 32, no. 3 (1999): 583–587.

14. Christopher Hayes, "Obama's Media Maven," *Nation*, February 6, 2007.

15. Jason Zengerle, "The Message Keeper: How David Axelrod Learned to Conquer Race," *The New Republic*, November 2008.

16. Ibid.

17. Quoted from *Chris Matthews Show*, "Obama America: 2010 and Beyond," January 18, 2010, http://www.youtube.com/watch?v=awBRPn WEIyc&feature=related.

18. Nayda Terkildsen, "When White Voters Evaluate Black Candidates: The Processing Implications of Candidate Skin Color, Prejudice, and Self Monitoring," *American Journal of Political Science* 37, no. 4 (1993): 1048; Jennifer L. Hochschild and Vesla Weaver, "The Skin-Color Parodox and the American Racial Order," *Social Forces*, 2 (2007):1–28.

19. "Volunteers for Obama Face a Complex Issue," *NYT*, October 14, 2008.

20. Pew Research Center, *Blacks Upbeat about Black Progress, Prospects*, January 12, 2010.

21. Kenji Yoshino, *Covering: The Hidden Assault on Our Civil Rights* (New York: Random House, 2006).

22. Lani Guinier, *The Tyranny of the Majority: The Fundamental Fairness in Representative Democracy* (New York: Free Press, 1995), 57–58.

23. Niara Sudarkasa, "Thomas Should Be Approved," *Philadelphia Inquirer*, July 28, 1991.

24. Maya Angelou, "I Dare Hope," *NYT*, August 25, 1991, E15.

25. U.S. Senate, *Hearings on the Nomination of Clarence Thomas to Be Associate Justice of the Supreme Court of the United States, Before the Committee on the Judiciary*, 102nd Cong., 1st sess. (September 17 and 19, 1991) (statement of Evelyn Bryant), p. 495.

26. Ibid., statement of Yvonne Thomas, p. 922.

27. Diane Pinderhughes, "Divisions in the Civil Rights Community," *PS* (September 1992): 486.

28. Lee Sigelman and James S. Todd, "Clarence Thomas, Black Pluralism, Civil Rights Policy," *Political Science Quarterly* 107 (1992): 231–248. Press Release, ABC News Poll, September 16, 1991. *Hearings*, part 2, p. 506 (see note 25).

29. Pew Research Center, *Blacks See Growing Values Gap between Poor and Middle-Class,* November 13, 2007, http://pewsocialtrends.org/assets/pdf/Race.pdf.

30. Scott Helman, "Obama, Clinton in a Tight Battle for Black Vote," *Boston Globe*, July 13, 2007; and Michael Dimock, "Black Enthusiasm for Clinton and Obama Leaves Little Room for Edwards," Pew Research Center, August 30, 2007, http://pewresearch.org/pubs/583/blacks-john-edwards.

31. Carl Hart, Charles Ksir, and Oakley Ray, *Drugs, Society, and Human Behavior* (New York: McGraw-Hill, 2008).

32. See Fredrick C. Harris, *Survey on Race, Politics, and Society* (Center on African-American Politics and Society, Columbia University, September 2008).

33. Henry Louis Gates, "A Conversation with William Julius Williams on the Election of Barack Obama," *DuBois Review* 6, no. 1 (2009): 15–23.

CHAPTER 6

1. Pamela Gentry, "The President Addresses African-American Unemployment?" *Black Entertainment Television News*, April 29, 2009, http://blogs.bet.com/news/pamela/2009/04/29/the-president-addresses-african-american-umemployment/.

2. Unemployment statistics are from the U.S. Bureau of Labor Statistics, http://www.bls.gov/news.release/empsit.t02.htm.

3. Barack Obama, "The President's News Conference," June 23, 2009, The American Presidency Project, http://www.presidency.ucsb.edu/ws/index.php?pid=86323#axzz1dkH7q8W2.

4. Barack Obama, interview by April Ryan, American Urban Radio Networks, December 21, 2009, The American Presidency Project, http://www.presidency.ucsb.edu/ws/index.php?pid=88310&st=African+American&st1=#axzz1dkH7q8W2.

5. For further discussions about targeted universalism and the jobs bill see Jason Reece, Christy Rogers, Matthew Martin, Stephen Menendian, and Caitlin Watt, "Targeted Universalism and the Jobs Bill," Kirwan Institute for the Study of Race and Ethnicity, March 2010.

6. Barack Obama, "LGBT Pride Month at the White House," Office of Public Engagement, The White House, June 29, 2011, http://www.whitehouse.gov/blog/2011/06/29/lgbt-pride-month-white-house.

7. Terry Shropshire, "Obama Tells Blacks to Stop Whining and Complaining and Start Fighting," September 25, 2011, Rollingout.com, http://rollingout.com/politics/obama-tells-blacks-to-stop-whining-and-complaining-and-start-fighting/.

8. "Black History Month 2011," The White House, http://www.whitehouse
   .gov/black-history-month-2011?page=1.
9. E. E. Schattschneider, *The Semisovereign People: The Realist's View of
   Democracy in America* (Hinsdale, IL: Dryden Press, 1975).
10. Charles V. Hamilton, "What Blacks Want from Carter," *NYT*, Decem-
    ber 4, 1976.
11. Charles V. Hamilton, "De-racialization: Examination of a Political
    Strategy," *First World: International Journal of Black Thought*
    (March–April 1977): 5.
12. Charles V. Hamilton, "The Politics of Deracialization in the 1990s,"
    National Political Science Review, 3 (1992): 177.
13. "The Herman Cain Guide to Race and Politics," The Root, http://www
    .theroot.com/multimedia/herman-cain-guide-race-and-politics.
14. Lani Guinier, *The Tyranny of the Majority: The Fundamental Fairness
    in Representative Democracy* (New York: Free Press, 1995), 57.
15. Richard Fenno, *Going Home: Black Representatives and Their Constitu-
    ents* (Chicago: University of Chicago Press, 2003), 33.
16. Ibid., 36.
17. Ibid., 141.
18. Krissah Thompson, "Can Obama Hold on to African American Voters
    in 2012?" *WP*, October 17, 2011.
19. Thulani Davis, "Black Mayors: Can They Make Cities Work?" *Mother
    Jones*, July 1984, 32.
20. James Melvin Washington, ed., *A Testament of Hope: The Essential
    Writings and Speeches of Martin Luther King, Jr.* (New York: Harper-
    One, 1986), 268–278.

Index